BOOKS AND RELIGIOUS DEVOTION

for alone, as the one only true

...ntres all of His teaching he...

...enly power, in all who ...

...rebelliously anywhere.

...Story is Truthful every

..., Coös County, New Hamp...

9. Please read page 88 in

...Book. Thomas Connary

...k referred to, is gilt paper

...ite in beginning and end

...is world ends verysoon

...ever work for endless

...ast faithfully.

Thomas Connary.

...ös County, New Hamp...

...ys November 30th

...at all day. We now

...nough here to cover

...Mr. Joseph McGold...

...ork for us yesterday,

...wood, He will I th...

ALLAN F. WESTPHALL

BOOKS
AND
RELIGIOUS
DEVOTION

THE
REDEMPTIVE READING
OF AN
IRISHMAN IN
NINETEENTH-CENTURY
NEW ENGLAND

THE PENNYSLVANIA STATE UNIVERSITY PRESS
UNIVERSITY PARK, PENNSYLVANIA

Library of Congress Cataloging-in-Publication Data

Westphall, Allan F., author.
Books and religious devotion : the redemptive
reading of an Irishman in nineteenth-century
New England /
Allan F. Westphall.
p.   cm — (The Penn State series in the
history of the book)
Summary: "Examines the book collection of
Thomas Connary, a nineteenth-century
Irish Catholic New England farmer, to reconstruct
how Connary read and annotated his books.
Reveals how books can structure a life of devotion
and social participation, and presents an authentic,
holistic view of one reader's interior life"—
Provided by publisher.
Includes bibliographical references and index.
ISBN 978-0-271-06404-8 (cloth : alk. paper)
1. Books and reading—New England—History—
19th century. 2. Marginalia—New England—
History—19th century. 3. Connary, Thomas,
1814–1899—Library. 4. Books and reading—
Religious aspects—Christianity.
I. Title. II. Series: Penn State series in the
history of the book.

Z1003.3.N4W47   2014
028'.8097409'034—dc23
2014009572

The Pennsylvania State University Press is a member
of the Association of American University Presses.

It is the policy of The Pennsylvania State University
Press to use acid-free paper. Publications on
uncoated stock satisfy the minimum requirements
of American National Standard for Information
Sciences—Permanence of Paper for Printed
Library Material, ANSI Z39.48–1992.

This book is printed on paper that
contains 30% post-consumer waste.

Frontispiece: Detail of figure 6.

CONTENTS

ILLUSTRATIONS

The seeds of this research project lie in the collector's instinct. Having spent years researching the religious writing and devotional culture of the Middle Ages, I developed an additional interest in collecting early printed editions of medieval religious and mystical writers, primarily from England. These small-scale collecting endeavors concentrated on the writings of the so-called Middle English mystics, including Walter Hilton, Richard Rolle, Julian of Norwich, and Margery Kempe, writers active in the fourteenth century and the first half of the fifteenth. Many of these early texts were made available in print in the late nineteenth and early twentieth centuries, a time when English Catholic scholars promoted a new spiritual energy and did much to revive interest in England's religious past. I had long desired a scarce nineteenth-century American edition of Julian of Norwich's *Revelations of Divine Love* printed by the Boston printers Ticknor and Fields in 1864. I had placed the book on a "wants list" with one of the biggest online marketplaces for rare and used books, and in the spring of 2008, I received an email alert that the book was available from an American bookseller in the small town of Bridgewater, Vermont. Part of the online book description ran as follows:

> The contemporary binding is firm. However, the previous owner of the book dating to the 1870s and 80s has inserted handwritten notes of a religious theme into the book and pasted numerous newspaper clippings onto blank areas. These clippings, however, do not affect any of the original text and make for some interesting reading of that time.

I read the description with a mixture of curiosity and mild annoyance: curiosity, of course, about what a nineteenth-century reader (presumably American) would import into a copy of Julian's *Revelations* and what the "interesting reading" might be, but also some disappointment that the book came with such invasive readerly additions, when all I wanted was a tidy copy of a familiar medieval text printed in the United States at the time of the Civil War. Conceivably, the bookseller thought along similar lines: the repeated "however" in the description, the firm reassurance that the insertions did not obstruct the printed text, and the very moderate price of the book all betrayed the assumption (shared by me) that collectors of antiquarian books prefer the pristine, unblemished copy.

What arrived in the mail from Vermont intrigued me. The copy of Julian's *Revelations* once belonged to an Irish immigrant to the United States, and this individual, clearly a Catholic of strong religious devotion, had converted the book into a repository of miscellaneous objects, including several newspaper articles, some private letters, and extensive handwritten religious reflections of a didactic and rather idiosyncratic nature. An email exchange with the seller ensued, and within a year I had purchased more than thirty volumes from the same collection, all containing the same Irish American owner's imports and annotations. The seller could reveal little about the provenance of the collection: it was bought from an estate sale in Vermont, and the books "were all packed into a trunk and had obviously been there for some years." The truth of the latter observation was confirmed by the layer of fungal growth found on several of the book covers and by the fact that the books were inhabited by a thriving colony of minuscule book-feeding insects (probably the so-called booklouse of the Psocoptera order) that greeted me whenever a book was opened but then sought refuge behind the spine to feed on the paste used inside the binding. Moreover, according to the bookseller, several volumes from the same estate had already been acquired by other buyers and collectors. I was provided with the relevant titles, but I never had the opportunity to examine these "lost" books myself. (The appendix lists the full range of titles.) This study is an attempt to make sense of the phenomenon that was presented to me in this way.

If any term characterizes the inception of this project—and the trajectory of curiosity-driven research that was to follow—it must be "serendipity." This idea captures the progressive questioning that has advanced this project, leading into what was for me unfamiliar and unexpected research territories, such as the Irish diaspora, nineteenth-century Irish American print culture, the religious culture of New England, the local history of Coös County in New Hampshire, and the history of psychiatry in North America. There may be a tendency today to deemphasize the significance of serendipity in academia (although we continue to cultivate myths of chance discoveries in science and other areas), but in this study, the idea has to be foregrounded. What follows charts a serendipitous journey and my evolving understanding and appreciation of an acquired collection of annotated books.

Horace Walpole's peculiar eighteenth-century coinage, "serendipity," is derived from an ancient Persian tale and refers to a story about a journey.

I once read a silly fairy tale, called *the three Princes of Serendip* [a medi-eval Persian name for Sri Lanka]: as their Highnesses travelled, they were always making discoveries, by accidents and sagacity, of things which they were not in quest of: for instance, one of them discovered that a mule blind of the right eye had travelled the same road lately, because the grass was eaten only on the left side, where it was worse than on the right . . . (you must observe that *no* discovery of a thing you *are* looking for comes under this description).[1]

There can be no doubt that when Walpole coined his curious neologism, he had in mind the serendipitous discovery of the Sherlock Holmesian type: the three princes, sent out by their father King Jafer of Serendip to gain the practical experience that would complement their deep book learning, use their keen powers of observation to make subtle inferences from clues and traces which to others may go unnoticed or appear trivial. Thus employing skills in detection and inference, the three princes reconstruct that which remains unseen.

With time, the meaning of the term "serendipity" has broadened to describe processes of discovery beyond the methodology of the subtle, detectivelike inference from signs.[2] We might find patterns of serendipity in planned dis-coveries and in the systematic investigation of the research project, in which one may set out in search of something without knowing exactly what will be found. We may dip into the archives to examine a particular corpus of mate-rial, conducting directed research while more or less expecting to find the unexpected: "systematic, directed (re)search and serendipity do not exclude each other, but conversely, they complement and reinforce each other."[3] Another form altogether of discovery by serendipity is the happy accident in which something is found but unsought. This is the chance discovery—inad-vertent, unanticipated, fortuitous—happening when we do not look for it or seek insight of another kind.

The discovery of the collection of annotated books from Vermont mani-festly belongs to this last category of serendipitous finding. I allowed myself to become serendipity-prone—to follow, as it were, the path of the princes of Serendip—by trusting an early intuition that the material that more or less dropped into my lap presented some measure of cultural and intellectual sig-nificance. Developing this discovery into a structured research project, employing the finding academically and sagaciously (to use Walpole's term), meant to explain, theorize, categorize, and contextualize on the background of a serendipitous discovery. First, however, the process was one of sharing an experience with the original owner, of becoming intimate with the books and, through them, with the owner's pious and earnest voice. These books, which had lain dormant for decades, preserve traces of past passion and sincerity, and what follows is in part an attempt to reawaken the voice of a past reader and to mobilize a measure of sympathy with him (by which I understand a sympathy of comprehension that seeks to understand the motivations of his bookish labors, not so much a sympathy of either pity or approbation). Thomas Connary, the owner of these books, emigrated from Ireland to the United States in 1833 at the age of nineteen. In fact, like any good serendipitist, Connary himself ventured forth alone in a manner inadvertent and fortuitous. As will be clear in what follows, he embarked on an unplanned journey across the Atlantic by an unanticipated route; he went where chance brought him, assisted by people he did not know well.

The books of this strange and ambitious reader reminded me, as a medievalist, of the cultural mobility of a tradition of medieval spiritual writing and the appeal it can exert on much later generations of readers. As I will examine in detail, Connary's library contains a wealth of medieval spiritualia, and it is invariably the case that he inscribes his own voice alongside, often in dialogue with, those of past spiritual authorities. Here was found another, to me unexpected, dimension of the reception history of medieval devotional writings. From my research on medieval religious culture, I also knew that we have precious little to go by in terms of recovering past acts of reading and past reading programs, but this material presented a superfluity of traces of acts of reading from a reader who documented his responses to books and his methods for engaging with them to an extraordinary degree. Here was one of the comparatively rare cases of a comprehensive source material for studying the reading and annotation practices of an obscure, non-elite reader from the past. Although it is as complicated methodologically to reconstruct the processes and psychology of reading with this nineteenth-century American reader as it is with a religious reader in fifteenth-century England, the annotated books seemed to me to offer substantial insight into how books can structure the religious experience and devotional regimens of an actual reader. In particular, they told me something new about how books can be adapted in myriad creative ways to structures of belief and religious praxis in a household.

In Connary's collection, I found later developments of recognizable medieval forms of religious books. Connary's handwritten notes, for instance, captured reiterated routines of reading and reflection resembling the book of hours—that best seller of the Middle Ages—which structured people's daily religious practices with its conventionalized medley of texts, prayers, psalms,

and interplay of textual and pictorial components. Connary also imported
numerous and diverse items into his books, echoing the late medieval devotional miscellany, a popular form of textual anthology compiled from miscellaneous sources, often a product of the tastes of an individual compiler and
used by lay readers for personal religious guidance. Moreover, the way Connary's annotated volumes became carriers of relationship, reinforcing social
and familial bonds with injunctions to shared prayer, paralleled the medieval
"common-profit" book that circulated in small devout reading circles, often
carrying injunctions to pray on the behalf of others (such as a book's previous
owners or its donor). As I worked with Connary's collection, such shared
understanding of books across temporal and cultural removes presented itself
with increasing clarity. My approach became less bound by disciplinary or
chronological considerations, by any strict division between modern and pre-
modern or between print and manuscript textual cultures. What came to
interest me more was the complex material culture of the book artifact—specifically, the book's capacity to elicit passion and religious affect, to reinforce
patterns of friendship and kinship, to help structure a life of devotion, and to
preserve traces of past acts of reading and reflection.

Thomas Connary's identity as a devout Irish American Catholic was
unusually and intimately bound up with books, and he insists on and
explores the symbolic and iconic depth of the book's materiality. For him,
the book object can be imbued with spiritual and salvific power by a God
who is himself understood as a "Book," containing all wisdom and all moral
directive. Again, such notions are not foreign to a medievalist familiar with
the ubiquitous image of the book of God's creation and with scores of religious texts requesting that readers meditate on Christ's crucified body as a
book, his white skin signifying the manuscript parchment; his blood, the
ink; and the five wounds, the vowels of the text. More than anything, Connary's elaborate and spiritually motivated enhancements of his books remind
me of a reader in late medieval England, Margery Kempe (ca. 1379–ca. 1439)—
somewhat of an apparition in Middle English religious literature, yet another
chance survival to our time, and, like Connary, a lay reader of extraordinary
eccentricity and determination.[4] Two avid readers who also create narratives, both Connary and Kempe bring idiosyncratic propensities to acts of
reading, insisting on self-expression with a public dimension. Their writings
make use of calculated rhetorical maneuvers and remind us that readers'
documents are themselves texts to be interpreted. Ultimately, both individuals may serve as a reminder that one person's inspired mystic is another person's madman!

Perhaps, as can sometimes be the case with serendipitous discoveries, the thing found *was* the thing sought. A collection of books that preserve a consuming religious fervor and the remnants of an elaborately structured reading and writing program had presented itself to me. It was what I had sought, but from a place I had not foreseen. My discovery happened to coincide with burgeoning interdisciplinary research into the history of the book. An overwhelming recent interest in the social and material culture of the book and the history of reading had of course prepared me for the finding, and it influenced my decision to invest labor and some measure of identification to understand the phenomenon of Thomas Connary's library. In the pages that follow, I hope to contribute to these areas of scholarship by offering an illuminating and meticulous chronicle of one man's universe of books.

ACKNOWLEDGMENTS

Parts of chapters 2 and 4 have appeared as articles, and I want to thank the journal editors for allowing me to use this material. "'Laboring in my Books': A Religious Reader in Nineteenth Century New Hampshire" appeared in *Library: Transactions of the Bibliographical Society* 13, no. 2 (2012): 185–204; "'I am here': Reading Julian of Norwich in Nineteenth Century New England" appeared in *The Mediaeval Journal* 3, no. 2 (2013): 137–68.

I am most grateful to two anonymous readers for the Pennsylvania State University Press for particularly generous comments and guidance on the first draft of this book. Thanks also to colleagues at the Press for their hard work and faith in this project—James L. W. West III, Patrick Alexander, Laura Reed-Morrisson, and Robert Turchick.

Some parts of this material have been presented at seminars and colloquia in the Centre for the History of the Book at the University of Edinburgh, and in the Schools of English at the Queen's University of Belfast and the University of St. Andrews. I have benefited greatly from discussions with audiences in these places.

Finally, I thank my family—Katie Ruan, Lone Westphall, and Bent Westphall—for their unfailing help and encouragement.

"I Am Here"

Early in the morning on Tuesday, the seventh of January, 1890, Thomas Connary—an Irish immigrant farmer living in the town of Stratford, New Hampshire—sits down in his study to read in one of his most treasured books, the *Sixteen Revelations of Divine Love* by the medieval English mystic Julian of Norwich. As Connary, who is now in his seventy-sixth year, recounts, he occasionally looks up from his book at "her picture fitted by myself over the window facing northerly in the room I am now using for reading and writing purposes."[1] As has been his routine for more than three decades, he inserts numerous notebook pages with religious meditations between the pages of Julian's writing. Some of these handwritten pages show prayer and reflection emerging from his reading of Julian's visionary accounts. The following statement, written in Connary's somewhat idiosyncratic prose, allows us to reconstruct a specific reading situation, and it begins to convey the particular esteem that this devout farmer has for his religious literature.

> Tuesday, early in the morning clear and dry, January 7, 1890, I am working in my book, next to Titlepage of Revelations of Mother Juliana in 214 pages, see her picture directly over the northerly picture now of the window in the room in which I am busy much of my time as I am sighting northerly, for purposes purely heavenly thank God. Mother Juliana was an Anchorite of Norwich: Who lived in the days of King Edward the Third, and published in Boston by Ticknor and Fields in 1864. The publishers are protestants. I have had the Book most of the time since it was published. . . . No glossary is required in the Book for my use—I understand the full force of the Divine blessed holy Heavenly words without explanation thank God. . . . Books however many, cannot be heavenly if God will not bless them, make them pure with His own heavenly graces endlessly continually always forever, so with money, so with the whole of earthly property. Thomas Connary

For Connary, reading Julian of Norwich alongside a wide range of spiritual and didactic texts signifies precious moments of privacy, emotional reward, and prayerful reflection. Far more than just acquiring and reading his religious literature, Connary invests significant labor in filling his volumes with a plethora of material, such as newspaper cuttings, religious images, poetry, and, most noticeably, handwritten pages of religious prayers and reflections as well as diary records of daily events and personal reminiscences. The augmented volumes are the result of years of laborious accumulation—a process that appears to have begun in the late 1860s and continued until shortly before Connary's death in 1899.

These annotation practices and the manifold ways in which Thomas Connary interacts with books are the subject of detailed examination in this study. What can it mean to be inside one's books, to participate in them, and to be shaped by them? The following chapters focus on the writings of an eccentric reader and book collector in order to investigate the passion and fervent piety that he pours into his books. Connary's library allows us to explore the opportunities provided by the material book for structuring the practical, spiritual, and moral life of readers. His annotations offer ample evidence of how a book's physical properties can participate in the imaginative and spiritual life of a reader: more than anything else, they show how books can become the material conduits for a deeply felt relationship to one's neighbor as well as to the divinity. As this farmer-bibliophile works in his private room, he puts his books to many and varied uses, but the cumulative effect of his labors is to convert his library into a comprehensive proclamation of faith. In it, we find elaborate records of religious reading as an ingrained habit of everyday life, one existing alongside the routines of agricultural labor and the domestic duties of a nineteenth-century Irish Catholic living in New Hampshire.

Occasionally, when reading Julian of Norwich and many other books, Connary writes in the margins a brief yet pregnant comment: "I am here." This, I will argue, is particularly ripe with significance. More than merely marking a specific juncture in his reading, it is the assertion of someone determined to inscribe himself into the experiences recounted in the book, to testify to their veracity, and, finally, to convert the printed book into a signed testimony of a particular intensity of religious devotion. For Connary, noting that "I am here" means to assert affinity and proximity with past authors and their writings in a way that is concrete and aesthetic as much as it is existential and ethical.

Connary provides us with some details of his early life in a note he inserts into his book *The Council of the Vatican and the Events of the Time*, printed in Boston in 1872:

> March 25, in the year 1833, I left Castlemarket, my native home in Old Ireland, in the Province of Leinster, Kilkenny County, near Ballinakill in the Queen's County, expecting to return to my native home in three months of time: when on the way I met a few people who were on the way to America, I accompanied them, and worked for Mr Josiah Bellows 2nd, and his family, in Lancaster, Coos County, New Hampshire in June that year, my home from that time to this day has been in the United States of America.[2]

Born in 1814, Connary was only nineteen years of age when he left Ireland. He was part of the early wave of Irish immigrants who came to the United States before the trauma of the Great Irish Famine and who brought with them overwhelmingly positive memories of Old Ireland. Intriguingly, the above record provides no further explanation of motives, no details about the trials of crossing, no impression of the thoughts running through the mind of a nineteen-year-old finding himself in an unfamiliar land.

An obituary for Thomas Connary in the *Coös County Democrat* from the year 1899 provides some further details about this early phase in his American experience:

> When about nineteen years old he left his home for America, and came to the town of Lancaster, N.H., in the early part of June. He had but fifteen cents in his possession at this time. He hired himself to Mr. Josiah Bellows for the small sum of seven dollars a month, and after having served his time with this gentleman he went about ditching for the farmers. During the winters he threshed wherever he could get employment. At that time, as is well known, threshing was done by hand. He seldom or ever got his pay in money but accepted the tenth bushel as compensation for his hard labor. He kept up this mode of livelihood for several years, then he purchased a small farm in Northumberland, on which he had a log cabin for a dwelling. While here his beloved mother, one sister and two brothers, John and Simon, came from Ireland to sweeten his life and labors. He now seemed happier, having his mother for housekeeper. At the age of thirty he married a worthy lady whose

name was Lucinda Stone. The following year he demolished the log cabin and erected in its stead a homesome frame building, the first of this nature ever erected in the town. He lived in this town for five years, working chiefly for the neighboring farmers. He was always very intimate with his old employee, Mr. Bellows, speaking of him ever after in the highest terms and praise. There were born to them in Northumberland one daughter and a son. He sold his farm here and purchased the old Partridge homestead in No. Stratford, on which he spent the remainder of his life.

In 1846, Connary settled in the town of Stratford, Coös County, then a town of some 550 people located on the Connecticut River on New Hampshire's northwestern border with Vermont.[3] Comprising the two settlements of North Stratford and Stratford Hollow, the town was granted its charter in 1762 under the name of Woodbury; this charter was regranted in 1773 with the name of Stratford in memory of Stratford-on-Avon, probably via Stratford, Connecticut, from where some of its earliest settlers had come. In Jeannette R. Thompson's impressive *History of the Town of Stratford, New Hampshire, 1773– 1925*, published in 1925, we read the following about Thomas Connary, who was deeply involved in communal affairs: "Thomas Connary, one of Stratford's most worthy citizens, came here in the '40s, and held many important offices during the fifty years of his residence in Stratford. He was selectman and treasurer during the Civil War, and furnished much of the material for the town history of that period."[4]

In this rural New Hampshire setting, which prospered as a farming and logging center, especially with the coming of the Grand Trunk Railway in 1853, Connary lived in his family farmstead with his wife, Lucinda, and their five children, Simon, Mary, John, Joseph, and Anne, until his death in 1899. Connary played a central role in establishing the Catholic mission in Stratford, according to Thompson:

> T. Connary was the first resident Roman Catholic, and to his ardent zeal and fervent piety the present prosperous church owes much for its maintenance through its pioneer days. "Of Mr Connary it may be said with the utmost truthfulness that he has ever borne an irreproachable Christian character as citizen, neighbour, friend; and in business he has maintained the highest type, and no one has been more trusted and honored by his townspeople. Indeed the entire family are numbered among our best citizens." . . . Through Mr. Connary's efforts a Roman

Catholic priest from Montpelier, Vt., came to care for the spiritual needs of the men of that faith who were employed in building the Atlantic and St. Lawrence Railroad, in construction here during the late '40s and early '50s; and Mass was first celebrated in a little building a few rods east of the station. . . . Mr. Connary bought the land on which the present church stands in 1866; but, as a church had been built in Bloomfield, building here was deferred until 1887, when a church was erected at a cost of $3,000.[5]

We know that after starting out with nothing and accepting "the tenth bushel as compensation for his hard labor," Connary, once established, did well and managed his finances deftly. The census record of 1870 for the town of Stratford estimates the value of the Connary real estate at a full $6,000, one of the town's higher valuations. In January 1899 the obituary in the *Coös County Democrat* characterized him as a "deeply religious man" whose "confidence in God was unlimited," while noting that "he was very industrious and of good financial abilities. . . . His generosity to the church of his heart is well known often indeed depriving himself for this end." Connary's contribution to the Catholic mission in the area came not only in the form of donations for the foundation of the Catholic church in Stratford but also in the purchase of the land for the cemetery and church (established in 1879) in Bloomfield, Vermont, across the Connecticut River, a stone's throw from North Stratford. Today, the stained glass window in the Sacred Heart Church in Stratford carries the name Thomas Connary, in memory of the benefactor and the town's first resident Roman Catholic.[6]

Connary's adherence to the Catholic faith was deep and fervent, fueled during his adult life by the diligent reading of Catholic devotional literature. While he collected books throughout most of his life, in later years his identity as a devout Irish American Catholic revolved around, and even gained meaning from, the purchasing, reading, annotating, and sharing of religious books. Records show that Connary was a member of the Stratford Hollow Library Association and that he was one of the twenty-six original subscribers (at the subscription rate of $10) when the Library Hall was constructed in 1884 to house approximately four hundred volumes.[7] Most important, he gathered an impressive private library, predominantly of Catholic devotional, hagiographic, catechetical, and apologetic works, but also of dictionaries and general reference, as well as writing on the subjects of travel and topography, philosophy, and history.

We can only conjecture about the full extent of Connary's library, which must have comprised several hundred volumes (see the appendix). This study looks at a segment of his library that has survived—a collection of about thirty books, nearly all on religious themes, purchased by Connary while he was in the United States from the 1850s onwards, and annotated by him from when he was in his fifties until a few months before his death at the age of eighty-four. It is useful from the outset to list those of Connary's books that figure most prominently in the following discussion. All contain copious annotations and miscellaneous documents.

- James Balmes. *Fundamental Philosophy.* Translated by Henry F. Brownson. 2 vols. New York: D. & J. Sadlier, 1858.
- Elizabeth de Bodenham. *Mrs. Herbert and the Villagers: or, Familiar Conversations on the Principal Duties of Christianity.* 2 vols. (vol. 2 only). Baltimore: Fielding Lucas, Jr., 1853.
- Jean-Pierre Camus. *The Spirit of St. Francis de Sales.* New York: P. O'Shea, 1867.
- M. A. G. Chardon. *Memoirs of a Guardian Angel.* Baltimore: John Murphy, 1873.
- Frederick W. Faber. *All for Jesus: or, The Easy Ways of Divine Love.* Baltimore: John Murphy, 1857.
- *Fables of Aesop and Others.* Translated by Samuel Croxall. New York: Derby & Jackson, 1859.
- St. Francis of Sales. *The True Spiritual Conferences of St. Francis of Sales.* London: Richardson and Son, 1862.
- George Foxcroft Haskins. *Travels in England, France, Italy, and Ireland.* Boston: Patrick Donahoe, 1856.
- Julian of Norwich. *Sixteen Revelations of Divine Love.* Boston: Ticknor and Fields, 1864.
- Thomas H. Kinane. *The Dove of the Tabernacle.* New York: P. M. Haverty, 1876.
- P. R. Leatherman. *Elements of Moral Science.* Philadelphia: James Challen & Son, 1860.
- F. Lewis. [Louis of Granada.] *The Sinner's Guide.* Philadelphia: Henry M'Grath, 1845.
- *The Lives of Eminent Saints.* Boston: Patrick Donahoe, 1853.
- *The Lives of the Fathers of the Desert.* Baltimore: Fielding Lucas, Jr., no year.
- James O'Leary. *A History of the Bible, its Origin, Object, and Structure.* New York: D. & J. Sadlier, 1873.

• Thomas Canon Pope. *The Council of the Vatican and the Events of the Time.* Boston: Patrick Donahoe, 1872.

This group of annotated volumes constitutes a remarkably well-documented—and self-documenting—archive that enables us to map a series of activities centered on the presence and the use of books. Viewed cumulatively, these artifacts allow us to reconstruct moments of reading, a physical setting, and the variety of uses to which the books were put. These traces reveal a dedicated reader for whom the reading of religious works represents precious moments of privacy and intimacy, as well as the reinforcement of social bonds that exist within a closely knit circle of family and friends. For this farmer-bibliophile, books are, quite simply, a necessity of life. Working inside books—reading, annotating, decorating, and pasting notes into them—becomes a means of pious self-fashioning and a dramatization of lived spirituality.

The following passage, found on a handwritten note dated February 12, 1890, and pasted in Julian of Norwich's *Revelations*, is an extraordinary statement about the powerful iconic status that books held for Connary. Written with his eccentric turn of phrase, it reads as a poignant, profound, and highly personal equivalent of Thomas Jefferson's statement that "I cannot live without books," or Jorge Luis Borges's bibliophilic assertion, "I have always imagined that Paradise will be a kind of library."[8]

> I have many Books and cannot think that I can ever be really happy anywhere without them: you will see that I speak of happiness now in this small paper, and when I speak of happiness in it, I speak of eternal everlasting heavenly happiness alone in it. For this one business purpose alone I love my Books, and for no other business purpose, from time I was born to this Wednesday February 12, 1890, I have loved my Books well only for the power which they give to me to have a heavenly home with our divine Creator continually for unending eternity. This way alone of Book keeping is God's way to prosperity and heavenly happiness unending.[9]

This statement, found inside a book especially valued by its owner, is written late in life, as he looks back on his years of laborious accumulation and annotation. In it he begins to convey a sense of a redemptive culture of reading, in which material, utilitarian, and spiritual values are seen to enhance one another. It is this understanding of a redemptive discipline of reading which the following chapters will attempt to analyze in depth.

Studying Used Books: The Plan of the Argument

This study examines fine details of annotation practices and what I shall refer to as book enhancement. It does so to explore how a strikingly opinionated reader-cum-annotator from a somewhat neglected demographic in American cultural and bibliographic history materially manipulated his books to reflect and develop his religious beliefs and practices.

One might characterize the study of marginalia and annotation as microhistory that tends to focus overwhelmingly on what we might call (with an unhelpful epithet) elite culture and on the public and professional annotator. We have studies, for instance, of Gabriel Harvey, the quintessential Renaissance humanist reader, who read, admired, and annotated his classical authors as models of rhetoric in order to prepare himself for debate in the realm of political action. Much has been written about Samuel Taylor Coleridge's inherently social annotations—clearly an archive of shared events of reading—that were circulated among friends and collaborators and eventually published. And we know of the Danish philosopher-theologian Søren Kierkegaard as a skilled exegete through his marginalia: we can follow him combing through his copy of the New Testament for useful references as he prepares his ammunition against the Danish state church, deemed by him to be compromised by decorum, moderation, and complacency.[10] Marginalia can be public, assured, and produced by celebrated figures. But with Thomas Connary we have an example of "the common reader" (to use another unhelpful epithet) from a group that we too rarely regard as active creators or agents, often because so little evidence has survived. I will argue that in his library we witness a powerful statement of personal conviction not to be sneered at for its provincialism or for the simplicity—or, more accurately, rigor—of its theology. We see an intelligence purposefully staging itself, as books are imagined as instruments of social interaction in both domestic and public spheres.

This study has benefited from the recent burgeoning of interest in bibliography, the material culture of the text, paratext, book history, and the social history of literacy. These flourishing areas of study have clearly come into maturity.[11] Two studies in particular have given new attention to manuscript annotation and moved bibliographic and readership studies in an exciting direction: Heather Jackson's *Marginalia: Readers Writing in Books* and William Sherman's *Used Books: Marking Readers in Renaissance England*. Both are groundbreaking and absorbing books, and both have influenced my work with the Connary collection.[12]

Jackson's genre study of marginalia, based on more than two thousand annotated books from the past three centuries, provides a positive assessment of the
phenomenon of writing in books. She argues that such intervention by readers
may usefully be studied as documentation of varied social experiences of interest to historians, biographers, and critics. Countering a too-facile dismissal of
the genre of marginalia as sporadic, individualistic, and often quixotic, Jackson
shows it to be full of complex motivation and historical circumstance: it even
emerges in her study as a genre with a distinct social history, indicative of different psychologies of reading, as indeed does the condemnation of marginalia
(prohibitions against the marking of books abound from the mid-nineteenth
century on, with the establishment of the public library system).[13] In two case
studies, Jackson demonstrates convincingly how marginalia by S. T. Coleridge
and writing found in copies of Boswell's *Life of Johnson*, when examined carefully and cumulatively, provide revealing insights into habits of reading and
constitute valid evidence for the history of the book and reading.[14]

Where Jackson largely focuses on the British reading culture of the eighteenth and early nineteenth centuries, Sherman's *Used Books* provides a welcome exploration of readers' marks and writing from the fifteenth century to
the seventeenth. With a preference for the more capacious term "book use"
over "book reading," Sherman offers rich evidence of an early modern culture
of the book in which the recording of useful and meaningful notes in the
blank spaces of a book was normative. This was a culture, he notes, in which
the word "mark" (as in "mark my words") meant "making books [one's] own
by making marks in and around them" long before it came to mean "noticing"
or "observing."[15] As with Jackson's *Marginalia*, *Used Books* presents two
detailed case studies of specific readers' creative book modification and annotation: the commonplace book of the prominent Elizabethan lawyer Sir Julius
Caesar, used by him over six decades, and a 1571 copy of Ferdinand Columbus's biography of his father, thoroughly annotated by the well-known Elizabethan scholar John Dee. These case studies examine hybrid forms of reading
and writing that reveal both an "unexpected intimacy and vitality" of annotating habits as well as the centrality of such habits to scholarship and power
politics in Tudor England.[16]

Combining valuable case studies with pertinent methodological considerations, Jackson and Sherman thus reorient our understanding of the book
culture of past centuries toward a dialogic relationship between books and
readers, where books accommodate responses to text, and where readers regard
their annotations less as private records than as conventional and public—and
in some cases even collaborative. Both studies, it should be noted, prioritize

certain modes of interaction with the printed book. First, they scrutinize remarkable volumes annotated by remarkable individuals, most often with a publicly performative dimension. For Jackson, who favors what she calls a "period of sociability," Coleridge becomes the paradigm for the sociable or professional annotator in whose circle personally annotated volumes were exchanged, often to make a display of learning or critical skills, with annotations operating according to "well, if unconsciously, agreed conventions." For Sherman, too, examining reading and writing practices of (mostly prominent or professional) book users in Renaissance England reveals shared codes of communication: whether designed to organize knowledge, to structure worship, or to cultivate a public persona in the realm of Elizabethan connections and politics, we see the traces of a consistent habit of annotating as part of a collective elite culture of reading. Second, and not altogether unreasonably, Jackson and Sherman examine book markings with a discernable, even symbiotic, association between text and readers' markings. Book annotation can endorse, facilitate reference, function as a mnemonic aid, or talk back critically to the text and its author, but it is always understood to respond directly and often discursively to the text at hand. In Jackson's words, "the essential and defining character of the marginal note throughout its history is that it is a responsive kind of writing permanently anchored to preexisting written words."[17]

This study adds to the valuable work carried out by Jackson, Sherman, and others, and it follows Sherman in preferring terms other than "reading" and "marginalia." In the books under consideration here, annotated and enhanced by Thomas Connary, we find remnants of past reading and we come across extensive marginal annotation, but these form only part of a much broader spectrum of activities performed with and around books. Sherman's consideration of hybrid book forms that merge print and manuscript, public and private, production and consumption are of particular relevance to my study of one book user who values books as much for the text they contain as for their capacity to function as a storehouse for miscellaneous items.[18] The personalized library of Thomas Connary allows us to add further complexity to the reality of marginalia and book use and to see markings in books take a far greater diversity of forms than so far appreciated. His books constitute a complex record of use and reader response; the same material shows reading and book marking as structured, planned activities, but also as springing up spontaneously and as extravagantly unsystematic. Often this material defies the taxonomies developed by Jackson and Sherman and complicates their assumptions about writing in books as conventionalized, argumentative, corrective, or professional. Furthermore, Connary's writing in books often cannot be said to be directly responsive to the print in any clear sense (i.e., engaging directly or argumentatively with the ideas in a text), although in some cases it obviously is. Even less can it be understood in any straightforward way in terms of the distinction between public and private that is integral to Jackson's characterization of the genre of marginalia.

For Connary, the use of books is one of co-creation, in which the object is augmented and embellished as a precious devotional memorial. Interleavings (i.e., clusters of densely written notebook pages inserted between the pages of print), instead of marginal annotation, are far more conspicuous features of Connary's labors in books. For more than three decades, he performs the painstaking task of copious interleaving, inserting himself into books piously, prayerfully, and autobiographically.

It is inevitable that we resort to terms such as "eccentric" and "idiosyncratic" to convey the striking nature of the material evidence under consideration here. We might do well to remind ourselves of what Anthony Grafton refers to as the "obstinate, irreducible individualism" of the reader, and Jackson's observation that the collective profile of past readers "can only be a group portrait of individuals."[19] Indeed, when focusing on such singular evidence and conducting, as I shall do here, a detailed forensic exercise in order to partly reconstruct a reading history and a pattern of use, we should acknowledge that most conjectures about the use of books and past events of reading are epistemologically uncertain, with a somewhat solipsistic side to them. But, on the other hand, we should not be overly reluctant or embarrassed to use whatever material remains we may come across to assist us in the important endeavor of reconstructing past encounters with, and perceptions of, books. When we examine the archive of Connary's books and documents we find material that is irreducibly individualistic and eccentric, but also understood by the owner to have profound social implications. In reading and book collecting we find welcome opportunities for silence and introversion, but books can also prepare a reader for social interaction, assist in the management of a household, and reinforce social bonds. The discipline that Thomas Connary refers to as his "Book keeping" always takes place within a larger continuum of activities that situate him in public life and in networks of social and domestic responsibility.

The following chapters examine not only routines and methods of book collecting but also the complex motivations and the historical circumstances that underlie the use of books. By analyzing Thomas Connary's writing and annotation habits in depth, and regarding these as always engaged in a form of intertextual dialogue with the contents of his books, we can gain new insights into the religious culture of New England Catholicism, religious tension and tolerance, the publishing of religious literature, and the capacity of such literature to guide religious desire, social activity, and moral discipline. Such an approach means to follow Jackson, Sherman, and others in moving beyond one dominant tendency in current book history research that examines books owned, purchased, or borrowed as recoverable and the source for quantifiable information, while marginalizing the book *read* as private and irrecoverable. Indeed, this study will foreground the physical remains of past acts of reading in order to examine creative uses and appropriations of the book object. The aim is to offer an interpretive account of a complex process that produces an enhanced aesthetic around the material artifact of the book and explores its phenomenal depth.

Accounting for this process of creative book alteration leads one naturally to the term "appropriation." Jackson, for example, refers to the production of marginalia as "an act of self-assertive appropriation," and, as Matthew Brown notes, the term has become a dominant critical concept in readership studies, capturing more than any other a reigning paradigm:

> Readership history rightly suggests that readers in the past can be posited as neither fully dominated by the culture of a ruling elite nor fully free to make a text mean anything they want it to mean. A conceptual solution to this problem has been to cast reading as an act of appropriation. Readers are hemmed in by genres and traditions, and within such controlled contexts—even in a pious culture of humility and rote repetition—they actively appropriate textual matter. . . . Given this dialectic of freedom and control, of play and constraint, readership historians advocate, when turning to individual readers, a sensitivity to conscious uses and appropriations as means to measure the creative, critical, or submissive habits of readers.[20]

It is quite useful to see Connary's interaction with his books as a process of appropriation, and as a particularly creative mode of appropriation at that. But, like Brown, I wish to use the term "appropriation" guardedly, especially when this is taken, as it often is, to suggest the reader's subversive or consciously aggressive and transgressive approach to the book and reading. In his groundbreaking study of the rituals of reading among theocentric Puritans in early New England, Brown demonstrates in exemplary fashion how the concept of the reader's appropriation of textual matter can be nuanced through an analysis sensitive to historical, geographical, and theological factors.[21] In this study I take a similar path by devoting attention to the cultural, bibliographical, and theological contexts that surround Connary's archive of annotated books. Ultimately, the term "appropriation," as a single critical term, cannot capture the range of highly personal, often contradictory, modes of Connary's interactions with his books. Probably no one single term can do justice to the numerous ways in which the book artifact can function crucially, and signify diversely, within the rhythms and reiterations of spiritual life.

This examination of Thomas Connary's book enhancements is centrally concerned with four subjects: reading, paratext, obsession, and epiphany. In the remainder of this introduction, I briefly introduce my approach to these subjects and outline a plan of the argument.

Reading

I have already stated my preference for the term "book use" over "reading": in some cases reading can take second place to other forms of interaction with the book, some of which may give little heed, or none at all, to the contents of the printed text. This is certainly true in Connary's case, but he also reveals much about himself as a reader and about the flexibility and development of his reading processes. In the chapters that follow, we look first at what kinds of books he reads before proceeding to consider the question of *how* he reads and enhances his books. Chapter 1 provides an overview of the contents of Connary's library and examines the supply end of Irish American book production that catered to the practical needs and ardent devotional Catholicism of the post-Famine generation. Connary's library provides a comprehensive and highly personal representation of a rich diaspora print culture, and in it we find the names of most of the notable individuals in Irish American writing in the latter half of the nineteenth century, whether authors, translators, or publishers. The appendix lists the books known to have been in the possession of Connary and his family. This accumulation of books cannot be said to be truly representative of publishing output and collecting trends, but it nonetheless gives a good impression of the types of reading programs that helped shape the flourishing of Catholic communities in the decades following the first wave of Irish immigration into America.

This archive of books and annotations provides occasional glimpses of a systematic and attentive reader, one who is stirred devotionally and enabled theologically from repeated, in-depth reading. Such productive exchange between text and reader will be highlighted in this study, which is in part motivated by the observation that much current book history and readership study gives very little sustained or analytic attention to the text. We will examine those instances when we see Connary as an astute and critical reader in an impassioned dialogue with the content of his books. The approach is to read Connary's annotations closely alongside the passages that they gloss, to show how an understanding of textual content is a prerequisite to fully appreciating the reader's extensive and intertextual gloss of prayer and theological reflection. Two of the most treasured and densely annotated books in his library are in the genre of the spiritual auto-biography, and we will consider how these influence his thinking on salvation, social obligation, and the good life.

The purposes and practices of Connary's reading are diverse and overlapping. He reads husbandry manuals for knowledge about livestock and farming, and he relies on a range of practical and didactic writings for his management of the corporeal and moral welfare of his family. He consults a broad range of titles for general knowledge on geographical, political, and historical topics, while books on Irish culture and history kindle nostalgic longing and are instrumental in cultivating a sense of Irish rootedness in the Connary family. Catechetical and theological works are employed to bolster religious education in the household, and a devotional literature, often of a mystical flavor, fuels an already ardent Catholic faith. (These categories of reading material are surveyed in greater detail in chapter 1.)

Accompanying such diversity of goals in Connary's reading is a multiplicity of reading processes and reader response. With access to a considerable number of books owned and used by the same reader, we can make some assessment of the complex modalities of reading, and we may see how each instance of reading is part of an evolving routine, with different elements attended to and with varying levels of intensity.[22] It is difficult to assign Connary's reading habits to a single, unified category; he habitually and unproblematically merges oppositions to which scholars often resort in the attempt to understand past traditions of book use.[23] Connary reads both extensively *and* selectively, and he reads intensively, with texts becoming the focus of concentrated, even meditative reading. Sometimes he responds to the text as a whole, but more often his concern is with local particulars, his attention fixed on a paragraph or even a word, not on the broader picture.

However fragmented the evidence, the enhanced books yield some insight into the microprocesses of reading and into the distinction made in cognitive psychology between on-line and off-line processes in readers' experience and interpretation of the text.[24] On-line processes involve the immediate reading and comprehension of the text. Reading performed in the here and now may lead the reader to write occasional elaborations and corrigenda in the margin, to underline or otherwise mark as he or she goes along, to record reading times and other reading context, or to add spontaneous remarks that highlight and endorse specific passages. These are traces that indicate repetitions and the immediate experience of reading, sometimes showing that considerable mental effort is associated with the act of reading, and sometimes suggesting how reading can be a spur to imaginative, nostalgic, or meditative flights motivated by a passage or a few words. Such on-line reading is of a different nature than off-line processes that take place when reading is interrupted or concluded and more comprehensive consideration and interpretation is possible. At this level, antipathy or sympathy with a text or its author can be established and recorded, texts can be combined and integrated in myriad ways, or a work can be understood in the light of established dominant ideas.

In Connary's case, much of his interaction with books seems detached from any act of reading, and evidence is particularly rich for off-line activity, in which texts are routinely combined with, and assimilated to, a complex of strongly held moral and religious beliefs. Another form of off-line activity also documented amply in the material is the recording of details about the reading situation and programs of book use. Often book historians rely on such records preserved apart from the books read, in diaries, notebooks, book reviews, and the like, but with Connary we find observations of this sort carefully preserved inside books on interleaved notebook pages. Chapters 2, 3, and 4 examine a variety of on-line and off-line processes in Connary's reading activities, but they also show the difficulty of keeping these processes entirely separate. For example, it can be difficult to determine whether an inserted note that disagrees with a point in the text represents an on-line or off-line response, as these may differ very little in form and substance, and a handwritten record of date and time is oftentimes ambiguous, as it may indicate a moment of actual reading or another form of book use and enhancement disengaged from the act of reading.

To examine Connary's book uses, this study proceeds by a form of forensic bibliographic method. This involves paying close attention to factors indicating patterns of book handling and reading, such as underlinings, manuscript punctuation, forms of emendation, inserted bookmarks, wear and tear of pages and bindings, deposits on or between the pages, and imported elements such as decorative embellishments and additional text (print or manuscript). It means also investigating the circumstances of reading—by looking, for example, at contextual statements about the reading situation, datings, ownership records, notes about procurement, evidence of shared book use, and personalized indices and reading plans.

Approaching Connary's radically customized volumes through a type of in-depth bibliographic inquiry allows us to make inferences about the diversity of book uses and to form an impression of reading practices that are intensive and extensive, silent and vocalized, withdrawn and communal. Past acts of reading can never be transparent to us now, only partially reconstructed. However, it is one of the tasks of the book historian to make educated, plausible conjectures about reading habits by attending to the physical particulars of the material objects before us, by building on what a rich literature on reading history and reading processes past and present has taught us, and by carefully situating and historicizing books and audiences.

Paratext

Gérard Genette's famous typology of the paratext has brought with it a new awareness of how concrete textual presentation is crucial to the experience of reading and the production of meaning.[25] "Paratext" is defined as the accompanying textual elements, supplied by authors, editors, or publishers, that surround the main text and influence the reception of the text and its interpretation by the public.[26] Paratext consists of elements both internal and external to the book. The internal elements (the "peritext") include framing components, such as the cover, typesetting, authorial attribution, title, list of contents, preface, and illustration, while elements situated outside the book (the "epitext") cover a large complex of public or private contexts that surround a text and bear on its reception, such as interviews, reviews, correspondence, and private conversation. The latter is a far more blurred territory of implicit contexts with no precise limits, "circulating, as it were, freely, in a virtually limitless physical and social space."[27] For Genette, paratext as a conceptual category converges toward authorial intention: paratextual elements constitute the threshold into the text, guiding the reader's engagement with, and understanding of, the text, and they are inserted by the author or by the editor or publisher (a reason, perhaps, why both Jackson or Sherman bypass the theme of the paratext in their studies of readers' markings in books).[28]

This study argues that Genette's survey, which was never intended to be exhaustive nor directly concerned with development and historical context, can usefully be broadened to involve a broader range of phenomena that are in no direct sense authorial or editorial.[29] Paratext can perform other functions than to ensure that a text is read "correctly" according to the author's intention. It can include the co-creativity of the reader and those elements (sometimes highly distinct) inserted by the reader that impact and shape the reading experience and the full experience of the book. As Peter Stallybrass remarks, "if paratexts make readers, so readers both negotiate paratexts and make new ones."[30]

Thomas Connary is a reader who is highly responsive to the paratext of his books and who demonstrates extraordinary creativity in inserting his own paratextual framing. He fills the margins and the blank front- and endpapers with his own extensive writing; he comments on the author, publisher, printer, typography, book format, the year and place of publication, book binding, and number of pages; and he draws attention in various ways to prefaces, dedications, imprints, lists of contents, plates, and frontispieces. Furthermore, the very nature of the book medium encourages him to produce a voluminous paratextual expansion that is essentially a process of reconstructing the book through the addition of his own materials and written guidelines for reading. In the subsequent chapters, I refer to this more broadly as a process of book enhancement. Chapters 2 and 3 profile Connary's various annotations and book enhancement practices, and they examine the self-styled paratextual apparatus that he layers in books to guide his own reading and that of others. Paratexts proliferate in these enhanced books, and their relation to main text is one of adjacency and collaboration. They take the form of, for example, handwritten dedications and rededications, reading directives, and exhortations, in addition to an elaborate visual paratext consisting of decorative embellishment, framing and dividing lines, and imported plates and illustrations.[31]

All of these paratextual devices work to orchestrate reception and reading practices. They also make possible a multidimensional use of books in which reading directives and the highlighting of passages point to various points of entry into text and facilitate a dynamic navigation of books in which the boundary between text and paratext becomes indistinct. The reader's inserted paratext is the trace of another authority who proposes a new way of processing, ordering, and prioritizing text. This acquires further significance when the owner assumes shared uses of books, intending annotation as paratext to become an integral part of the medium and to determine the experience and actions of subsequent readers. This is the type of socially oriented peritexts characterized by Jason Scott-Warren: "Prompted neither by the author nor by the publisher, these are 'accompanying productions' which aim to influence how a copy of the text will be interpreted by the readers who will later share, or borrow, or buy, or steal, or inherit it. . . . they create a frame for future readers of that volume."[32]

Chapter 3 addresses in detail the social paratext of Connary's books—a particularly performative dimension of the paratext where we find him address-ing his family with dedications, reassurances, and directions.[33] This part exam-ines Connary's attempts to influence the reading activity of his closest social circle, and it extends Genette's idea of the epitext by suggesting that kinship can assert itself as an important part of the social epitext of annotated books: the affection for those closest of kin can be part of the exterior context through which a book is mediated to a reader, and it may become a determining factor in ensuring or constructing a proper reception. The books examined here are rooted in the domestic sphere and inscribed with paternal affection and a shared hope of redemption. When we consider the epitext of Connary's books and the context of the reading situation in a household, we see how closely texts, spaces, and relationships can interpenetrate.

In the following, I deal mostly with evidence internal to the book, using the forensic bibliographic exercise to provide an account of Connary's book enhancements and reading habits. But aspects of social context and the exter-nal epitext that structure the reading experience and enrich its meaning need to figure prominently as well. Among these are lineage and kinship, Irish iden-tity and the experience of emigration, the location of reading and the spatial arrangement of the reading room, and, finally but most overwhelmingly, Irish Catholic devotion. This factor of devotion becomes the overarching context and catalyst for the material enhancements preserved in the form of inserted correspondence, exhortation, and prayers. Devotion is the epitext—both pri-vate and social—which structures the mental world of a reader and which his volumes are made to incorporate.

Obsession

The Connary collection of annotated books immediately confirms the current scholarly orthodoxy that reading is not a passively receptive mode of con-sumption but co-creative, and it supports a widespread perception—expressed, for instance, by Adrian Johns in *The Nature of the Book*—that "an apparently authoritative text, however 'fixed,' could not compel uniformity in the cultures of its reception. In practice, rather the reverse seems to have happened."[34] This is a study of a reader with considerable agency, and, like other studies of enter-prising readers, it can provide nuance and challenge to general or statistical assessments of reading. Moreover, it allows us to understand aspects of readerly intensity and eccentricity in specific reception contexts and acts of reading.[35]

I have already offered commentary on the inescapable idiosyncrasy and uniqueness that characterize any systematic annotator of books. But with Connary we move further into a territory of eccentricity and even obsessive behavior. In her book *Marginalia*, Jackson dedicates a chapter to "fanatic" readers who establish special relationships with particular books that become "dangerously emotional," where the forms of interaction with particular volumes become, in her words, "manifestly over the top."[36] What is not always certain, though, is wherein fanaticism resides for Jackson and precisely how her case studies "define the outer limits of common usage."[37] Among her examples are three kinds of hybrid book forms: the commonplace book, which serves as a personal "filing system" with material culled from diverse sources; the "extra-illustrated" book, into which readers import decorative materials such as prints and magazine clippings; and, finally, treasured Bibles, which "[attract] supplementary materials, almost as an act of worship, certainly in a spirit of reverence."[38] What appears to be the common denominator for these kinds of volumes is that readers apply to them a particular measure of system and enthusiasm. With Thomas Connary, on the other hand, we abandon routine conventionality and the somewhat eccentric to observe a proper fanatic at work.

The final chapter of this study examines the association that can sometimes exist between book annotation and obsession. We enter the realm of the personalized and obsessive to study a reader whose confrontation and collaboration with books appears compulsive at times. For Connary, the prodigious expansion of his books is the material effect of a bibliolatrous obsession and a desire to cling to words and pious proclamations. Pursuing these ideas further brings us into a discussion of issues of psychopathology and mental distress and an exploration of how the enhanced, inscribed book may function as a vessel for nostalgia, personal retrospection, and the retrieval of traumatic memories. Furthermore, by drawing on sources such as U.S. census records and nineteenth-century psychiatric manuals, we are able to understand something about Connary's association with madness in the latter part of his life, when he increasingly came to feel the tenuous nature of physical and mental equilibrium.

Studying Thomas Connary's book use reveals inscrutable eccentricity and a reader for whom the tangible presence of annotated books can alleviate mental afflictions. This is a relationship with books rooted in substance and physical instantiation, as enlarged volumes are being felt, handled, and experienced in routine sessions. But it is also a relationship based on the idea—one not uncommon and with incalculable manifestations through the ages—that books possess redemptive power and are worthy of important ritualized activity. At the core of the obsessive behavioral patterns characterized in this study is a deep consciousness of the book and its rich signifying power.

Epiphany

Laboring in books—writing marginalia and providing other forms of augmentation and decorative enhancement—means to become a co-creator, to infuse a book with additional meaning. In book use is found a space for textual and discursive meaning, and through it Connary maps his thoughts on subjects of theology and the moral life. But laboring in books is equally an aesthetic and devotional exercise, a prayerful activity that acknowledges God's power and presence. Upsetting any bifurcation between surface and depth, interior and exterior that we may instinctively bring to such material, we will examine a mode of book use that fuses spirituality and the sacred with an attention to the manufacture and materiality of the printed book. The treasured object of the book, in its inscribed and augmented state, can preserve the owner's past experiences of clarity and religious intensity.

The following attempts to reawaken the voice of this book collector—a voice that would not speak to us were it not for the accidental survival of his books and papers. For that reason, the writing that follows will be punctuated by quotations from Connary (and longer quotations than is the norm in our scholarship) in order to give a sense of a distinct voice and a distinct vocabulary forged by him for the activity of reading and handling books. Most notably, the five main parts of this study will be interspersed with short sections in which I allow Connary to recount his own religious, epiphanic experiences, while offering some comment on how the experiential dimension lies at the heart of his Catholicism and spiritual self-articulation. From early adulthood, Connary purports to have had a series of spiritual experiences of a felt relationship to the divinity, and these are recorded with considerable precision and narrative force in his annotated books. By structuring this exercise around extensive quotation of Connary's own words, I hope to go some way toward bringing back to life a past reader and a remarkable book-centered devotion with some interesting mystico-theological nuance. In particular, the aim is to convey a sense of an idiosyncratic voice on the margins of history. Connary establishes his own language to capture what, for him, is the essence of devotional literacy and spiritual authenticity.

A reader can assert himself as author, and Connary tells and recounts and provides a considerable extension of the book's signifying power. This study examines aspects of nonprofessional authorship and says something more broadly about the range of opportunities provided by the material book for recording and communicating religious fervor and personal history. But it is necessary to confront the constructed nature of the evidence under investigation. Connary's writing is conditioned by memory, yearning, and narration, and it is as notable for its intensity as for its careful rhetorical craftsmanship, which draws on metaphorical and quasi-mystical registers. One voice entirely dominates the material, holding and asserting interpretive power. It is a voice of unquestionable sincerity, yet also, we need to recognize, one that offers its univocal, idealized depiction of a redemptive reading discipline and seeks to disseminate a distinct language for epiphany and Christian eschatology.

The following chapters shift the focus from a conventional understanding of the author and a perceived fixity of print toward a reader-oriented study of devotional and didactic writing. They explore in detail how books (always spelled in Connary's notes with a capital *B*) are precious inscribed objects, and how the process of inscribing them becomes a form of partaking in the nature of the divine and a mode of prayer. Pursuing such ideas further means that we need to think about dimensions of presence, the sacred, redemption, affective and somatic reading experiences, epiphany, and deixis—dimensions that we are perhaps rather ill-equipped in the present intellectual climate to bring into our study of book history and the history of reading.[39] It is a central claim of this study that such dimensions are crucial to our attempts to understand the power of physical objects to materialize belief and to reconstruct the actual uses, individual and social, of religious writing in print and manuscript culture.

1

IRISH AMERICAN PRINT CULTURE IN THE
NINETEENTH CENTURY: A PRIVATE LIBRARY

This Book was printed for me.

**—Thomas Connary, undated note on the title page
of Camus, *The Spirit of St. Francis de Sales***

A Collector and Reader

This chapter provides an overview of the books in the library of Thomas Connary, purchased, read, and annotated by him in the United States in the latter half of the nineteenth century. The focus will be on him as a member of the Irish expatriate in America and, especially, on the underexplored part of American book history and reading history which is the Irish diaspora print culture. Chapter 2 examines Connary's complex practices of book use, but first I want to consider what the contents of his library tell us about the type of reading material made available by Irish American book publishers catering to Irish expatriate communities.

The surviving collection of books and papers amassed by this farmer from rural New Hampshire provides a particularly interesting perspective on the energetic publishing program through which a trickle of Irish Catholic book publications in the first decades of the nineteenth century became a veritable flood in the 1840s and '50s and thereafter, emerging from the Irish Catholic printing centers in America such as Boston, New York, Philadelphia, and Baltimore. This was a print initiative preceded, and in large measure made possible, by a Protestant print and marketing revolution from the early years of the nineteenth century, in which Bible and religious tract societies became large-scale, nonprofit manufacturers and distributors of print. Endeavoring to reach every American with Protestant Bibles and didactic tract literature, this movement paved the way for the mass production of print in America through the use of the latest manufacturing technologies, especially stereotype printing.[1]

Thomas Connary systematically acquired the products of early Irish and Catholic publishing houses in America in a way that was motivated by a sense of nostalgia for "Old Ireland" as much as by the perceived practical, catechetic, and devotional needs of the head of a larger household. While one should always exercise caution in claiming the representative nature of such personal collections, which are the products of individual tastes and the contingencies of availability, such caution may be particularly urgent here: the sheer number of books collected by Connary, of which just a smaller part can be surveyed here, might well have been outside the reach of his fellow Irish Americans of lesser means, and certainly of those with less determination.

The library of Thomas Connary is characterized above all by its clear utilitarian function and orientation toward practical and devotional guidance within a domestic setting. It shows how mundane concerns of household management and a general active interest in history, politics, and geography blended with spiritual ambition and an interest in moral instruction to provide a rationale for the acquisition of books and other reading materials. There is little place for recreational reading material, by which we may understand publications indulged in for the sake of pleasure (including lighter popular fiction, but not exclusively) rather than moral or religious edification. We also find very little of the earliest pre-Famine body of Irish American writing, which is a particularly rich and resourceful literature of folklore, history, novels, poetry, comedy, and satire and has been expertly surveyed in Charles Fanning's *Irish Voice in America*.[2] Far more prevalent in Connary's library is the Irish immigrant print output of the 1840s and '50s—a uniquely American tradition of ethnic writing designed to guide the Irish in their new setting. This literature was often prone to humorless didacticism and a sentimental moralizing rhetoric, but it also offered real guidance and emotional appeal to many, especially as much of it sought to kindle a devotional Irish Catholicism.[3]

The appendix provides a catalogue of the contents of Connary's library, and it conveys an impression of the reading material generally provided to an Irish immigrant readership with a view toward nourishing and reinforcing Catholic identity. Four books in Connary's possession were especially representative of the owner's interests as a book collector and reader, and characteristic, too, of the wave of Irish American publishing that sought to make suitable Irish Catholic literature obtainable in affordable editions. Published by some of the key houses catering to Irish readers in America, these titles give a sense of what was most often the strongly pious nature of these publication initiatives—as well as of the rather tense sectarian context, in which a diasporic print culture existed to offset predominant Protestant literature, often perceived to be anti-Catholic.

F. Lewis [Louis of Granada], *The Sinner's Guide*
(Philadelphia: Henry M'Grath, 1845)

Thomas Connary's copy of *The Sinner's Guide*, by the famed Dominican theologian and preacher Louis of Granada (1505–1588), is a cloth-bound, dark brown octavo volume with debossed ornament on the front and back boards and a gilded spine depicting a cross surrounded by elaborate floral ornament. The binding shows signs of heavy and frequent use. As the book was regularly pulled from the shelf, its binding shows considerable shelf wear and the head of the spine is missing.

Originally entitled *Guía de Pecadores*, Louis's voluminous exhortation to virtue and obedience was published in Badajoz, Spain, in 1555. In his admiring 1913 entry on Louis of Granada in the *Catholic Encyclopedia*, J. B. O'Connor finds in the *Guía* "a smooth, harmonious style of purest Spanish idiom which has merited for it the reputation of a classic, and an unctuous eloquence that has made it a perennial source of religious inspiration."[4] Indeed, being marked in its English translation by a particularly intimate style of repeated appeals to the reader, homely analogies, and frequent invocation, the work stands out among a flood of early Spanish ascetic and penitential works, and it achieved considerable popularity throughout Europe. Its significant influence on the practical morality and prudent regulation of St. Francis of Sales (1567–1622) is discernable in several works in Connary's library, including St. Francis's *Spiritual Conferences* and *Introduction to the Devout Life*.

The Sinner's Guide is one of many titles in Connary's library that are translated works, often of much older Continental European religious texts. Other translations in Connary's collection include *The Practice of Christian and Religious Perfection* by St. Alphonsus Rodriguez (1532–1617) and James Balmes's (1810–1848) *Fundamental Philosophy*, along with four titles by St. Francis of Sales that were often reprinted by American Catholic presses. Together with a wealth of translations of contemporary Catholic works, mostly German and French, these writings were esteemed on account of their unambiguous didacticism and/or devotional spirituality. They bear witness to what was a publication and translation initiative targeted at Irish Catholic expatriates perceived to be urgently in need of spiritual and moral edification.

Published in Philadelphia in 1845 by Henry M'Grath, who brought out numerous Catholic devotional and apologetic works, *The Sinner's Guide* is referred to by Connary as "an old Book," and he notes that "I had the same work in my native home, Old Ireland." This title is thus one of the many that Connary was familiar with from his early years in Ireland and which he (re-)

acquired when he settled in the United States.[5] The earliest annotation by Connary in the volume is a decoratively swung ownership inscription on the first page of the preface: "Thomas Connary's Book, Stratford Town, Coös County, New Hampshire June 27 anno 1876." It is possible that the book was purchased a long time before such inscription, as is often the case.

That Connary's copy of *The Sinner's Guide* was particularly precious to him is evident from a brief handwritten note dated January 12, 1881, and inserted into the book before the title page: "I will continue to love this Book as a good Book, as long as God will be good in every respect—it plainly represents divine Truth in every respect." Connary spent considerable time and effort on decorating this volume, which contains more than fifteen inserted pages, double-sided and densely written, of prayers, religious reflections, and miscellaneous recordings, many of which will be discussed in the following chapters. The flyleaves and endpapers accommodate a particularly rich selection of Bible quotations, prayers, poetry, newspaper fragments, and printed illustrations of the Passion and Resurrection of Christ, all written or pasted in by Connary.

Thomas H. Kinane, *The Dove of the Tabernacle*
(New York: P. M. Haverty, 1876)

Thomas H. Kinane (1835–1913), parochial vicar of Templemore, North Tipperary, and dean of Cashel from 1888 to 1913, published his most famous devotional work under the somewhat fanciful but memorable title *The Dove of the Tabernacle; or The Love of Jesus in the Most Holy Eucharist* with J. F. Fowler in Dublin in 1873. The text appeared the same year from P. M. Haverty in New York, a bookseller, importer, and publisher of Irish-related material (including the popular *Haverty's Irish-American Illustrated Almanac*), and it quickly went through several editions in Europe and America. (The twenty-eighth edition was published with M. H. Gill in Dublin in 1884.) Kinane's work was an immediate best seller, undoubtedly due in no small measure to its strong promotion by the *Irish Catholic Magazine*—and the fact that it appeared with the authoritative testimony of no fewer than fourteen members of the Irish episcopate, as well as a glowing preface by Patrick Leahey, archbishop of Cashel.

A contemporary review in the *Irish Monthly* characterized *The Dove of the Tabernacle* as "the work of zeal achieved amidst the labours of a rural parish" and commended it for the "fullness and accuracy with which the Scripture arguments for the Real Presence are expounded in what is meant to be merely a simple popular treatise of devotion."[6] Being first and foremost intended to inflame pious sensitivity and fervent devotion to the Sacred Heart of Jesus, Kinane's work presents, in a detailed yet accessible manner, scriptural arguments for the Real Presence, wrapping these in ardent prayers and exclamations. Didactic and catechetic expositions are followed by pious resolutions and admonitions to self-scrutiny, such as the following:

Resolution.

MY dearest Jesus! Thy church, where Thou dost ever dwell, is as holy as the Sanctuary at Loretto. Year after year, O Lord, we read, with sighs and tears, of some sanctuary profaned, some altar or tabernacle containing the "Holy of Holies" desecrated. I adore Thy patience. To try to make reparation for all, and for my own irreverences, I resolve never to be guilty, either in word, or look, or dress, or gesture, of anything unworthy of the sanctity of Thy house, and always "to reverence Thy sanctuary." "Thy church, O Lord, is the house of God and gate of heaven" (*Gen.*, xxviii. 17).

Divine Host! Make me faithful to this resolution.[7]

Not only does Connary provide affirmation by signing his name below this declaration in Kinane's text (as he does to declarations throughout the volume), but he also repeats in the margin in his own hand the sentence which must have intrigued him: "My dearest Jesus! Thy church where Thou dost ever dwell, is as holy as the Sanctuary at Lorette. Thomas Connary."

Connary's copy of *The Dove of the Tabernacle*, printed by P. M. Haverty in 1876, is a dainty and compact sixteenmo size (17 × 10 cm) of 323 pages, bound in red cloth with decorated black borders to the boards. At the center of the front and back covers is the central insignia of the Sacred Heart wrapped in the Crown of Thorns, from the top of which appears the Cross amid flames. On the front pastedown is evidence of how Connary obtained this volume: the original price sticker reads, "Nicholas Williams, Catholic Bookseller, Boston, 75c." The covers of the volume are rubbed and show severe wear to edges and spine; the hinges have cracked and several single pages have separated. One of Connary's many penned notes in this volume is written on the final endpaper and dated "3 O'clock in the afternoon, June 30th 1896," stating that "children destroyed a portion of this Book. Now I mark it again as my own beautiful Book." Judging from the amount of wear and damage, this was one of the books in most frequent use by Connary. Its status as a devotional best

seller commended by Catholic Ireland must have been of particular significance to him. Over twenty years, from 1878 to 1898, he inserted into the volume more than thirty handwritten pages of prayers and elaborate decoration,
as well as appeals and religious exhortations intended for reading by his family.

James Balmes, *Fundamental Philosophy*, translated by
Henry F. Brownson (New York: D. & J. Sadlier, 1858)

The first English translation of the Spanish Catholic priest Jaume Llucià
Balmes's (1810–1848) *Filosofia Fundamental* was that published by D. & J. Sadlier from their offices in William Street on lower Manhattan in New York.
First offered for sale in 1856, Balmes's comprehensive systematic philosophy
was regularly reprinted by the family-owned publishing house through the
latter half of the nineteenth century, with approximately one new print
appearing each decade.

When the brothers Denis and James Sadlier moved from Ireland to New
York in 1832 (one year before Connary made the journey) to publish works
addressing the spiritual and educational needs of an exponentially growing
Irish community, they founded what by the early 1850s would be the largest
publishing house in America.[8] Among its earliest publishing endeavors were a
Catholic Bible (the Douai-Rheims version), a German-language New Testament, and Alban Butler's *Lives of the Fathers, Martyrs, and Other Principal
Saints*. The Sadliers also eventually acquired the *New York Tablet*, an important
Catholic weekly newspaper in which a large proportion of the stories and
novels of the prolific Mary Anne Sadlier, James Sadlier's wife, appeared in
serial form. Romantic in expression, her writings were inspirational and edifying to many Irish American Catholics.[9]

With Balmes's *Fundamental Philosophy* we are at the more intellectually
challenging end of the Sadlier range. In this comprehensive exposition of the
scholastic system of thought, Balmes adopted and adapted the philosophy of
St. Thomas Aquinas to the intellectual debates of his day. Devoting his early
university years to the exclusive study of St. Thomas's *Summa Theologica* and
commentaries thereon (only occasionally allowing himself to indulge in Chateaubriand's *Genius of Christianity*), Balmes produced an elaborate rationalist
system of epistemology, ontology, and metaphysics designed to put logic back
on track after what was seen as a dominant and damaging strand of Cartesian
skepticism in European thinking.[10] Other notable writings by Balmes include
a translation, with an introduction, of the maxims of St. Francis of Sales (1840)

and the important *Protestantism and Catholicity Compared in Their Effects on the Civilization of Europe* (1844; also in Connary's library). The latter was his intellectual and restrained, even tolerant, critique of Protestantism, which quickly saw translation into French, Italian, German, and English.[11]

That Thomas Connary was interested in Balmes's biography is evident from a newspaper clipping dated, in Connary's hand, March 18, 1882, and pasted to the final contents pages of the first volume. Written by an anonymous "veritas" from Ellsworth, Wisconsin, it lists in encyclopedic style the main achievements of the "learned theologian, profound philosopher, and enlightened publicist." This is one of numerous paste-ins in the volume from different papers and magazines on subjects as varied as the death of Captain Nelson, who accompanied Henry M. Stanley on one of his African expeditions; the disposition of the ideal farmer's wife ("ever presenting the bright side, and concealing nothing but her own sorrow"); and the unprecedented crisis between the Egyptian Khedive and the British government following the British dismissal of the newly established Fakhri cabinet in January 1893.

Connary's copy of Balmes is in two large, compact octavo volumes totaling 1,081 pages, bound in blue cloth with blind-stamped pattern on the boards and gilt title on the spine. The volumes contain much of Connary's own writing in the form of religious reflections, transcribed poetry and letters to and from local postmasters, as well as several addresses to his children that instruct them to preserve his books and annotations. The annotations and inserted pages date from March 1871 to March 1897, with a particular concentration in the summer of 1881. The earliest marking is in the form of an ownership note on the first page of the introduction: "Thomas Connary's Property, Stratford, Coös County, New Hampshire—March 28th 1871." Some marginal notations serve to direct Connary's reading, as we see for instance on page 1: "see and read pages 31 and 32, Chapter IV, Section 51 of this Book." But, such directives aside, very few of the annotations or inserted pages pertain directly to content in the text. The fact that the two volumes show little wear, apart from moderate shelf wear, suggests that Connary may have done little regular reading of Balmes's *Fundamental Philosophy*. However, when Balmes formulates the epistemic certainties of his commonsense philosophy (offered as an antidote to the Cartesian project of universal doubt), they resonate very strongly with the assured proclamatory tone in which Connary's writings assert belief and moral conviction. Especially appealing to Connary is Balmes's firmly declared adherence to the Catholic faith throughout his *Fundamental Philosophy*, not least when the Spanish author concludes that "[a] careful study of the objections brought against Christianity, lays bare a truth confirmed by the history of eighteen centuries; the most weighty objections against Catholicity, instead of proving any thing against it, involve a proof which confirms it."[12] Later I will suggest that the tolerance of intellectual and religious difference that characterizes Balmes's writing finds a parallel in the reflections of Connary.

George Foxcroft Haskins, *Travels in England, France, Italy, and Ireland* (Boston: Patrick Donahoe, 1856)

If the family-owned Sadlier publishing house was one of the key providers of spiritual and educational material to a rapidly growing Irish American Catholic community, that founded by Patrick Donahoe, who emigrated from Ireland to Boston in 1821 at ten years of age, was surely another. This indefatigable entrepreneur and deft salesman established his flourishing Boston business by producing a vast range of affordable Catholic publications and a very popular news magazine (and, additionally, offering a wide range of Catholic devotional paraphernalia). One of his characteristic publishing initiatives was his series of Catholic Books for the Poor, consisting of a selection of thirty-two-page pamphlets in the small thirty-twomo format (14 × 9 cm), each with the life of a saint, "embellished with a splendid engraving," and priced at three cents. It was Donahoe's declared ambition to remain dedicated "in the endeavor to reproduce, in a cheap form, many of the very valuable works issued from time to time in Europe, which, from the high price when imported, or otherwise, are out of the reach of the majority of Catholics of America, and also . . . to extend and bring out, at a small price, the copyright works of American writers."[13]

One example of Donahoe's European Catholic material is Louis Gaston de Ségur's polemical *Plain Talk about the Protestantism of To-Day*, published in 1868, which bears the imprimatur of the bishop of the diocese of Boston and the testimony of the archbishop of Baltimore: "Plain Talk I regard as an excellent Book for circulation. It will do an immense good." Appearing with the characteristic ten pages of the publisher's advertisements at the rear of the volume, the preliminary title page also becomes a place of advertisement, carrying a price of 25 cents, and the further reduced prices of "twenty-five copies, $5; fifty copies, $10; one hundred copies, $15." One of the advertisement pages states triumphantly about Ségur's *Plain Talk*,

The Cheapest Book Ever Published!!!

MR. DONAHOE has endeavored for years to furnish books at as cheap rates as the Protestant booksellers, and much lower than the publications of the Catholic publishers. This he has been enabled to do, from the fact that his publications are manufactured in his own buildings, and receive his personal superintendence. It is a mistake, therefore, to say that "Catholics have not cheap books." It may be that other publishers do not issue cheap books, but the charge against our establishment is not correct. And if the "gropers after truth" will give us a call, or send by letter, they will find our books are cheaper than any in the country. We challenge comparison. Remember, we allude to **OUR OWN PUBLICATIONS**.

This is the confident voice of one of North America's most successful and enterprising nineteenth-century publishers catering to the rising Catholic population, and it shows how the highest significance is attached to the availability and affordability of books within the divided religious scene of New England. For an ambitious publisher like Donahoe, it became a matter of principle to match the achievement of Protestant societies like the American Tract Society and the American Bible Society, which had considerable success in making books cheap and plentiful through power printing, stereotyping, and systematic distribution.[14]

The vast majority of Donahoe's publications can be classed as devotional and catechetic. Most of these were offered in inexpensive octavo or twelvemo cloth-bound volumes, with a few titles—chiefly standard Catholic prayer books likely to be valued as aids to personal and public devotion—offered in a wide range of bindings. One example of the latter is *St. Joseph's Manual, Containing a Selection of Prayers for Private and Public Devotion*, published by Donahoe in 1853 in a small, sturdy eighteenmo volume (16.5 × 10 cm) of 696 pages, and offered for sale in seventeen different binding options, ranging from "strongly bound in sheep" priced at fifty cents to the *de luxe* "velvet, mountings with morocco case" at ten dollars.[15]

In 1856, Patrick Donahoe published *Travels in England, France, Italy, and Ireland*, by the Rev. George Foxcroft Haskins (1806–1872), in a 292-page octavo volume.[16] Haskins, who converted to Catholicism in 1840 and was ordained a priest in 1844, was founder and rector of the House of the Angel Guardian in Boston, a school for orphan and destitute Catholic boys aged nine to sixteen. He obtained considerable state funds and donations for his welfare initiatives, with many donations coming from the non-Catholic community and demonstrating his function as a "liaison between Catholics and secular leaders."[17] On more than one occasion, Haskins toured England, Ireland, France, Italy, and Belgium with a view to visiting orphanages, reform schools, and other charitable institutions, and these tours provided the material for his two travel books.[18]

In the Boston of Haskins's day, as Peter Holloran has shown, social welfare and charity for children had become determined by the sectarian divide between Protestants and Catholics and the formation of a dual institutional system. It is this background of sectarianism, and a common rhetoric of overt indignation, which set the theme for Haskins's *Travels*. In fact, as Haskins asserts in his introduction, the very rationale for the publication is to offset the Protestant travel descriptions that dominated the market:

> The Catholics of this country, though for the most part poor, are fond of reading. Many religious works, and some few histories, and tales, and political essays are the principal books within their reach. Books of travels they have none. With regard to the customs and doings of other nations they have little means of obtaining information except from Protestant tourists. But their productions, even the best of them, are so well seasoned with sneers and misrepresentations, perhaps unintentional, of the practices, ceremonies, customs, &c., of Catholic countries, that, instead of being instructive, they are pernicious and dangerous.[19]

The descriptions that follow predictably laud the superior virtue, philanthropy, and religious observance of the Catholics whom Haskins encounters on his tours, while what is diagnosed as Protestant ignorance and decadence is described in a manner aloof and patronizing. An anecdote relates an encounter in the Church of the Annunciation in Florence with an American artist who dismisses a group of monks as "a set of rascals," and this provides Haskins with

> one among many facts that have convinced me of how little value are the opinions and judgments of Protestants, though otherwise intelligent and agreeable men, on all questions touching the faith of Catholics. Is it that, with all their pains and money expended in the attainment of a collegiate education, they have, after all, only acquired a vast amount of IGNORANCE? Is it that all their intelligence, and refinement, and polite accomplishments, are a mere external whitening? Is it that, though adopting Christian names, they are, in fact, no better at heart than the

equally polished and accomplished gentlemen of the age of Cæsar Augustus?[20]

As a counterweight to Protestant worldliness and spiritual laxity, Haskins notes that any "reflecting and unprejudiced tourist in Ireland" cannot help but admire the people's "shining virtue" and firm and inflexible attachment to the Catholic faith.[21] Haskins represents a widespread understanding among many contemporary Irish Catholic clergy in America of a natural convergence of an Irish identity and genuine American ideals, rather than a collision of disparate cultures. Indeed, at the center of his American teleology is the incorporation of Irish ethnicity—of these "apostles of Christianity," "destined to be the pioneers and heralds of the true faith."[22] When it comes to ensuring the inviolable conservation of the American Constitution, Haskins insists that the Irish are the "essential auxiliaries," having "abjured and cast away the constitution of England": "Fuse them into the American character, and I know of no people on the Earth that would stand forth on the pages of history at once so dignified, so virtuous, so brave, so illustrious."[23]

There is little if any evidence that Connary thought along the lines of the opinionated Haskins, or sympathized much with his rhetoric of sectarianism and indignation. As the next chapters will show, Connary's interests lay elsewhere, especially in silent, pragmatic assimilation into New Hampshire village life and its institutions, in local church life, and in the day-to-day management, practical and spiritual, of a sizeable family homestead.

Connary's copy of Haskins's *Travels* is an octavo volume in quarter leather and maroon cloth binding, with blind-stamped border design to the boards and gilt lettering on the spine. It is evident that Connary accorded no special value to the thirteen pages of advertisements at the rear of the volume, because copious newspaper and magazine clippings have been pasted across advertised titles (the subject of some discussion in the next chapter). The annotation and leaves inserted by Connary are much less extensive than in, for instance, Balmes's *Fundamental Philosophy* or Kinane's *Dove of the Tabernacle*. They consist mostly of his routine prayers, religious assertions, and some diary recordings, with no direct association to, or commentary on, Haskins's text.

Periodicals and Newspapers

A note by Thomas Connary in *The Sinner's Guide* (and found in several other volumes) states that "I had the same work in my native home, Old Ireland,"

and it provides some insight into the tandem nature of European and North American Catholic print enterprises. Donahoe's declared aim, as we saw, was to "reproduce many of the very valuable works issued from time to time in Europe." For Connary, the reacquisition of Catholic literature was motivated in part by nostalgia, by a desire to be once again with the books available in "Old Ireland" that helped structure early religious education, and in part by a perceived need for spiritual guidance and catechetical instruction in the new setting of his New Hampshire family homestead.

We need to recognize, too, the central importance of newspapers and magazines, from which Connary pasted innumerable clippings—on a wide range of subjects—into his books wherever blank space allowed. The key publication here is the *Boston Pilot*, which was to become the official newspaper for the Archdiocese of Boston, published weekly since 1829 and an important organ for Catholic opinion, particularly with the Irish in New England.[24] From 1838 until his death in 1901, Patrick Donahoe was the editor and proprietor of the *Pilot*, which remains in print to this day as one of America's oldest Catholic newspapers. An advertisement at the back of Haskins's *Travels* of 1856 offers a subscription to the newspaper "at the low price of $2.50 a year" and advertises the *Pilot* as "a journal devoted to the welfare of the Irish race in America. It contains news from all parts of Ireland, and other countries, and is a faithful guide to the emigrant in his new home." Also represented in Connary's compendium of newspaper and magazine items are clippings from the *Boston Weekly Globe* (published from 1873 until 1892, when it was absorbed by the *Boston Daily Globe*), as well as the more local *Coös Republican* (published 1855–81, from Lancaster, New Hampshire), and the *People and Patriot* (1883–92, from Concord, New Hampshire). In the copy of Julian of Norwich's *Revelations*, we find inserted correspondence to and from the *Pilot* and the *Coös County Democrat* pertaining to Connary's settlement of subscription fees and the purchase of almanacs.[25] In the same volume is found Connary's own duplicate copy of a letter dated November 24, 1884, that was sent to the publishers of the *New England Homestead*, opening thus: "Though I have now much more papers and books than I have time to read I send thirty cents to you in this, that you may let me have in justice to yourselves for it a few numbers of your paper."[26]

Worthy of note is the diverse nature of Connary's newspaper and journal subscriptions, which included papers from both sides of the sectarian divide as well as widely disseminated New England papers and more local, parochial periodicals. Connary might well have been heeding advice such as that in Rev. John O'Hanlon's *Irish Emigrant's Guide for the United States* (published by

Donahoe in 1851 and in Connary's library) concerning household reading and
newspaper subscription: "The trifling expense of a dollar to two or three a year,
will not be an object with most men, and the amount of intelligence communicated both to himself and the members of his family, will amply compensate
him for the outlay. It should be observed that if this paper be a religious one,
he should subscribe for that published in or near his own diocese, if only to
encourage the efforts of a local Catholic press."[27] Connary reads periodicals as
someone with the responsibility for the practical and spiritual management of
a household, but also, it appears, as someone who strives towards some balance in the loyalties and affiliations of his subscriptions. The appendix provides a fuller list of the newspapers, periodicals, and other miscellaneous
papers referred to and purchased by Connary.

Reading for Guidance and Edification:
"Book Keeping" in the Connary Household

When we turn our attention from Connary's use of newspapers and periodicals to the range of books acquired by him, we notice the predominance of
what we may tentatively categorize as a literature of religious guidance and
practical guidance on matters such as farming and household management.
Needless to say, any distinction between practical and religious guidance is not
an absolute one: in fact, much of the interest of this archive of reading material
stems from precisely the way in which the categories overlap, and are understood by the owner to overlap, within his extensive reading program.

In the area of practical guidance, we find writing useful to someone with
responsibility for the moral and corporeal welfare of a household. Titles referred
to by Connary as *Youth's Director* and *The Duties of Young Men* would have
guided the instruction of adolescent and young adult family members.[28]
Equally practical, if rather more mundanely so, is a selection of books on agriculture and livestock, including *The Farmer's Treasure: A Practical Treatise on
the Nature and Value of Manures,* by Frederic Falkner, and two titles referred to
as *The Farmer's Own Book* and *The Complete Farmer.*[29] In addition, we find in
Connary's library an array of titles that would have provided broader guidance
to life in America and the immigrant experience. Among these are a number
of introductions to American history and society, as well as the voluminous
New Hampshire as It Is, comprising information on geography, demographics,
and industrial and humanitarian assets, together with numerous biographical
sketches of distinguished individuals.[30]

The volume referred to as "O'Hanlon's 'Guide,'" in all probability John O'Hanlon's *Irish Emigrant's Guide*, would have provided detailed and practical guidance for life, work, and social participation in the adopted country. As Hanlon equips his fellow Irishman with a realistic and pragmatic manual for survival, he urges both the acknowledgment of the "most noted and objectionable traits of Irish character" (a certain "want of determination," some "intemperance," an occasional "lack of sober reflection," and "a tendency to crowd into cities and be engaged in large bodies on public works"), as well as the "preservation of religious principles and independence."[31] The self-reliant and industrious Irish expatriate is encouraged to participate in American life while preserving his religious character and maintaining his sacred rootedness in the family. This ideal of peaceful assimilation is embodied in the life of Thomas Connary, and it is framed by O'Hanlon in terms of purposefulness and a predetermined naturalization. Recalling Haskins in his *Travels*, O'Hanlon opines that

> of all other strangers, the educated Irishman finds himself most at home in the United States,—he seems to have been destined by nature for a participation in the active and business pursuits of the country, and in the benefits and advantages derived from its laws and institutions. His innate feelings and disposition, moreover, seem to be almost congenial to the habits and general character of the people amongst whom he is called upon to reside; and no man takes a deeper and more abiding interest in the honor, prosperity and institutions of the country of his adoption. Even the uneducated classes of Irishmen are actuated by like motives and impulses.[32]

When we turn to Connary's collection of religious guidance literature—the overwhelming majority of his books and clearly where he invested most of his efforts as a book collector and annotator—we find a body of complex and diversified discourses that cuts across literary genres. Predominant are texts of didactic, catechetical instruction and Bible history. Connary refers several times to "my little illustrated Catechism of 183 pages" and "Catechism of the Council of Trent."[33] James O'Leary's *A History of the Bible, Its Origin, Object and Structure*, printed by D. & J. Sadlier in New York in 1873, provides a compendious 483-page introduction to the scriptures. These are all titles that would have strengthened Connary's religious knowledge and aided him in the religious instruction of his household: they reflect the didactic and catechetic priorities of someone functioning as a kind of estate manager with a degree of pastoral responsibility within his tight-knit family unit. O'Hanlon, in his *Irish Emigrant's Guide*, envisages precisely such a role for the head of the household: "It will be the duty of all heads of families to place those under their charge within the rank of religious instruction, to see that they are careful in discharging the duties of religion required of them, to keep them from the contamination of evil influences, particularly those that might endanger or weaken the ties that bind them to our Holy Church" (178).

Two other texts in Connary's library that would help construe such domestic religious instruction are Bourdaloue's *Sermons and Moral Discourses in the Important Duties of Christianity* and Comtesse Elizabeth de Bodenham's *Mrs. Herbert and the Villagers: or, Familiar Conversations on the Principal Duties of Christianity*. The latter two-volume work was praised in 1824 by the English *Catholic Spectator* as likely to "commence a new era in the History of British Catholic Literature" and as an important contribution to the "art of dramatising instruction."[34] Structured according to the sacraments and the Ten Commandments, Bodenham's text consists of a series of dialogues in which the maternal figure of Mrs. Herbert addresses the confusion and misunderstandings of villagers with her exemplary Christian learning, humility, and patience. It is not difficult to imagine how the extended didactic counsels in the text could serve as applicable models for religious instruction within the household.

Another significant portion of Connary's works of religious guidance consists of devotional works, hagiographic works, and prayer books. These varied literary forms were designed to enhance pious sentiment and structure a life of prayer. Classic titles such as Julian of Norwich's *Revelations*, St. Francis of Sales's *Spiritual Conferences*, Thomas à Kempis's *Imitation of Christ*, and *The Life and Revelations of Saint Gertrude* lend themselves to private concentrated reading, as evidenced by the rich annotation and many inserted pages of religious reflections. The book entitled *Memories of a Guardian Angel*, translated from the French of Guillaume Chardon, provides another interesting example of Connary's devotional literature. Consisting of eighty-eight brief ruminations on themes from the Christian life and its spiritual tribulations, the work draws on a range of patristic writings, saints' revelations, and "the safest mystical writers" to expound Catholic teaching on the ministry of guardian angels. Inserted handwritten pages in this volume indicate that it provided Connary with much consolation and reassurance. A note from 1875 on the first page of the text offers interesting clues to the possible shared use of the book in the Connary household; it also indicates that Connary purchased the book, originally published in Baltimore by John Murphy, from the well-stocked bookshop of Patrick Donahoe.

Thomas Connary's Book.

Stratford, Coös County, New Hampshire, October 5, 1875, Received this day from Mr. Patrick Donahoe of Boston, Massachusetts, which I wish to use and have the member of my family circle use as a pure blessed treasure always, never to be sold for money or measured by frail temporal treasures of any kind under any circumstances.

Thomas Connary.

Several other volumes indicate similar patterns of shared reading in the Connary household, and these will be the subject of further discussion in chapter 3. Some of the volumes evidently shared between family members relate the lives of saints and have been thoroughly annotated by Connary, often with handwritten addresses and appeals to his children. Two such titles are *The Lives of Eminent Saints*, published by Donahoe in 1853, and *The Lives of the Fathers of the Desert*, from Fielding Lucas Jr. in Baltimore (undated).

One final important group of Connary's works of religious guidance reminds us that this was a time of pervasive religious and social controversy: it consists of titles from the rich array of Catholic apologetics and religious polemic readily available to Catholic audiences in America. Not all of the religious polemic that we find in Connary's library is as restrained as Gaston de Ségur's *Plain Talk*, which opens thus: "My *plain talk on Protestantism* is with Catholics, rather than with Protestants. It is not an attack, nor a controversy either; it is intended as a work of *preservation and self-defence*."[35] Unambiguous controversy and real asperity of language are found in *The End of Religious Controversy* by the English Catholic bishop and polemicist John Milner (1752–1826), a work that Connary refers to frequently (mostly by title only) in his notes. Published in 1818, but written about twenty years before, this tract spurred a flood of embittered answers in the form of pamphlets and counter-polemics in the decades that followed. We can also include in the category of Christian polemic *Discourses Addressed to Mixed Congregations*, by John Newman (who was appointed cardinal in 1879) which Connary has in the edition printed by Donahoe in 1853, as well as Haskins's *Travels*, so rich in defense and Protestant criticism. An American polemic in Connary's library is the 472-page *Controversy between Rev. Messrs. Hughes and Breckenridge, on the Subject "Is the Protestant Religion the Religion of Christ?,"* a lengthy exchange as tedious as it is puerile between the Catholic clergyman who was to become the archbishop of New York and a distinguished Presbyterian minister who had served as chaplain of the House of Representatives. Originally a debate carried out in various Catholic and Presbyterian newspapers, this was published in

book form in 1833 by various publishers in Philadelphia and reprinted numerous times in the United States.[36] In the early part of the correspondence,
Hughes indicates the centrality of the publishing media to the dissemination
of the debate: "'The Presbyterian' will continue to publish until one or the
other of us, think proper to decline the contest. I, on my part, shall have the
whole re-published in one of *our* papers, so that the Catholics may receive the
enlightenment of your arguments."[37] Connary's copy of this voluminous controversy is that published by Eugene Cummiskey of Philadelphia in 1864
(sixth edition); on the front flyleaf, he notes, "February 4, 1865 bought of
Patrick Donahoe Boston. Price $1.50."[38] As I shall discuss in chapters 4 and 5,
Connary, who acquired a rich selection of polemic and defense writing, shows
little direct concern with schism and reciprocated animosity. He appears
instead to be interested in shared teaching between Protestants and Catholics.
Perhaps as a result of settling as the first Catholic resident in a small New
Hampshire town, his predominant interest is in the nature of the different
creeds and in the common ground for the devotional life.

Connary's activity of "Book keeping" is largely guided by the practical
requirements for religious instruction and a desired integration of temporal
and spiritual governance. If Connary's library is designed to resolve any potential crisis or dilemma, it is how to be truly and deeply spiritual while being
devoted to the effective management of a household and agriculture—in other
words, how to reconcile an inward spiritual ambition with care for the physical, spiritual, and moral lives of one's dependents. A process of book collecting
that is preoccupied with such questions generates its own logic, one in which
the "farmer's treasure" can allude both to Falkner's agricultural manual and to
Kinane's *Dove of the Tabernacle*, the small-sized devotional book that was one
of Connary's most precious possessions and has survived filled to the brim
with inserted pages of prayers, religious reflections, and exhortations.

Another feature of such "Book keeping," as noted above, is the relative lack
of recreational reading. The genres of poetry, novel, and short story are largely
absent. Rather surprising, perhaps, is the fact that we find none of the moral
and didactic stories of Mary Anne Sadlier, whom Charles Fanning has characterized as "the fictional advisor to the Famine immigrants."[39] Perhaps Connary found the depressing urban setting of many of her novels, which often
have the disillusioned protagonist return to live in Ireland, to be at odds with
his own, largely positive, American experience.[40] More likely, however, is that
Connary simply was not drawn to the fictional mode of writing, preferring
instead to be informed and instructed through the more unambiguous means
of reference works, history books, and devotional and didactic tracts.

We find in his library a copy of Aesop's *Fables*—a genre didactic by definition, intended to instruct and delight—and it is clear that at least parts of this text were read carefully as a source of moral edification. Edward W. Martin's *Secrets of the Great City: A Work Descriptive of the Virtues and the Vices, the Mysteries, Miseries and Crimes of New York City*, steeped in heavy-handed didacticism and not without sensationalism, suggests that reading for entertainment and moral strengthening could go hand in hand. Another title referred to by Connary, *Exploration of the Valley of the Amazon, Made under Direction of the Navy Department*, appears to appeal to a curiosity about strange and exotic places and suggests occasional priorities other than a strictly didactic one. The same can probably be said about the rich selection of reference works—dictionaries, historical overviews, topographical guides, and the like—that we know was also in Connary's possession.

I have characterized the contents of Connary's library as a literature of guidance, comprising diverse modes of instruction and a variety of textual forms. The overwhelming majority of texts can be classified broadly as devotional, catechetic, or didactic religious literature, a literature that could help produce configurations of religious and moral discipline and ensure a workable balance between an inner spiritual life and practical worldly management. Towards the end of his *Irish Emigrant's Guide*, O'Hanlon emphasizes the importance for the Irish immigrant of securing private property and the essential "requisites of life": "[O]nce his homestead has been secured in the country, he will live contented and respected, and have the satisfaction of seeing his family grow up around him prosperous and industrious, and removed from the pestilential examples and practices of city life."[41] Secure in his New Hampshire homestead and surrounded by family, Thomas Connary dedicated the last decades of his life to the precious and laborious process of "Book keeping," in which books were collected, arranged, decorated, and annotated. As we shall now explore in detail, this Irish immigrant farmer's library serves as a guide to, and is an elaborate product of, lived religious experience.

EPIPHANY

"Seeing Very Plainly"

Thomas Connary witnessed something remarkable in Stratford on Tuesday, January 17, 1888.

> Read my words of description of the Blessed and Holy Virgin Mother and her Blessed and Holy Company as I saw them very plainly, in this, my own house, on the 17th, of January in the year 1888. . . . I will now give in this a few of my thoughts in viewing the Blessed and Holy Virgin Mother of Jesus Christ, with a few of her Blessed and Holy companions then and there I was much more than very happy thank God. I felt very sure then, that God and His whole heavenly creatures were fully with me for endless Eternity.

These reminiscences, which are recorded, signed, and inserted between pages 54 and 55 of St. Francis of Sales's *Spiritual Conferences*, demonstrate remarkable concreteness. In what must be understood as a corporeal vision, Connary sees the blessed company "in this, my own house," and he asserts the central hermeneutic category for his felt religious experiences, namely that of seeing "very plainly" (a phrase repeated in all of the recorded experiences). This is the succinct record of literal visualization and physical detail, clearly dated, and it shows minimal effort to move beyond the dimensions of the "then and there" in the direction of speculative or abstract reflection. Yet some move toward the abstract *is* implied, for it is through this vision that Connary finds unequivocal affirmation of his own salvation. The phrase "I was much more than very happy" gives some indication of the deeply emotional nature of the experience and also of the difficulty of conveying it adequately through the resources of conventional language.

We know that Connary records the same experience in his book *The Council of the Vatican* on November 24, 1890. This shows that he returns reflectively to such episodes over time and records them for his family as the culminating experiences that bring life and devotion into sharp focus. Facing page 25 of *The Council of the Vatican* (in a chapter on the attendance of the bishops of Ireland at this twentieth ecumenical council), we read the following thoughts about the same occurrence:

Now I will say here, that God's heavenly visit to this, my Stratford home, Tuesday, January 17, 1888, was to prove to my full satisfaction, that I was then with Him as one, for Endless eternity. Now I cannot ever fear death, here or any where thank God, and my advice to all is this: Never disobey God. Now all must see everywhere as fast as possible that our best human creatures never will disobey God anywhere, their happiness is heavenly pure. Sin is being wrong, is hateful, is senseless, is brutal. Thomas Connary.

This is where Connary brings together the account of a perceived visionary experience and some theological reflection. The precise interpretive path is difficult to discern: the full meaning of the appearance of the Virgin and company seems to have been immediately or intuitively understood, rather than the result of logical reasoning or prolonged contemplation. And the implications are soteriological and ethical, as Connary derives from the visionary impression a deeper understanding and reassurance concerning his own salvation and God's moral law. In other words, the corporeal vision becomes a mode of instruction for Connary, being also a privileged vision of inclusion in the company of the elect.

As is true of all of Connary's recorded religious experiences, there is no reason to understand the nature of his "plain seeing" as anything else than a concrete corporeal vision. The experiences are not presented as imagined apparitions, or as visions cultivated through prolonged interior meditation on images, holy persons, or specific events, like the Passion of Christ.[1] Manifested to Connary in the "then and there" of familiar surroundings, the appearance of the Virgin and company provides proof "to my full satisfaction" of a role in the divine plan and mission.

2

"LABORING IN MY BOOKS":
THOMAS CONNARY'S BOOK ENHANCEMENTS

> My work [is] in papers large and small—in news-
> papers—in numberless Books large and small of all
> kinds, and of every kind and sort, firmly embodied in
> the most beautiful material temporal property we
> now have everywhere in this world as most purely
> precious and necessary for us to have in it.
>
> **—Thomas Connary, note dated January 29, 1889,
> between page 214 and the end flyleaf of Julian of
> Norwich, *Sixteen Revelations of Divine Love***

Enhancing "the Blank Paper Surface Room"

The collection of Irish American literature surveyed in the previous chapter motivates Thomas Connary to be at his most creative as he decorates and annotates individual books in complex ways, making them the portable signifiers of his own religious identity. One question that needs to be addressed from the outset is how best to account for this type of material evidence. What Connary refers to as "laboring in my Books" involves a complex process of annotating and inserting handwritten notes, newspaper cuttings, drawings, letters, devotional prayers, and meditations. For want of a better term, and following a suggestion by Heather Jackson from her book *Marginalia: Readers Writing in Books*, I will refer to this as a process of book enhancement.[1] Jackson acknowledges the absence of an apt term in our critical discourse and discusses several examples of the decorated and/or annotated book, introducing terms "that seem just about right for certain cases, but none that is adequate to the set as a whole. Among those rejected are fetish, icon, talisman, portfolio, album, scrapbook, and shrine. It might be that we need a new word altogether: bibliofile, perhaps, or BEPU—Book Enhanced for Personal Use."[2]

Connary, as we will see, makes of his printed books what we may term composite volumes, or devotional miscellanies, which contain a wealth of material. To term his additions to his books "annotations" or "marginalia" fails to capture the diversity of practices in which he engages. Indeed, I will make use of most of the terms rejected by Jackson, attesting to the complexity of Connary's engagement with the physical book. But I will be consistent about the terms "book enhancement" (the process) and "enhanced book" (the product) to describe the volumes that make up Connary's library. By an "enhanced book" I have in mind a book that has been physically and materially enlarged— that is, a book that is made more voluminous through the addition of pages and miscellaneous objects. But I also have in mind the enhancement of a book's symbolic and iconic properties. Ultimately, these understandings of the term "enhanced book" cannot be separated: laboring in books, and investing them with spiritual and imaginative power, is to turn books into prayers and testaments of personal faith and even to designate them as vessels of sacrality.

Thomas Connary began his project of laboring in books rather late in life, and it appears to have marked for him the culmination of a life of active and devoted Catholicism. The pattern of Connary's annotation and enhancement practices looks something like this: starting from the early 1860s, we find little else than ownership inscriptions and occasional notes regarding purchase (price, method of procurement, etc.). When we enter the 1870s, Connary provides sporadic annotation—mostly in the form of transcribed poetry, biblical quotations, and extended prayers—much of which addresses members of his own family. It is from the final years of the 1870s, when Connary is in his sixties, that his book enhancement acquires momentum, and he begins to insert his own handwritten religious reflections into his books. He spends time decorating his volumes in the early years of the 1880s, and numerous items of poetry—either transcribed or cut out from various newspapers and Catholic magazines—find their way into the volumes as well. The addition of densely written pages of religious and moral affirmations becomes particularly abundant throughout the eighties and nineties; the last dated page found is from June 10, 1898, six months before the owner's death at the age of eighty-four.

In the material examined for this study, we see approximately four decades of Connary's being with, and being inside, his books. His handwriting remains characteristic and clearly legible throughout, but also changes with the phases of life. The relaxed, decoratively penned, almost calligraphic annotations and ownership inscriptions of the late 1850s and '60s stand in some contrast to the steady and controlled hand of the 1870s and '80s. Generally, careful spacing and fluency of line characterize the handwriting here, but it occasionally becomes crowded to the point that spaces between words are nonexistent, or it shows sweeping extensions and enlarged letters that betray deep emotional content and intensity of religious sentiment. Toward the end of the 1890s, we see the handwriting of an aged individual, somewhat shaky at times, with inconsistencies in letter size and pen strokes applied with erratic pressure.

The discipline of "laboring in my Books" appears to have been pursued with mounting dedication and passion. Principally, this activity takes the form of the infilling of blank spaces with myriad items, all intended as part of a comprehensive proclamation of faith. This is an activity internal to the printed book, and among the many additions and items found inside his books are the following: handwritten marginalia with prayers and addresses to family members; annotations to the printed text; manuscript punctuation in the printed text; pen trials and doodles; underlinings; ownership inscriptions and signatures; inserted notebook pages with prayers, theological reflections, family history, and miscellaneous observations; letters and postcards; transcribed correspondence, poetry, and short stories; business and visiting cards; newspaper and magazine cuttings; printed advertisements; extra-illustration (i.e., illustration derived from sources outside the book itself) and drawn images and religious symbols; pressed flowers; textile borders; voting tickets; decoupage decoration; comprehensive lists of other books owned; and notes concerning printers, booksellers, and prices.[3] Such enhancements occur across the library, with most of these additions present in each individual book. We thus see composite volumes saturated with a superfluity of traces of their owner, in a manner suggesting a *horror vacui*—an obsession with filling the empty space. But more accurately, the book enhancements reveal a fascination with the opportunity that the blank space (in Connary parlance, "the blank paper surface room") provides for self-articulation and for inscribing oneself quite literally into the range of religious themes and experiences recounted in the books.

Crucially, Connary's library of enhanced books serves as a reminder that reading and book use are spaces of relative autonomy: a reader can make of a text what he or she wishes, can ignore directives for the act of reading, and can appropriate or subvert a text by inscribing in it multiple, sometimes contradictory, utilities. One example among many occurs between pages 80 and 81 of his edition of the *Spiritual Conferences* of St. Francis of Sales, where Connary has pasted a number of handwritten pages, dated by him September 28, 1896 (fig. 1). Here, amidst St. Francis's ruminations on the theological virtue of hope, we find six inserted pages containing Connary's own record of time and weather conditions ("10 o'clock in the morning clear and beautiful"), a long meditation on the importance of obedience toward God, some notes about an enhanced book given by Connary as a gift to Postmaster Riley Brown, and a

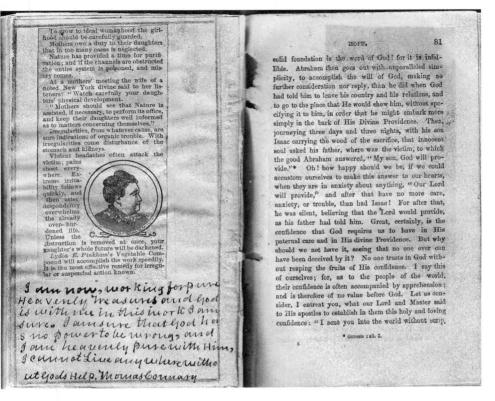

FIG. 1   St. Francis of Sales, *Spiritual Conferences*, pages 80–81

printed advertisement for Lydia Pinkham's Vegetable Compound, a so-called women's tonic for the relief of menstrual and menopausal pains.

Although I will later suggest how particular book genres and formats condition Connary's responses and the amount of book enhancement, there is very little that prepares us for such unpredictable, even arbitrary, interpolation in this religious book. For Connary, however, such interaction with books is compelling. In his labor in books, he finds a moment of redemption and emotional reward, which exists meaningfully alongside a rigorous routine of physical labor, social activity, and religious discipline. Four of the most notable types of book enhancement in Connary's collection are decorative embellishments, newspaper cuttings, prayers, and diary notes. Although these modes of book enhancement are presented individually below, they in fact come together as one unified merging of text and image, print and manuscript, the spiritual and the worldly, enlarging the signifying power and the range of uses of each volume.

Decorative Embellishment and Extra-Illustration

One of the most complex and creative disciplines of Connary's book enhancements consists of decorative augmentation. Every single volume contains
some feature of aesthetic embellishment, whether in the form of a few added
notebook pages with a border carefully ruled and drawn in colored crayon, or
an elaborate program of inserted and hand-drawn images, decorated title
page, and calligraphic handwriting. Throughout, such creative effort is motivated by a desire to turn books into homely and intimate objects. When Connary inserts pressed flowers from his farmstead between the leaves of his books,
or pastes pieces of textile and cloth of special meaning to him onto their pages,
or inserts a printed advertisement for passage tickets to and from "Old Ireland," then he is making the volumes distinctly his own and treasuring them
as signifiers of identity and a sense of belonging. Out of the many striking
examples of Connary's decorative enhancement, I would like to examine three
in some detail.

The small collection of devotions to the sacrament of the Eucharist, *The
Dove of the Tabernacle*, was acquired by Connary in 1878 and was in frequent
use by him over a period of about twenty years. Opposite the title page, surrounding a picture of Christ displaying his wounded heart, Connary has
pasted borders and crosses of grey cardboard, thus turning the page into a
devotional aid, a kind of shrine dedicated to the Sacred Heart of Jesus (fig. 2).
On the back of the same page are even more elaborate decorative borders cut
from cardboard and colored with blue crayon, as well as a cutting from Donahoe's *Pilot* with a poem entitled "Time," on the *ubi sunt* theme. On the preceding flyleaves are several other clippings, including a short article from the
Pilot that extols the benefits of farm labor as opposed to employment in the
city (plagued as the latter often is by strikes, poor lodgings, meager pay, etc.).
Such decoration, in which images and inserted journal fragments are surrounded with decoupage-style borders or other forms of embellishment, gives
a sense of the creative involvement that is part of the physical activity of
"laboring in my Books."

A similar level of creativity has been applied on the three front flyleaves of
The Sinner's Guide, which present an interesting medley of handwritten Bible
quotations, didactic appeals to family members, newspaper clippings with
devotional verse, and extra-illustration. Three full-page Bible illustrations from
a cycle of engravings printed by John Philp in London have been pasted to the
blank pages, showing the *Ecce homo* scene, the Burial of Christ, and Christ's
appearance before Mary Magdalene. It is difficult to think of a more fitting

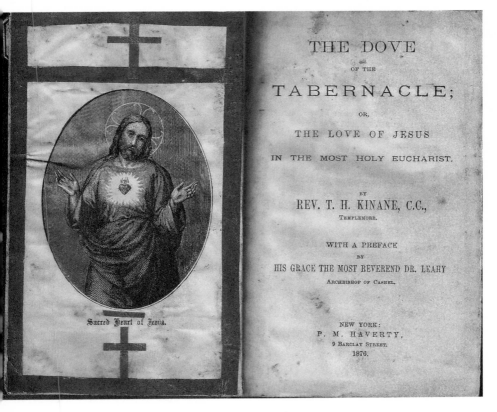

FIG. 2   Thomas Kinane, *The Dove of the Tabernacle*, title page

visual paratext to prepare for the theme of sin and penitential self-scrutiny than the image of the scourged Christ confronted by the hostile crowd. The image provides a suggestive linkage to the main themes of the otherwise unillustrated text, but it is also able to function independently as a visual aid to meditative introspection.

It is noteworthy that the most elaborate decorations, which show forms of decoupage with pasted drawings, images, fragments of cloth, and so on, occur most often on the blank leaves opposite the title pages. Given Connary's overwhelming interest in paratextual and printing details and the general physical makeup of the book, there is a certain logic to the fact that the title page, with its record of author, publisher, place, and date, elicits the most elaborate degree of creative enhancement. Following the pasted-in illustrations at the front of *The Sinner's Guide*, the page opposite the title accommodates a complex merging of decoration and image with religious statements (fig. 3). At the top of the

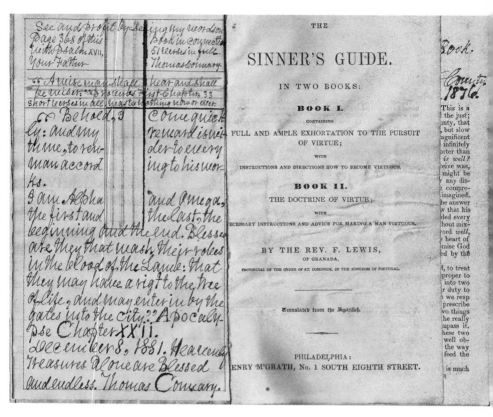

FIG. 3   F. Lewis [Louis of Granada], *The Sinner's Guide*, title page

page, Connary refers his family to his own annotation elsewhere in the same volume: "See and profit by seeing my words on Page 368 of this Book in connection with Psalm xvii, 51 verses in full. Your Father Thomas Connary." (At the bottom of page 368 is then found Connary's transcription of the Psalm, "with the holy, thou wilt be holy"—actually Psalm 18:25 of the Douai-Rheims version.) At the top center of the page is drawn a cross in black ink and blue and yellow crayon, in the bar of which is written a line from Proverbs 1 ("A wise man shall hear and shall be wiser"), and at the foot is found the longer quotation from Revelation 22:12–14. The page is signed and dated December 8, 1881, and concludes with the assertion "Heavenly Treasures alone are Blessed and endless." The central image of the Cross on the blank page facing the title *The Sinner's Guide* thus provides a graphic structuring device for the three items of biblical text from Psalms, Proverbs, and Revelation, all of which stress wisdom and righteousness before God, with clear warnings against the sinful life. The miscellaneous items of quotations, exhortations, inserted verse, and extra-illustration function as an elaborate preface to the book's call to the virtuous life.

In such examples Connary produces a saturated, yet decorative and balanced, *mise-en-page*, becoming in the process a cowriter and coproducer, as responsible for the layout of the book as the typesetter was. It is not uncommon to see Connary extend a book's pagination by providing his own page numbers in manuscript on the flyleaves and pastedowns, thus producing a continuation of the purchased book. It is as if he is reminding the printer that although the printed text has concluded, pages that accommodate additional text and meaning still remain.

One further example of extra-illustration is found in the small volume *The Lives of Eminent Saints*, printed by Donahoe in Boston in 1853. At the end of the Life of St. Bridget, between pages 142 and 143, Connary has imported a small color print showing Christ's Entry into Jerusalem together with the printed biblical text—one of a number of such prints issued by the Catholic Publication Society in New York (fig. 4). This insertion is part of an accretion of devotional memorabilia found in many of the smaller volumes. We know from several written dedications in the volume that Connary, at various moments, gave this book as a gift to his son Joseph and his daughter Anne: the illustration of Christ's Entry carries the short note "Memento mei to Joseph T. Connary From his Father Thomas Connary. May 14, 1883." Addresses and petitions such as this, found throughout Connary's library and the subject of more discussion in the next chapter, do much to establish the status of books as valued and personal objects within the Connary household.

An important part of the book additions includes the foreign elements that are often referred to as "extra-illustration." Jackson reminds us that a preferred term in British libraries for such additions is "grangerized," a word that refers to the English clergyman and print collector James Granger, whose 1769 *Biographical History of England from Egbert the Great to the Revolution* invited the interleaving and pasting in of supplementary illustrative material, mostly in the form of engraved portraits.Granger initiated a fashion that quickly caught on, as many books published in the eighteenth and nineteenth centuries lent themselves to "grangerizing" by incorporating designated blank places for the relevant illustrations that the readers were to seek elsewhere.[4] The terms "extra-illustrated"

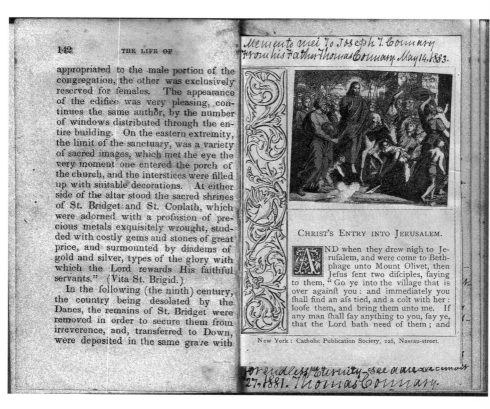

FIG. 4   *The Lives of Eminent Saints*, pages 142–43

and "grangerized" are potentially but not necessarily synonymous. Where "extra-illustrated" is a broad term for the incorporation of any amount and type of illustrations from extraneous sources, a book that invites "grangerizing" would tend to circumscribe carefully the form and amount of illustration and addition that it is designed to absorb. (For example, such a book might provide printed frames within which additional images could be inserted.)

For Connary, who is extra-illustrating—or, more aptly, extra-decorating—his volumes with an array of materials (image and text, print and manuscript), the book does not end with the printed text. In particular, the blank front and end flyleaves invite an enhancement with layers of decorative and textual embellishment to form an elaborate parenthesis to the printed text, though it is never of parenthetical significance. This is a type of creative devotional accretion not dictated in any direct way by the theme and nature of the text.

Newspaper and Magazine Clippings

It is useful to see one part of Connary's book enhancement labors as partaking in a well-established tradition in American popular culture of producing scrapbooks, a process where readers cut out and paste down illustrations and reading material from newspapers and magazines. In a valuable recent study, Ellen Garvey demonstrates how nineteenth-century scrapbooks functioned as "democratic archives" in which readers "wrote with scissors" to claim ownership of their reading in a time of abundant output from the proliferating print media.[5] Connary certainly seems to have done much of his reading with scissors in hand, always ready to cut out useful material and preserve it inside his books, fusing the functions of scrapbook and printed book.

Each of Connary's books contains numerous newspaper and magazine paste-ins that integrate decorative and utilitarian functions. These are sourced from a wide range of periodicals and Catholic magazines (mostly the *Pilot*) and are used extensively to fill the blank spaces of his books and to provide a referential intertext. The inserts are often framed by elaborate colored borders or by Connary's own handwritten annotations. The number of such clippings varies considerably from book to book: *The Council of the Vatican* contains thirty-five items, ranging from short notices of a few lines to full-page articles, while only ten items (mostly short devotional poems clipped from the *Pilot*) find their way into the small devotional volume entitled *In Heaven We Know Our Own*. These magazine fragments almost never cover the printed space; in a few instances, the printer's advertisements at the back of volumes have been covered. Inhabiting blank space and providing useful reference, these cuttings offer revealing insights into the interests and reading habits of a nineteenth-century Irish American farmer with the responsibility for the welfare and financial management of a large household.

Page 24 of *Memoirs of a Guardian Angel* provides some space for enhancement and acquires a very harmonious and balanced appearance through the addition of a brief article neatly framed in striking yellow crayon (fig. 5). I quote the article in full, as it provides an example of the didactic thread that prevails in these clippings.

A Bishop's Opinion of Balls and Dances

Speaking of balls and dancing the Lenten Pastoral of the Bishop of Wheeling, West Virginia, says: "Apart from the immodest dancing, the questionable characters that congregate at such places, the late hours kept, the lone walk home, and other dangerous features make these balls fruitful of most sad and sinful consequences. How many a fair name has been blighted; how many a life forever embittered; how many a family brought to shame by these nocturnal revelries! Parents, we entreat you, for the love of God, withhold your children from all such gatherings. See that poor girl, on whose brow, once fair with gems of holy purity, is now written the stigma of disgrace and shame. Ask her *where, how* she fell; and doubtless she will point to the ball-room and the dance-house. Or watch that young man, whose lecherous looks betray the hidden corruption, and inquire into the story of his short but checkered life. But a while ago he knelt monthly at the holy table, and received the pure delights of virtue and innocence. But the dizzy round of the dance, the sensual music of the siren who there presides, the consequent excitement of his low, animal passions, have corrupted his heart and well-nigh driven him to despair.

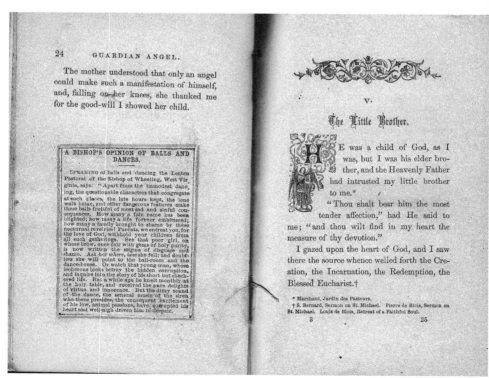

FIG. 5   M. A. G. Chardon, *Memoirs of a Guardian Angel*, pages 24–25

It is possible that Connary was drawn to such writing as much for its rhetorical flourishes as for its rather stifling didacticism, which may perhaps have been instrumental in his own instruction of family members. The theme of moral edification is found throughout the range: a cut-out pasted on page 202 of *The Sinner's Guide* contains "Good Rules of Conduct," while pages 158 and 159 of *Historical Selections from the London Rambler* preserve two short pieces entitled "Good Manners" and "A Word for the Boys." Several articles pertain to the nature and disposition of the ideal wife, while a short piece stuck to the back of the title page of Bishop Camus's *Spirit of St. Francis de Sales* muses on the theme of "Precept and Example."

A wealth of devotional verse and prose enriches every single one of Connary's books in the form of small magazine fragments scattered throughout the volumes wherever blank space appears. This collected material of hundreds of short compositions constitutes a corpus of now-forgotten parochial amateur poetry. On a flyleaf in *The Lives of the Fathers of the Desert*, we find Anne T. Clarke's short verse composition for the *Pilot* entitled "Hymn to Our Blessed Lady in Her Assumption," while the top margin of page 32 of John Newman's *Discourses* barely leaves sufficient space for a brief "Acrostic for Ash-Wednesday," beginning with the lines "*Remember, man, that thou art dust.*" Some pieces of verse are not without appeal, such as the version by C. C. Lord of Hopkinton in New Hampshire on the familiar theme "April Showers Bring May Flowers," found on an end flyleaf in Haskins's *Travels in England, France, Italy, and Ireland*.

Another related body of cuttings indicates an active interest in Church history and matters doctrinal and ecumenical. Of the many on this theme are two articles appropriately deployed in *The Council of the Vatican*, one offering a brief summary of the nineteen ecumenical councils and the other relating details of a visit by Bishop Conroy, the apostolic delegate, to Boston in 1878. A short article on the history of the Catholic community in New Hampshire occupies two end flyleaves in Julian of Norwich's *Revelations*.

Other thematic clusters include notices relating to monetary issues, with specific articles about inflation, interest rates, coin minting, and the history of money, banking, and personal finance. Among many, we find a short piece on the world's oldest banknotes inserted in Julian's *Revelations* and an item in *Memoirs of a Guardian Angel* assessing the benefits of purchasing by cash or credit. As with most other such clippings, these are sourced from the *Pilot* and other Catholic periodicals, indicating these publications' attempts to equip Irish immigrants with basic competence in personal financial management. The pecuniary themes of these articles coincide with similar interests in Connary's own inserted writings, which touch on issues of state finance, inflation, the issuance of bills of credit, and the financial management of his own household.

Practical issues of housekeeping, agriculture, and corporeal welfare are the subjects of numerous clippings, as are themes of general history, geography, and the amazing. The following is a selection of article captions that gives some flavor of the often colorful subjects that spurred Connary to excise items from periodicals to paste into his books: "Men of Mighty Muscle," "The Richest Man in the World," "A Yankee Sailor Who Has Twenty Wives and Fifty Children," "Difference between Peerage Nobility and Nobility of Blood," "The World's Smallest Nations," "Bologna University Library—Book and Print Robberies," "Death of a Noted African Explorer, Capt. Nelson," "Frigid Mary Anderson—How She Did Not Marry an English Duke," "Kidnapped by Bandits—Wealthy Sugar Planter Taken Prisoner," "Bishop Healy Gives the Pope a Pair of Moccasins, and the Pope Wears Them," "The Monasteries of Mount Athos," and "Myths, Legends, and Folk Lore of Eastern Europe and Asia" (this latter occupies five pages of front flyleaves in the *Fables of Aesop and Others*).

We need also to acknowledge a pronounced interest in the morbid in these fragments—in murders, accidents, disasters, executions, and so forth. At the end of *Fables of Aesop* are found no fewer than twenty-five pages of advertisements for the publishers Derby & Jackson of New York, and these are used by Connary to assemble a potpourri on the themes of death and ethical conduct. A rather jarring combination of printed fragments is found in this selection, which begins with a series of obituaries of people in the town of Lancaster, New Hampshire, for 1886 (several of whom were acquaintances), followed by a poem entitled "The Baby's Prayer," ending with the lines "For when earth is wrapped in winter, / In the heart of the Lord 'tis spring." Then follow two didactic pieces, one on ministering angels and one entitled "Be Content," which juxtaposes "the many defalcations and criminal frauds" of the financial and business world with the vocation of the farmer, "the highest employment for any member of the great human family." Concluding this assemblage is an article covering six pages of advertisements on a long-lived theme, "Hanging as a Means of Punishment—Does It Prevent Crime and Increase Morality?" For the author, "Howard" (presumably an allusion to the great British penal reformer John Howard), the execution of Roxalana Druse in Herkimer County, New York, in February 1887 provides an occasion for reflecting on what is perceived as the inhuman manner in which executions were conducted. The botched execution of Mrs. Druse on an upward-jerking gallows, which achieved public notoriety at the time and made chilling headlines, became an important factor in the introduction of the electric chair, first used in New York's Auburn Prison in 1890. In his article, "Howard" partakes in the debate of the time by advocating the application of "discoveries and advancements of science" in order, as he puts it, to "humanize and revolutionize the barbarity of the scaffold"—his position is not one of the denunciation of the death penalty per se. Connary himself remains silent on the matter of the death penalty: all we know is that he took an interest in the subject as part of an active and broad interest in social and ethical issues.

One last curious instance of Connary's added items should be mentioned— this one actually defacing the portrait of the Irish political leader Daniel O'Connell that opens Donahoe's advertisements (fig. 6). At the rear of Haskins's *Travels*, where a blank leaf faces the first page of the advertisements, two very different items on religious matters excised from the *People and Patriot* have been pasted to cover the large portrait of O'Connell. One ponders theological questions, "piercing, probing, to the core," and the other is an

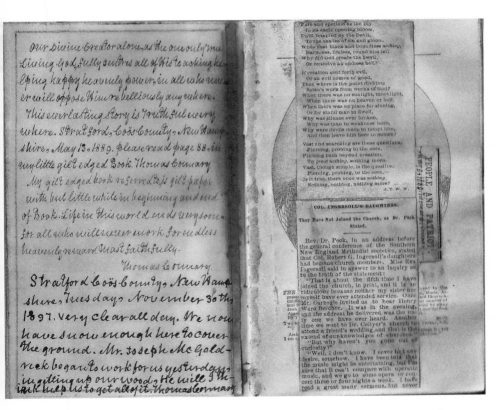

FIG. 6   George Haskins, *Travels in England, France, Italy, and Ireland*, advertisements at the back of the volume

anecdotal piece on the famed American orator and political leader Robert G. Ingersoll's daughters, who, preferring the opera and concerts, feel no calling to attend church regularly. We may speculate that Connary had no need for Donahoe's advertisements here, as he probably had them elsewhere, perhaps as separate pamphlets. The list of advertisements would no doubt have been useful to Connary, who often refers to books received from Donahoe by mail and makes no mention of ever calling at Donahoe's offices in Boston.

The many pasted newspaper clippings show a reader who wanders across the books of his library, underlining, highlighting, inserting in them what captures his interest, and ignoring or even defacing what does not. As Connary enhances his volumes with a selection of newspaper fragments, sometimes arranging these into thematic clusters, he also orchestrates a range of utilities for his books. Haskins's *Travels* can be read as a travelogue by an opinionated Irish American clergyman, or it can be consulted for miscellaneous printed religious items, some of them devotional and some of an anecdotal nature. The *Fables of Aesop* provides didactic guidance through entertaining narratives, but it may also meet various reference needs or offer matter for reflection and spiritual consolation in the form of a medley of short articles on ethical conduct and the end of life.

An important part of Connary's discipline of book enhancement is to facilitate such multiple uses, where the same book may be consulted for utilitarian, didactic, edifying, and devotional purposes. The type of readerly enhancement characterized here may also enable Connary to compensate for a dimension almost absent in the range of book titles he acquires. It is through the addition of magazine clippings that he allows himself to indulge in the incredible, morbid, and anecdotal. If utilitarian and didactic titles dominate in his library, these textual, scrapbook-like augmentations add an important component of a broader recreational reading.

Diary and Miscellaneous Records

Two striking features of Connary's book enhancements are the self-referentiality of the annotations and their tendency to convey a vivid impression of daily life through additions that resemble diary recordings. Fascinated by the possibility for inserting new meaning, Connary adds significantly to his library as part of an endeavor to suffuse it with a sense of identity, community, and belonging. Here we can begin to explore the nature of book enhancements as a form of autobiography that maps activities and personal history, which is a dimension largely absent from previous studies of book markings such as those by Heather Jackson and William Sherman.

Many of the newspaper fragments inserted by Connary provide information on local events in Stratford and its purlieus in which Connary had some form of involvement. Parochial notices and information on town events and administration occur often. Thus on the final of the front flyleaves of *In Heaven We Know Our Own,* dated in Connary's hand December 26, 1894:

> The grand bazar, held last week for the benefit of the Sacred Heart church, closed last Saturday evening, and the "guess" goods were all disposed of. The fair was not as lucrative as last year, but considering the short time in which Father Marshall had to prepare for the event, it has proved to be a success, and much money was realized from the venture. We understand that a parsonage is to be built for the priest the coming year. Father Houlihan has been in town since the fair opened. The Catholics must have realized $500.00 from the fair.

Stuck to the contents page of *The Council of the Vatican* in September 1884 we find the following notice about a social gathering in neighboring Lancaster: "There were between two and three hundred at the dance in Joe Connary's new barn last Tuesday night. Adna and Carlos Schoff played violins and Elmore Schoff played the organ. All seemed to enjoy themselves. Refreshments of cake and coffee were served. Thanks to Mr. and Mrs. Connary for the good time we all had."

If Connary partook in such conviviality, or if he was home enhancing books, we cannot know. But the events provide some indirect indication of Connary's involvement with the affairs of the town: the grand bazaar was held at the Sacred Heart Church in Stratford, which had been erected on land purchased by Connary for the purpose of building the town's Catholic church, and the barn dance was thrown by Joseph T. Connary, Thomas's son, born in 1856. (Connary subtly indicates that he was present at the last event: where the article states that "about 200 assembled on their 100 feet barn floor," he replaces "200" with "204" in his own pen, reflecting an habitual preoccupation with numerical exactitude.)

Printed notices of such local events find their parallel in the inserted notebook pages that occur throughout the Connary library. Many of these handwritten additions are of the almanac and diary type, with notes on the weather, local celebrations, and the cycles of farming and harvesting. They also contain stories of the purchase and exchange of books, the cycle of church life, church building and maintenance, the participation in the sacraments, visits made by the Connarys or by others to the Connary homestead, funerals, town meetings, and the like.

A handwritten note in *The Council of the Vatican* is dated May 28, 1882, and produced after Connary's attendance at Pentecost mass in Bloomfield, Vermont with his sons Simon, Joseph, and John: "Very Reverend Father Patrick McKenna pastor—Son Simon and myself received the Blessed Sacrament profitably I hope—next mission Sunday there June 25, 1882." Following details of the mass is an extended series of prayers and meditations on the subject of human sinfulness, after which Connary records several fond memories of his deceased daughter Anne. He then goes on, in characteristic sequence, to outline a reading and book enhancement program for that specific day, which includes reading his diary for the year 1863 together with his books *The Council of the Vatican*, Boudreaux's *God Our Father*, and a book he refers to as *Pictorial Bible and Church History Stories*. The entire entry is characteristic of the way in which Connary establishes the setting carefully (the date and time, weather conditions, the events of the day) before he describes the precious pastime of book reading and enhancement. But more than that, it offers insight into the sequence of ideas and feelings that pass through his mind on that afternoon in the spring of 1882. The associative leaps that take him from sacramental participation with his sons, via reminiscences about his deceased daughter (deeply pious, according to Connary), to an interconnected train of moral reflections are conveyed in carefully composed sentences with little separation and punctuation, and they are preserved on treasured paper left behind by his daughter, as he specifies in some detail. Although his thought processes can take off in a number of spatial and temporal directions, they all come together meaningfully for Connary, all converging on inscription in books.

Invariably, records on daily events blend into religious meditation and assertion in a way that suggests how local community, topography, and domestic responsibility always enrich Connary's spiritual life. The following are typical observations that function as the prolegomena to Connary's extensive religious writing in books: "Thursday, dark, calm and rainy. August 18, 1887— yesterday was clear and beautiful all day, we drawed home one load of oats"; "Wednesday, January 31, 1883, cloudy windy and mild, eleven o'clock in the forenoon, I am working faithfully in this paper"; "April 10, 1878, seven in the morning here, wind northerly and purely musical in tone."

Between the final contents page and page 1 of St. Francis of Sales's *Spiritual Conferences*, Connary has inserted eight pages in 1883 that again blend religious thoughts with miscellaneous records. The conclusion to this inserted booklet can be seen in figure 7. A substantial part is addressed to his children and shows how books can function as storage for personal history and genealogical records. Like a family Bible passed on from one generation to the next, accruing records of births, deaths, marriages, and baptisms, Connary converts the volume that houses the spiritual wisdom of St. Francis of Sales into a depository of family history and precious reminiscence:

> My Father Simon Connary born in Ballycallen, 4½ miles westerly from Kilkenny City, Kilkenny County, Leinster Province Old Ireland, February 20 1785, died Lisdowny, in said County and province, December 12, 1825, aged 40 years, 2 months, 8 days if I count my figures right. I, Thomas Connary, was born in Aquaregar, near Lisdowny, May First day, 1814,

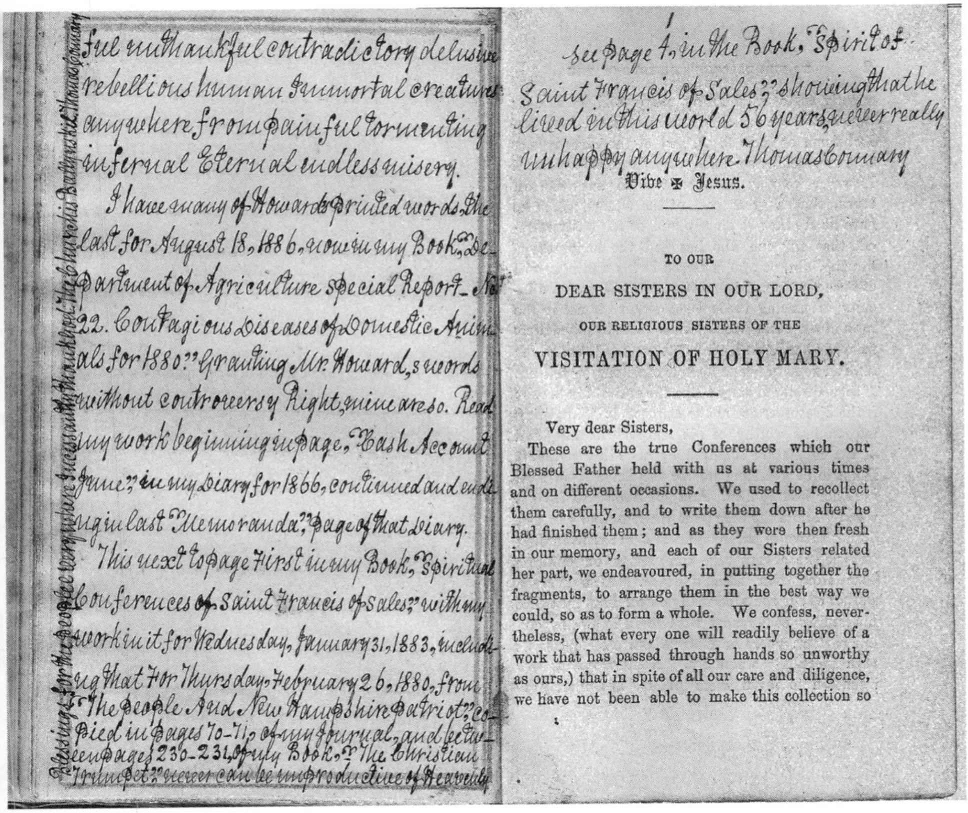

ful unthankful contradictory delusive rebellious human Immortal creatures anywhere, from painful tormenting infernal Eternal endless misery.

I have many of Howard's printed words the last for August 18, 1886, now in my Book, "Department of Agriculture Special Report_No 22. Contagious Diseases of Domestic Animals for 1880." Granting Mr. Howard's words without controversy Right, mine are so. Read my work beginning in page, "Cash Account June," in my Diary for 1866, continued and ending in last "Memoranda," page of that Diary.

This next to page First in my Book, "Spiritual Conferences of Saint Francis of Sales," with my work in it for Wednesday, January 31, 1883, including that for Thursday, February 26, 1880, from "The People And New Hampshire Patriot," copied in pages 70-71, of my Journal, and between pages 230-231, of my Book, "The Christian Trumpet," never can be unproductive of Heavenly

see page 4, in the Book, "Spirit of Saint Francis of Sales," showing that he lived in this world 56 years, never really unhappy anywhere. Thomas Connary

Vive ✠ Jesus.

TO OUR

DEAR SISTERS IN OUR LORD,

OUR RELIGIOUS SISTERS OF THE

VISITATION OF HOLY MARY.

Very dear Sisters,

These are the true Conferences which our Blessed Father held with us at various times and on different occasions. We used to recollect them carefully, and to write them down after he had finished them; and as they were then fresh in our memory, and each of our Sisters related her part, we endeavoured, in putting together the fragments, to arrange them in the best way we could, so as to form a whole. We confess, nevertheless, (what every one will readily believe of a work that has passed through hands so unworthy as ours,) that in spite of all our care and diligence, we have not been able to make this collection so

FIG. 7 St. Francis of Sales, *Spiritual Conferences*, page 1 my Family homestead was in Castlemarket in said Kilkenny County, near Ballinakill, in the Queen's County, during the full time we lived in Ireland after my Father's death. Castlemarket is near Ballinakill Roman Catholic Church, in Ballyragget parish. I left my Castlemarket home and family early in the morning March 25, 1833, expecting to go to the County Kerry to remain there at school a few months, then to return to my Castlemarket home and Family. As my thoughts that day were very firmly united prayerfully with our Divine Creator under His Directing Powerful Wisdom I saw the Town of Lancaster, Coös County, New Hampshire, early in June 1833, after living thankfully with my dearly beloved Cousin John Castigan and his Family in Saint Nicholas, Canada, I have not since seen my Castlemarket home. In our Ballyuskil Church our King blessed me, 53 years away from my native home—19 years of age in May 1833.

This is one of many similar and overlapping accounts elsewhere in the library that record biography and reminiscences from "Old Ireland." Connary here preserves, in a book he deems likely to remain with his family, his memory of that fateful day in March 1833, when, in a somewhat happenstance manner, he intended to leave home to pursue school for three months, but joined company with "a few people who were on the way to America." Books are considered the safest storage for such precious details of family history and genealogy—details which often seem shaped by the embellishing imagination and which must be designed to induce a consciousness of family roots among other and future members of the family.

It can often be difficult to discern any direct correlation between specific titles in Connary's library and the type of information he stores in them. Miscellaneous records and family history provide some striking insight into the thoughts that appear to him in specific moments and reading situations. As we see, being deeply immersed in books and in the experience of reading can trigger imaginative or nostalgic flights in which reading itself is paused to pursue the different activity of documenting and communicating before an anticipated intimate audience.

Prayers and Religious Assertions

Densely written pages of religious meditations are by far the most abundant and consistent feature of Connary's work in books, and the decorative prayer page on what was a blank leaf in *The Dove of the Tabernacle* is a fine example (fig. 8). The page contains extensive writing to effectively fill up the entire space: it is divided into two compartments framed by blue borders, with the top compartment containing the standard christogram of western Christianity, the I. H. S. monogram for Jesus Hominum Salvator (Jesus savior of mankind), with the crossbar of the "H" carrying the Cross.[6] In the large compartment below, Connary has transcribed a prayer to obtain special graces and divine protection, opening with the invocation "O, God, who hast vouchsafed to consecrate the standard of the life-giving CROSS with the precious blood of thy only begotten Son." Underneath this is the following affirmation addressed to his family:

> Dearly beloved children—Divine Truth is God's unchangeably perfect grammar of just necessary charitable words in all languages, therefore as

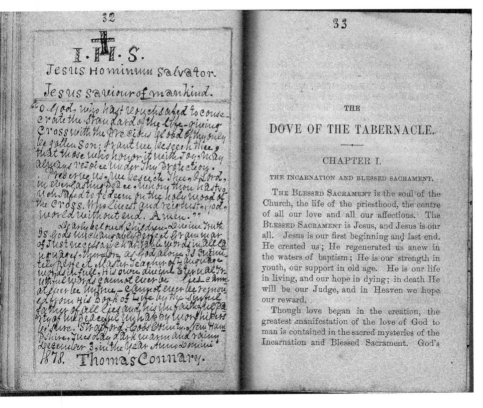

FIG. 8   Thomas Kinane, *The Dove of the Tabernacle*, pages 32–33

God alone is infinitely perfect Master Teacher of language words in full, His own divine Eternal truthful words cannot ever be lies—cannot ever be untrue—cannot ever be removed from His Book of Life by the sinful father of all lies and his unfaithful party of unpeaceful unhappy worshipers be sure. Stratford, Coös County, New Hampshire, Tuesday dark warm and rainy December 3, in the year Anno Domini 1878. Thomas Connary.

Religious declarations of this sort are ubiquitous in Connary's enhanced books. They occur most comprehensively in the devotional works, such as *The Dove of the Tabernacle* and Julian of Norwich's *Revelations*, and significantly less in other genres. Invariably, the prayers tend to group themselves in clusters around the opening and closing pages of each volume, where they provide a highly personal framing, or gloss, of the contents of the book. Connary evidently wrote up most of the prayers and devout proclamations separately in notebooks, but in tandem with his program of reading, and he produced them for insertion between specific pages of his books to complement and enrich the print. Numerous instructions tell where precisely to add pages into the books that were being read at a specific moment, and it is clear that a purposeful exchange is often intended between print content and devotional annotation.[7] In the case of *The Dove of the Tabernacle*, the correspondence between the handwritten prayer page and the theme of the book is evident: Connary's prayerful invocation to the Cross and holy blood of Christ introduces the fervent Christocentric piety and devotion to the Sacrament of the Eucharist that are the main theme of Kinane's book, dedicated as it is "to the most sacred and adorable Heart of Jesus."

To call Connary's religious annotations "prayers" is in most cases something of a misnomer. His writings demonstrate very little in the sense of ardent plea or invocation of God; there is some expression of thanksgiving and praise, but little petition for guidance or graces from God, and even less of what we may term affective Christocentric prayer that reflects on details from the life of Christ to excite pious fervor. Instead of apostrophizing his God, we find Connary proclaiming, affirming, and testifying—always bearing witness to the august benevolence of God and the universal possibility of salvation, always denouncing falsehood, malignity, and impurity.

The printed authority of Newman's *Discourses* appears with Connary's own, highly personal gloss, as on the verso of the title page: facing Newman's dedication to the Reverend Nicholas Wiseman is a written rumination on the theme of the transience of the created order, which encircles an imported newspaper fragment on the same theme (fig. 9). Connary's handwriting spirals around the newspaper clipping, so a reader must rotate the book to read his words. As usual, daily observation functions as a prelude to religious reflection:

> Stratford, Coös County, New Hampshire, Monday morning cloudy with light sprinklings of snow here, January 17 in the year 1881—I now assure the whole human family everywhere in space, that the one only True Living God and His own peaceful faithful orderly family of immortal creatures will ever please to be really beautiful and Happy for endless Eternity. . . . I am working fast and very faithfully, to show the fact that God and His own Eternal Heavenly Pure Government Law of Exact Divine Justice never can be overruled anywhere. Thomas Connary.

They are sustained themes articulated in idiosyncratic prose and with a compulsive force that dominate these prayers, namely, the truth of the divine law and the moral rectitude necessary for the salvation of the Christian soul.

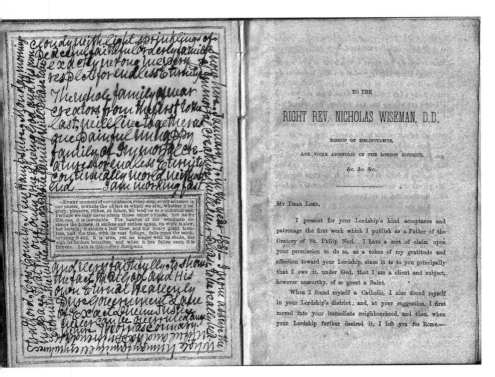

FIG. 9   John Henry Newman, *Discourses Addressed to Mixed Congregations*, verso of title page

The above admonition reads like a signed declaration, intended as guidance and caution to the members of his family who read this copy of Newman's *Discourses*, and even to "the whole human family everywhere in space." Connary's very own discourse, that of someone who has obtained special insight into the workings of salvation and the urgency of conforming human will to God's moral law, frames the *Discourses* of the cardinal.

Connary's thoughts continue to revolve around the theme of eternal salvation and human volition, understood by him as humankind's innate capacity for correct moral action made possible through "the human power we have from God as our Gift."[8] In a note inserted between the front flyleaves in *Mrs. Herbert and the Villagers*, Connary employs his distinct terminology to communicate his surety concerning the eternal nature of what is termed God's "Theological Law": "Here in this world, we have political law, and much sin mixed into it, this we know. Theological Law is God's Law, as He teaches it to all who are willing to believe him. We are sure that God is in every respect right, and we obey Him as well as we can obey Him, we cannot do any better than we can do. Every thing proves fully the existence and purity of God, and His Law."

We might reasonably say that Connary's statements are characterized by theological rigidity and a striking solemnity of proclamation. They provide his books with a reiterated and uncompromising moral rigor, which has the cumulative effect of a forceful statement of personal religious conviction. As is so often the case with his prayer and admonitory annotations, they tread a fine line between the personal and sincere, on the one hand, and the bizarre and fanatical, on the other. His sentences are often as enhanced as his books, characterized by syntactically tortuous articulations and filled to the brim with descriptive adjectives and superlatives. Through prayers and affirmations he pours religious fervor and high moral seriousness into his private library and manifests his passionate devotion to Catholicism: "I am now strictly a Roman Catholic with God and his Holy and Blessed family of heavenly pure immortal creatures. Now I must say that for all of the money of this world, I cannot ever be, for one moment, any better than a pure Roman Catholic." This declaration is found, unsurprisingly, on one of the first pages pasted into *The Dove of the Tabernacle*—this much-valued book of ardent, devotional Catholicism in which the main emphasis is on devotion to the Holy Eucharist.

Connary's handwritten religious prayers and ruminations come in all shapes and sizes, from short assertions—for example, "I am for Heavenly pure endless Peace. Thomas Connary," written in a margin of Peter Fredet's *Modern History*, or the official-sounding statement in *Mrs. Herbert and the Villagers*,

"now with this pen in my hand, I can truly say, that God is here and everywhere as well as in heaven"—to the large-size, densely written nine leaves
(eighteen pages of writing) imported as a pamphlet into the second volume of
Balmes's *Fundamental Philosophy*. The tendency is for these enhancements to
become more frequent and elaborate in the late 1880s and throughout the
1890s, where they demonstrate the most insistent scrupulosity of articulation
and arrangement. In fact, we might regard them as a form of retirement project that labors to preserve the culmination of a life of devoted Catholic piety.
Looking back at decades of book enhancement in the spring of 1890, Connary
remarks in his copy of St. Francis of Sales's *Spiritual Conferences* that "I have
written much as an old farmer, in my own very busy way, much more than I
thought of writing when I began to write." Writing in 1893 at the age of eighty,
he records his determination to continue in hard labor, but by this he now
understands withdrawn, bookish labor, a necessary substitute in old age for
manual labor:

> I sincerely hope, that all who can ever see my work in this paper, will be
> well guarded by God and by His heavenly family of Immortal creatures
> against human imperfection and defilement forever. I am not writing
> for a temporal purpose, God who knows everything, believes me fully,
> and I am more thankful to Him than I can ever speak, I am full to over-
> flowing with a desire to be with Him for endless Eternity. Failing in
> ability to work in manual labor, I have said often to the members of my
> family, that I would in this way, and in every such way, live with our
> Divine, bountiful Creator and with His heavenly family of Immortal
> creatures.

This striking record registers both thanksgiving as well as a desire to inter-
cede on others' behalf through the laborious activity of "Book keeping." I shall
have more to say in the following chapters about this rationale of intercession
and mediating prayer, which lies at the heart of Connary's book enhancement
project. For now, we may note his overwhelming, joyful desire to be united
with his God, which is inscribed into nearly all of the specimens of Connary's
religious writings discussed above. Inserted between pages 330 and 331 of *The
Council of the Vatican*, and dated May 28, 1882, is a note that exemplifies the
distinct parlance with which he conveys the desire for salvation and certainty
about the divine power. Again, direct praise and invocation of God are not the
most common discourse types in Connary's written statements, but here they
function powerfully to express assurance, determination, and gratitude:

Until I will be called home by thyself fully, from this perishable very necessary probationary world, mercifully lead and direct me in every respect in all of my powers and faculties as one of thy most faithful peaceful servants truly, in justice mercy and charity to the whole family of immortal creatures everywhere incessantly—here we have the full benefit of thy endless eternal infinitely perfect working Power and Plan, with no remuneration from us to thee, constantly coming in our favour, fully measured exactly right in every respect by thyself alone in moments—in hours—in days—in nights—in seasons, and in years annually continued, and to be annually continued right in every respect exactly long enough to be exactly right in every respect everywhere in space.

Planning Reading

The surviving collection of Connary's annotated books preserves some vivid records of reading situations along with detailed plans for structured reading programs, through which we can map, in some outline, the sequence in which the books and his writings in books are to be read. Next to the title page in *The Lives of the Fathers of the Desert*, Connary pastes a series of notes dated October 28, 1893, that contain his peculiar commingling of daily observations, religious meditations, and bibliographic notes. He notes that "Mrs. Dunbar and Miss. Trasy are here, they go to Island Pond today, and Lucinda is gone with them to visit for a short time." Then follows one page of reflections on moral behavior and the end of time, beginning with the declaration "the whole of Temporal Life very soon comes to an end, then if we use all of our time right we have heaven with God and His family for endless Eternity." We read next the following record: "I have my watch from Lancaster, New Hampshire, permanently fixed by Jeweller Kimball for me, price for fixing it is two dollars, I am told by my son Joseph Connary." Finally, in the same cluster of inserted pages, Connary turns to the subject of his "Book keeping": "Now I turn to my Book, 'Children of the Patriarchs,' in 288 pages, and my pen and ink work in it in pages 14, 20, 100, 232, 236. Read next my paper next to page 254 of my Book of Fables in 358 pages, with my Book of Fables in 224 pages, with that of 344 pages of Beautiful parables. Thomas Connary." Characteristically, books are here identified by numbers of pages or their subject rather than by title, and often the reading directives refer as much to the annotation inserted within books as they do to the printed text itself.

The beginnings of Connary's inserted pages often detail the scene of his reading and book enhancement program for a particular day, an activity that often commenced early in the morning. Thus on a note inserted between the title page and the dedication of *The Dove of the Tabernacle*: "August First 1896, clear and cold in the morning, we have finished our haying work for this year yesterday thank God. Now I turn to pages 620. 621 of my Book Volume 1.2.3 in the Lives of Saints—there you will see a beautiful picture of Jesus, Mary, and Joseph." On another documented occasion, we know that Connary worked with his two books *Preparation for Death* and *The Spirit of St. Francis de Sales*, and it is in the latter that he preserves a note beginning "Monday, 11½ O'clock in the forenoon, December 15, 1881, we have more snow here now than we had before this season—warm light sprinklings of rain-clouds, unmoved in calm repose I copy a little of my work now in paper between pages 8, and nine of my Book 'Preparation for death.'"

In some volumes, even more elaborate reading programs are outlined with lists of specific chapters in books and the order in which they should be read. Such directives make it possible to map entire reading plans and to get some idea of the scope of Connary's library, since reference is always made to multiple other titles that were enhanced in a similar manner. An example among many occurs in the *Spiritual Conferences* of St. Francis of Sales, on the back of the title page (fig. 10):

> Please read very often from page 68 to page 80 of this Book Thomas Connary. Please read in this Book page 141. Read pages 148, 149. Also 166, 167, 168. My last theological work is in my Book Governmental Instructor, and in my Book A New General English Dictionary printed in London, England, in the year 1744, the pages of the Book are not numbered, my page referred to is next to page lettered MOS. I wish all to remember that my theological work cannot be wrong, Thomas Connary. My next theological work is in beginning of Book Juvenile Companion, small, pages 300, date June 1890 . . . Please read in this Book page 196 to page 214. Read page 54 in this Book—Cordiality. Read page 93 of this Book.

These are the remaining traces of a carefully planned reading program that records with remarkable specificity the extent and sequence in which both printed text and inserted notebook pages ("my theological work") should be read. Directives such as these may collaborate with a text's list of contents and other paratextual features to facilitate multiple navigational strategies within a

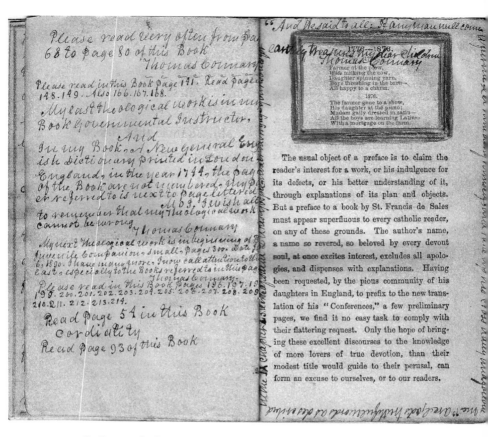

FIG. 10   St. Francis of Sales, *Spiritual Conferences*, verso of title page

book. They also suggest a process of piecemeal, reiterated, and ruminative reading in which specific passages or pages are singled out for special attention, probably with a view to memorization. Frequent underlining and obvious wear and thinning on the pages referred to in these instructions indicate that at least some of Connary's many reading plans were actually carried out in his daily routines of devotional reading and writing.

Equally detailed are a series of records, dating from March 1881, found opposite the first page of John Newman's *Discourses* (fig. 11). These instructions again indicate the simultaneous reading of "pen and ink work" together with the printed word. I quote from this extended plan, which outlines a program of book enhancement and then proceeds to detail a reading list that comprises entire books, newspaper fragments in books, and handwritten pages.

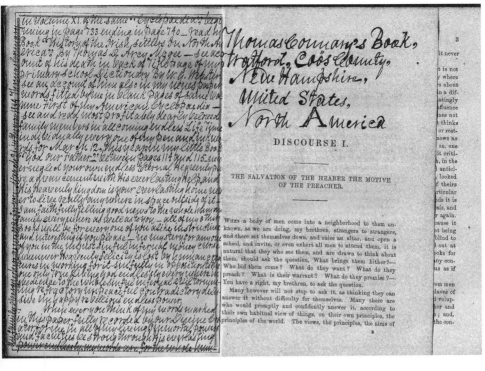

FIG. II   John Henry Newman, *Discourses Addressed to Mixed Congregations*, page 1

A broad interest in religious matters and the creed of other Christian denominations is apparent in this and other outlines.

I mark five of my Books in this order.

1. "Newman's Sermons"—page 107—see my paper between pages 108 and 109.
2. "The Lamp 1860"—newspaper printed words.
3. "Volume 2, of "Gordon's America"
4. "Charity in Conversation"—in back of contents page vii, and first Introduction page.
5. "Day Star of American Freedom"—in back of one of the first blank pages . . .

Read my little Book "Stories and Parables of Saint Bonaventure"—read in said volume 2nd of "Gordon's America" and in volume 1rst of it, an account of Mormonism, also an account of Mormonism beginning in page 130, ending in page 142, of my Book: "Religious Creeds and Statistics By John Hayward"—see my newspaper account of the Mormon Church and troubles in first blank pages of Volume First of my "New American Cyclopedia," and in volume xi of the same "Cyclopedia," beginning in page 733 ending in page 740—read my Book "History of the Irish Settlers in North America," by Thomas D. Arcy McGee—see account of his death in back of Titlepage of my Primary School Dictionary By W. G. Webster—see an account of him also in my newspaper words fitted by me in blank pages of same volume first of my American Cyclopedia.

This set of complex, interweaving instructions conveys a sense of the distinct language that Connary applies to the discipline of "Book keeping." It also gives an impression of a peculiar, self-devised readerly methodology, in which a route is mapped through distinct items of print, manuscript, and image in a way that carries meaning to the reader, but whose underlying rationale remains somewhat obscure to outsiders.

In a highly relevant recent discussion, Peter Stallybrass observes that the complex and unpredictable ways in which readers approach a text can often limit the significance of paratextual features such as an index, preface, or a list of contents. As readers may access text randomly and reshape the function of books, we cannot simply assume a straightforward reading according to the directives in the main text: "a totalising view of paratexts, in which each element is added up, misrecognizes how one paratext can be used to skip or evade another."[9] The implication of Connary's approach to reading is precisely that it exposes in a rather extreme way the limits of the printed paratext, as he appears to be guided primarily by his own highly idiosyncratic system of reading routes and text excerption.

One thing is certain: for Connary, reading "Books" means reading enhanced books. It means reading printed text, manuscript annotation, and newspaper cuttings preserved in the enhanced book, often in conjunction with material external to it, such as biblical text, periodicals, diary records, and religious images. All these various components blend meaningfully to form a complex and integrated program of reading. Although there is occasional mention of full-scale linear reading in which a book is read through from cover to cover, the directives cited above indicate that the norm for Connary is the frequent but discontinuous consultation of selected titles and the interpolated material within. Several instructions for reading give some idea of how Connary planned his reading in sessions involving the printed text, his own annotations, and text from the Bible. This is a process of eclectic and piecemeal reading in and around the printed text, in which an interest in a specific theme, like the biography of authors or the history of other churches (such as the Mormons), guides the trajectory of reading, more so than any internal organizational structure of a single book volume. Often such a thematic emphasis leads Connary to disregard the print in favor of a system of cross-referencing with attention focused on the book enhancements themselves. At other times, however, he shows himself to be not just an acute and concentrated reader of the entire printed book, but also a critical one.

A Reader's Responses

So far we have seen how Connary's writing in books can generate a life of its own, being cross-referenced from one volume to the next, with annotations glossing other annotations, often with an uncertain relationship to the printed text. As such, this material may confound our customary expectations about what it means to annotate a book: we may reasonably expect writing in books to complement the text through supplementation, various sorts of referencing, displays of learning, corrigenda, or polemical engagement. But with Connary's book enhancements we are reminded of how the transition from ascertaining *what* is being read to *how* text is read can be fraught with considerable difficulty.

However, there are many instances in which Connary's notes gloss the print in a very direct way—instances in which his handwritten additions register critical engagement, and in some cases disagreement, with the text that accommodates them. Chapter 4 argues that Connary conducts repeated and in-depth readings of the works of Julian of Norwich and St. Francis of Sales and that he was deeply influenced by the theology and spirituality of these authors. But first we examine a few preliminary cases where Connary proves himself a particularly responsive, if highly dogmatic and eccentric, reader, and where he engages discursively with passages in his books in ways that reveal much about him as a religious and reading individual.

We see a particularly opinionated reader in Samuel Croxall's edition of the *Fables of Aesop*, where Connary's stern disapproval of Croxall's morals does not preclude an underlying esteem for the author and his book: "I am much more than very sorry to have to see and feel that many of Samuel Croxall's words in Fable Book of 358 pages are sinfully wrong in every respect as his long windy

preface signifies beginning and ending with the Greek Monk Maximus Planudes—I am thankful for his Book and have nothing in my mind for him but
purely just faithful charitable feelings of affection."[10] The Anglican clergyman
Samuel Croxall's (1688–1752) edition of Aesop's *Fables* appeared in London in
1722. In his preface, Croxall opens with an unequivocal dismissal of the classic
biography of Aesop offered by the thirteenth-century Byzantine grammarian
Maximus Planudes, and then launches a rancorous attack on the then dominant edition of the fables by Roger L'Éstrange, expressing harsh anti-Catholic
sentiment throughout. Regarding L'Éstrange's edition as highly inappropriate
to Americans who are "born with free blood in their veins and suck in liberty
with their very milk," Croxall's is an obvious bid to discredit L'Éstrange as "a
tool and hireling of the popish faction" who promotes "pernicious principles"
detrimental to youth.[11] These are sentiments offensive to Connary's Catholicism, but he is not one to continue in a spirit of stinging polemic: at the end
of Croxall's preface, in a note signed "fifteen minutes before eleven o'clock in
the forenoon of December 8, in the year 1884," he notes simply that Croxall
"proves to my full satisfaction that he has hurt himself as a sinful deceiver
much more than he hurt the monk" (i.e., Planudes).

However, Connary's main interest resides not with the prejudiced Croxall,
but with Aesop's fables themselves and their didactic applications. In the same
note, Connary states, "I read the Fables cxxxix, in pages 252 and 253, with
pages 265, and 266, cxlvi, including the Applications for both in this Book,
with much pleasure as exactly right in every respect everywhere—in pages 57
and 58 of it, Fable xx, with its Application as Teaching never can be right anywhere as I very plainly read the whole open infinitely perfect endless Eternal
School Book of Creation." Fable xx, which Connary dismisses as "never right
anywhere," tells the story of a lamb abandoned by its mother and brought up
by a goat, and it concludes, "it is they whose goodness makes them our parents, that properly claim a filial respect from us, and not those who are such
only out of necessity."[12] The precise nature of Connary's objection to this
moral explication remains rather hazy, and he records no more than his own
categorical disapproval. What meets with his approval, on the other hand, are
the fables entitled "The Husbandman and His Sons" and "The Old Man and
His Sons," the titles alone suggesting the particular resonance to a farmer for
whom household and business management were constant concerns. In the
first of these fables, an old man desirous to ensure the continuation of his
agriculture tells his sons that a treasure lies buried somewhere in a field. The
sons find no treasure per se, but, having tilled the entire land in search for it,
manage to produce an abundant crop. The moral application extols the disci-

pline of agriculture and asserts that "labour and industry well applied, seldom fail of finding a treasure."[13] In the second fable, a father teaches the power of unity to his sons torn apart by dissension, and the reader is instructed that "those of the same blood and lineage have a natural disposition to unite together, which they ought, by all means, to cultivate and improve."

Apropos of these fables, Connary registers no discursive or argued response but proceeds by way of categorical approval ("exactly right") and rejection ("exactly wrong in every respect"). What is clear, however, is that his focus on fables relating to the experience of family unity parallels the many embedded notes in his books that either talk of family affairs or directly address members of "my dearly beloved family." Connary appears to esteem the didactic value of the fable genre within his own tight-knit family unit, but when the application of a fable can be seen to denigrate the power of filial bonds (as with the story of the lamb brought up by a goat), he claims for himself reliable powers of discernment and rejects it unreservedly. In this case, the appeal is to his family and any other reader of the *Fables of Aesop*: "I write a few words in this, that you may know how to guard against improper teaching everywhere in Books, and everywhere outside of Books."

If an absence of direct discursive engagement characterizes Connary's interaction with the fable genre, we do note some such engagement in his annotations in P. R. Leatherman's *Elements of Moral Science*, printed by James Challen & Son in Philadelphia in 1860 and not reprinted since. In his notes, Connary demonstrates some subtlety of argument and takes issue specifically with the author's teaching on moral obligation. He notes several times in the margin "wrong reason here" and "wrong again," and then writes substantial correctives and dogmatic assertions that encircle the printed text in multiple layers (fig. 12).

On page 15 in Leatherman's theologico-philosophical investigation, we read the following on the subject of moral duty: "Our object is to acquire knowledge of the Moral Law. In our investigation of the various subjects of which we must necessarily treat, we should have some standard by which to determine whether our views are true and false. We should neither be guided by the dictates of conscience, nor by what we may suppose the laws of nature teach us, in determining what is right and what wrong in morals. The Sacred Scriptures are the only infallible guide in morals." With the sentence beginning "We should neither be guided by the dictates of conscience," an asterisk marks the beginning of Connary's correction: "Wrong reasoning here—understand the Holy Bible wrong and you do not understand Endless Eternal Infinitely Perfect necessary government just Law as God Himself perpetually teaches

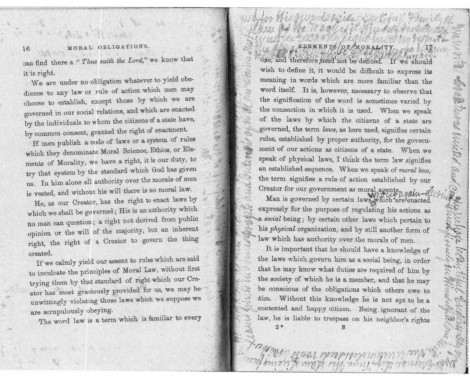

FIG. 12   P. R. Leatherman, *Elements of Moral Science*, pages 16–17

His own Exact one only Law to all who choose Him as the one duly True Living God everywhere in His own Infinitely perfect Creation—His Law and reasoning power live in Himself for Himself and for His own Dutiful Creatures. Thomas Connary."

This statement, which displays eccentricity of thought and articulation, is contained in a single prolonged sentence enveloping the text that it refutes. Theological precision is not found in great measure in Connary, but we may glean a little about his preoccupation from such annotation. As with Leatherman's disquisitions, Connary is concerned with the fundamental principles of morality, and less with the level of practical application and actual rules of conduct. What makes him react strongly is Leatherman's claim that scripture can be relied on as the singular and infallible guide to moral action and his consequent distrust of "the dictates of conscience" in deciding right from wrong. In opposition to Leatherman, Connary insists on the fallibility of the human hermeneutic capacity: since there is a real danger that the Bible be misinterpreted, it cannot be relied on solely, or even principally, for moral absolutes. Instead, for Connary, the ultimate obligation of "Dutiful Creatures" is understood to be within the dictates of the "Divine Just Law," the "Law" that Connary affirms in nearly all of his pages, but never talks about as represented paradigmatically by the scriptures or by the example of Christ's moral living. The crucial factors for Connary remain those of human conscience and volition: insight into God's moral law is available to those who actively choose God and reject sin. Choosing God means to partake in the absolute and indubitable benevolence of a God who is "exactly right in every respect," a God who is characterized as "the infinitely perfect endless Divine giver of every good gift, nothing bad can ever come from Him, nothing bad can ever come from Him anywhere."[14] When Leatherman looks outside of human conscience to the Bible for moral absolutes of right and wrong, this proves irreconcilable with Connary's ironclad conviction of one supreme and benevolent "Law" in which the elect partake. For Connary, divine "Law" remains universal, singular, and unified, so when Leatherman treats of "laws" (in the plural), this motivates Connary to provide another spiraling *corrigendum*. I quote Leatherman first, followed by Connary's response:

> Man is governed by certain laws, which are enacted expressly for the purpose of regulating his actions as a *social* being; by certain other laws which pertain to his *physical* organization, and by still another form of law which has authority over the morals of men.[15]

> Wrong again—during the whole beautiful Endless Day of God's Eternal Life Time His Law Living full in Himself alone as one only Law of Endless Life Time for Himself and for His own Docile Dutiful Family of Immortal Creatures united and combined firmly in Himself alone with the numberless seeds roots branches leaves fruits incomes profits and interests of that one Divine Just Law as He Teaches it Himself perpetually must be Exactly Right in every respect—the opposite must be exactly wrong in every respect I know positively. Thomas Connary.

Leatherman's observations about the several laws that govern the individual are here replaced with one single image of universality and incorporation, a grand lyrical proclamation, in which the entire cosmos partakes in God's unified and "Exactly Right" Law. The striking image of total incorporation, in which the elect live under the domination of "the Law" together with the "numberless seeds roots branches leaves fruits incomes profits and interests," effectively fuses Connary's proximity to the agricultural world with the monetary sphere that absorbs so much of his thinking. The significance of the Bible as a moral guide clearly takes second place in relation to this vision of the "Docile Dutiful Family of Immortal Creatures"—the glorified recipients of the divine Law, uninclined to do evil.

As these examples indicate, we cannot separate Connary's book enhancements from his moral and theological opinions. All enhancements, whether written or image-based, on spiritual or worldly themes, can be seen as ways of rehearsing a limited repertoire of religious perspectives and deeply felt convictions. Connary's written responses tend to occur when he finds his own principal themes reflected in the texts, whether by affirmation or negation. In such cases, text passages provide the opportunity for reiterating his creed, sometimes in a way that shows great relevance to the print and some occasional theological sophistication (as when engaging with the finer casuistries of Leatherman's philosophy). But more often the response appears peculiar and somewhat bizarre, leaving the precise relation between printed text on the one hand, and enhancement and annotation on the other, indeterminate.

With these observations in mind, we need to acknowledge the inherent difficulties in understanding Connary more profoundly as a reader. We can assess him fairly comprehensively as a book enhancer—as an interactor and collaborator with the material book. But as a reader of books he responds by means of the dogmatic assertion (whether he is endorsing or disagreeing) and provides very little discursive engagement with the text that could reveal deeper insight into the process of reading, its practices, reiterations, and modalities. Although clearly an impassioned and opinionated reader-cum-annotator, Connary the reader is silent about much and remains, to a certain degree, an enigma. To what extent, for instance, does he read a text in a progressive arc from cover to cover? Were the majority of his enhanced books subject to reiterated, selective, piecemeal reading, and were some not read at all? And what about Connary as a social reader: is reading only, or predominantly, a private, withdrawn activity, or was it also thought of as a social event that involved reading aloud and responding collectively to books? These are questions that will be considered further in what follows, but definitive answers do not present themselves readily.

The Autonomous Reader

The preceding discussion has investigated strategies of book enhancement that provide direct and reflected response to the printed text. But it is also clear now that we need to acknowledge the extent to which there is often no explicit exchange between book and enhancement, the material book becoming simply a medium for a self-styled *bricolage* of miscellaneous observation and family records. Two further examples, peculiar and visually striking, provide further illustration of method and complexity.

In *The Council of the Vatican*, the back of the title page and the facing first page of the preface show the way in which Connary deconstructs what we habitually think of as the unity of the printed page by deploying in it disjunct items with unclear relation to the printed text (fig. 13). Here, on the blank leaf facing the preface, is inserted a lengthy newspaper summary of a lecture on the achievement of Christopher Columbus given by the Rev. Edward McGlynn, pastor of St. Stephen's Church in New York (undated). Opposite it, Connary has written one of his innumerable appeals to his children to be firm in faith and avoid sin. Kinship and the domestic setting remain the all-important context—the social epitext—for the reception of the enhanced volume. Connary's exhortation surrounds the printed preface in characteristic fashion, and

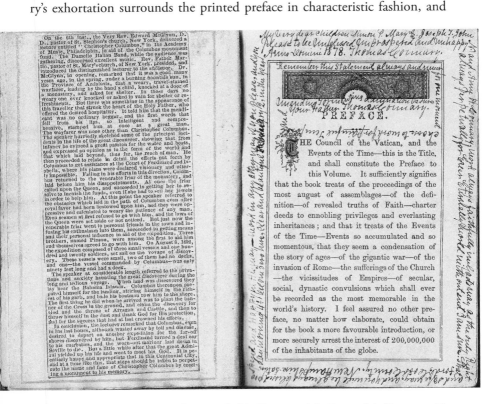

FIG. 13   Thomas Canon Pope, *The Council of the Vatican and the Events of the Time*, page iii

ends: "Stratford, Coös County, New Hampshire, Saturday morning 4 below zero here, clear and beautiful February 2, in the year Anno Domini 1878. Thomas Connary. Remember this statement always and never for one moment choose to work for painful temporal and unending tormenting damnation be sure. Your Father Thomas Connary."

Similarly saturated with annotation and enhancement are pages 16 and 17 of Newman's *Discourses*, which contain the end of "Discourse I" ("The Salvation of the Hearer the Motive of the Preacher") and the beginning of "Discourse II" ("Neglect of Divine Calls and Warnings"). The following handwritten prayer appears on page 16, where it barely avoids the print and is apropos of Newman's themes of obedience and salvation (fig. 14): "I sincerely and most humbly Pray, that God may help me incessantly, as one of His own universal faithful peace makers, in cheerfully and peacefully harmonizing all of my own powers with His Divine Unlimited Heavenly Eternal Power, exactly in such a way and manner for endless Eternity as will continue to be most pleasing to Himself."

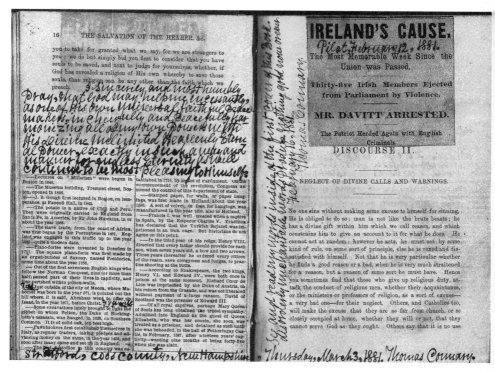

FIG. 14   John Henry Newman, *Discourses Addressed to Mixed Congregations*, pages 16–17

Underneath the prayer is pasted a newspaper clipping with a medley of trivia, ranging from the year the potato was imported into Europe (ca. 1563) to the invention of "stamped paper for walls" in Holland (ca. 1555). Intriguingly, the following information has captured the attention of Connary, who adds "read" and "free will" in the margin: "Just outside of the city of Mecca, where Mahomet was born in the year 571, is pointed out the hill where, it is said, Abraham went to offer up Isaac, in the year 1781 before Christ." Connary's brief yet telling addition of "free will" at the end of this entry connects with his rich corpus of notes that focus on human volition and on the urgency of conforming one's will to the moral law of God. Heading the opposite page is a newspaper headline from the *Pilot*, dated (by hand) February 12, 1881, on the ejection of thirty-five Irish members from the British Parliament, "The Most Memorable Week Since the Union Was Passed." Extending down the left-hand margin of the page is one of the many reading directives that refer not to the print but to an inserted magazine cutting and surrounding annotation: "see and read my words inside of the first cover of this Book. disorderly uncharitable words produce nothing good now or ever. February 16, 1881. Thomas Connary." The page referred to—the front pastedown on the inside cover—contains extensive writing and a printed summary dated January 15, 1881, of a speech given by the Irish Republican and social campaigner Michael Davitt on "the three F's": "Fixity of Tenure, Free Sale, Fair Rents." These pages in Newman's *Discourses* show Connary at work on enhancing the book from the middle of January to early March 1881, and inserting into it an assemblage of prayer, reading directives, miscellaneous references, and writing related to the Irish cause, focusing especially on British oppression and landlordism. It is the achievement of the creative annotating reader to produce a text (or multiple texts) within a page—a text (or multiple texts) within a text.

The true pleasure of the text can be found in the scope it offers for self-articulation and pious proclamation (themselves forms of self-annotation). For Connary, this means converting books into multipurpose objects where writings and varied materials at hand are inserted in a book's vacant space. Notes from 1889 found in Julian of Norwich's *Revelations* observe that "we have no diary's for sale in this town this year," and the book contains a correspondence between Connary and the Pilot Publishing Company in which Connary reminds them to send a "Pictorial Catholic Home Almanac" that has been delayed. Such occasional scarcity of books and paper may have led Connary to make even more imaginative use of his printed books as scrapbook-style repositories of miscellaneous material.

At first sight, the impression may be that a book is enhanced merely because it offers space to do so, and because of its perceived physical durability. Connary notes, for example, that his densely annotated and heavily worn *Spiritual Conferences* of St. Francis of Sales "is a good Book well bound and can be safely retained in my Family continually forever."[16] The book, in other words, can be appreciated for properties other than the text it contains, and it is sometimes uncertain whether Connary actually read a given text. As we all know from experience, the purchase, possession, or borrowing of a book provides no conclusive evidence of actual reading. But the case of Connary opens up one further caveat as we attempt to recover the experiences of reading: even a book annotated, inscribed, and enhanced is not *de facto* proof of actual reading. In some instances, even when a book shows signs of heavy wear with the pages coming loose, the top of the spine missing from frequent handling, and the binding separating, it need not have been a book read.[17]

Far from being troubled by such *aporia*, Connary ultimately claims the freedom that is the reader's. He shows himself to be an unusually diligent, attentive, and systematic reader of texts: numerous pages of notes record discursive and critical engagement with the printed word. But equally often, his creative book enhancements record no direct response to this printed word but are parasitic upon it. They constitute an elaborate paratext that thrives in the ample blank spaces, threatening at times to suffocate the printed text with something more pertinent.

Such creative *mise-en-page* and multiplicity of texts truly reveal Connary to be the poacher *par excellence* of the printed book, using the materials at hand to turn his volumes into miscellanies of factual reference, devotional edification, and family history. In the two examples above, the pages feature not one text but a multitude of texts, and all become, in a sense, primary texts. The newspaper fragments and the marginal annotations, both of which appear decontextualized, acquire relative autonomy, paradoxically so because of their location in the print margins. Here, what Connary terms the "blank paper surface room"—the empty page or the blank areas on a printed page— becomes the ultimate response inviting structure.

In using the metaphor of the reader as poacher, I refer of course to Michel de Certeau's famous essay "Reading as Poaching," first published in French in 1980.[18] This essay is a particularly wide-ranging and historically sensitive contribution in a body of recent reader-response criticism that explores reading as active and co-creative. In it, de Certeau offers thoughts on how the practice of reading can rework, or "re-employ," various elements of a text in unpredictable ways, for diverse purposes, and under varying social and institutional constraints. De Certeau's observations regarding the appropriating reader, who puts textual matter to creative and unanticipated uses, resonate strongly with Connary's book handling practices: "The reader takes neither the position of the author nor an author's position. He invents in texts something different from what they 'intended.' He detaches them from their (lost or accessory) origin. He combines their fragments and creates something unknown in the space organized by their capacity for allowing an indefinite plurality of meaning."[19]

De Certeau's rather liberal evaluation of the reader's freedom is a welcome and influential corrective to any approach that too readily assumes the inconspicuous or passive reading habits of nonprofessional readers. Part of its aim is to foreground what Matthew Brown later referred to as "appropriation's selective aggression," through which the reader may be "claiming literary property as one's own."[20] In a recent application of de Certeau's thoughts to the study of privately owned codices of late medieval religious texts, Ryan Perry has drawn attention to what he terms "a capricious dialogism" between the reader and the text read, through which "improvisational and enigmatic readings and patterns of use will arise, with the reader appropriating the matter of the book into the service of her own ideologies, incorporating the text into well-established rhythms and customs of everyday life and belief, as opposed to acquiescently taking direction from the author."[21]

As suggested in the introduction, the terms "appropriation" and "poaching" can help us understand much of what is going on in Connary's enhanced books. Nowhere are these concepts more relevant than with the tendency of the enhancements to generate their own self-annotation and system of cross-reference, referring exclusively to themselves while disregarding the print. Such is evident in the following instructions, which indicate routine reading *between* the pages—that is, reading the handwritten notes embedded in the books: "Read all of my work beginning in page 276 of my journal, with that between pages 342 and 343 of Book 'Milner's End of Controversy,' in connection with this, next to last contents page in my Book, marked in back 'Council of the Vatican.' Thomas Connary."[22]

Another insert that facilitates a process of reading outside or around the main text is found in Vanbrugh Livingston's *Inquiry into the Merits of the Reformed Doctrine of "Imputation."* Stuck to the front flyleaves and parts of the contents pages is a short story entitled "An Hour of Terror" written by an N. J. Cotton for the *Coös County Democrat.* The chilling tale of horror and suspense is too long to fit in the front of the book, so it continues at the rear of the volume, where it occupies three end flyleaves. Such book enhancement can serve no other purpose than that of recreational reading, and it opens up the possibility of navigational strategies within the book other than just a reading from beginning to end. Meaning is understood by Connary to reside in the margins as much as in the printed text itself, and recurring prepositions such as "between," "around," "next to," as well as "first in" and "at end of" (on the front and end flyleaves, respectively) direct attention to textual and decorative enhancements in a book's "blank paper surface room."

Connary's own book-writings at times become primary texts, generating elaborate auto-commentary, with the inserted additions neatly framed and set off from the print. At other times they function in the mode of the discursive footnote, which, as Jacques Derrida observes, "is also a text unto itself, rather detached, relatively decontextualized or capable of creating its own context, such that one can read it quickly and directly for itself."[23] To be sure, with Connary's writing in books we are at the opposite extreme from the type of marginalia that offers *corrigenda* or glosses to the print but nothing personally revealing. Instead we see personal glosses glossing each other and carefully cross-referenced from one volume to the next—but not responding to the print at the center of the page.

This form of book enhancement shows a poacher of the entire book (not merely of texts) who devises his very own criteria for the use of books, and it contradicts to some extent some widely disseminated initiatives in the literature of the time to circumscribe reading processes and promote traditional reading habits. As David Nord has shown in his study of early nineteenth-century American evangelical printing, the promotion of wholesome Christian literature often went hand in hand with the promotion of a particularly intense and structured form of meditative reading. The reading directives in much religious tract literature, Nord shows, explicitly sought to combat cursory, random, or light reading and insisted that the ruminative and continuous reading of a book from cover to cover was essential if reading was to be virtuous and function as an essential means of grace.[24] This is, of course, an idealized form of devout reading, and readers were free to set their own standards for what constituted efficacious reading, as Nord also demonstrates. With Connary we see the enterprising and autonomous reader, undoubtedly more intensely pious than many writers of didactic tracts had in mind, but also one who is capable of inserting material for random, nonlinear, and leisurely reading pursuits within a multifaceted reading program. This is the reader who, in the words of de Certeau, "invents in texts something different from what they intended," a reader who labors across the organized printed surface, combining and re-employing textual matter in countless ways.

Having acknowledged Connary's selective reading and free interventions, we should note the clear coherence often detectable between print and enhancement, and the way in which the design features and genre of a book determine reading, utility, and the density of annotation. We see Connary always experiencing and commenting on format, typesetting, *mise-en-page*, and paratextual framing, and these dimensions directly influence the nature and scope of his interaction with specific books. A small book on a devotional subject matter, easy to carry around, is far more likely to attract substantive annotation and enhancement than, for instance, a large, two-volume book on local history and topography. Unsurprisingly, we notice a heightened degree of spiritual and didactic intensity in the annotations inserted in devotional and mystical texts: such intensity is often absent from the nonreligious books, where the enhancements tend rather routinely to reproduce prayer, admonition and miscellaneous records. And it is in his religious literature that Connary labors with the utmost intensity to add graphic embellishments, making these an integral part of a book's design features and textual presentation.

In all these cases, whether he is working with books on religious or secular themes, we might perhaps best understand Connary as enhancing books in the sense of collaborating with them, rather than subverting or appropriating them, or performing upon them the "silent aggression" of the "poacher." He makes of his books what he needs, and this involves turning the book artifact into both an event and a monument, imbued with context and sincerity. The meticulous dating and signing of the hundreds of handwritten pages in the books capture multiple events of reading, and the succinct note "I am here," recorded in the margins of selected volumes, inscribes these with the immediacy and address of the letter or the signed declaration. The following chapter explores further the process of enhancing not just the utility of his volumes but also their signifying power as iconic objects.

EPIPHANY

The Lamp

"Now I say read my Diary page for November 23 last, when in my bed early in the evening here, I plainly saw in one of my hands a lamp of fire burning. I put the fire out moderately as a lamp—I found no lamp to put away: it was gone. No dream in this reality be sure." This brief account, dated Sunday, August 28, 1892, is found on the note inserted opposite the title page in Bishop Camus's *Spirit of St. Francis de Sales*. As with Connary's vision of the Virgin and her blessed company, this one is recorded elsewhere in Connary's books, where it is glossed in greater depth as to its moral implications. Thus in Philippe's *Six Hundred Thousand Combatants*:

> November 23d, 1891, I made this Record, when about ten o'clock in the evening I began to sleep, then Immediately, I sat up in bed, and plainly saw in one of my hands a lamp burning, I stopped the blaze by blowing it moderately. As I plainly saw the Lamp burning in my hand, then I found the Lamp gone. This I mark now as a reality pure and heavenly, as God is my Judge here and everywhere. No more persecution for obedience to God, I sincerely hope. I cannot ever think that sin can be right anywhere. We may think that sin is very necessary some times. I say now that sin never was necessary, never can be necessary. In doing business we must be very firm for the right, and very reluctantly punish the wrong in persons who should be no more than very willing to believe us, and never for one moment desire to have such persons severely punished. All cannot in the beginning of Life see the best way to Live, but God continually shows the right way to all who are thankfully willing to believe Him.

Specificity of place and time pervades all of his spiritual experiences: the "then and there" of Connary's visions of the holy Virgin and of the lamp of fire burning are always made manifest, whether "in this, my own house" or "when in my bed early in the evening here." Again, the hermeneutic category for these showings—"seeing very plainly"—is underscored repeatedly. So predominant is the corporeal dimension that the first recording above makes no mention of any spiritual content, nor does it show an evolving understanding of a theological significance. When Connary returns to relate the account, slightly later in *The Six Hundred Thousand Combatants*, he derives from his experience affirmation of his moral perspective, although the interpretive connection remains opaque: his declarations remain largely void of ratiocinative engagement.

Anyone with interest in the spirituality of the English Middle Ages will inevitably be reminded of that remarkable description we have, from the fourteenth-century English mystic Richard Rolle, of a vision also centered on the overwhelming experience of sensible fire.

> I first felt my heart begin to warm. I felt it truly, not simply in my imagination, but just as though my heart was burning with a physical fire. I marvelled, you may be sure, at how this burning in my soul leapt up, and at its unanticipated comfort. It was so vivid an experience that I often put my hand against my chest just to see if I could feel any cause for the heat outwardly! But once I knew that it was purely a matter of inward, spiritual nature, and that the burning sensation was not from a carnal love or concupiscence, I realized it had to be a gift from my Creator. Accordingly I was glad, and melted with a desire for a greater experience of love.[1]

We have no indication that Thomas Connary read Richard Rolle, who had yet to be made widely available in print at this time, nor that he had much knowledge of the late medieval vogue of affective devotion to Christ and his Passion of which Rolle was an influential and ebullient representative. Of particular importance to Rolle is the demarcation of sensible from spiritual impression: his is a famous example of the priorities of the medieval discourse of *discretio spirituum*, the discernment of spirits, that distinguishes what he terms "bodily cause utwardlye" from what is properly supernatural and occurs "of gostely [spiritual] cause inwardlye." Connary, by contrast, shows little interest in such a discipline, making a more elementary distinction between dream, on the one hand, and reality or "plain sight," on the other. Glossing his impression as reality pure and heavenly, Connary finds here an experiential, quasi-mystical affirmation of his moral perspective and of the reality of God's direct moral guidance. His own language of literal visualization thus provides another dimension to the themes that predominate throughout his writings—namely, the absolute, and absolutely benevolent, nature of God's moral law, and the urgent need to abandon sin.

3

REDEMPTIVE READING IN THE CONNARY HOUSEHOLD

> My dearly beloved family members and full family connections in all coming time, please make every Book, word, picture, figure, numeral, and pen mark which I will leave with you, read, and count in favour of the most pure undefiled Eternal endless Heavenly love, justice, peace, and unlimited charity, with our Divine Creator's incessant Help—keep them, and yourselves clean, in harmony with Divine harmony.
>
> —Thomas Connary, note dated May 16, 1883, inserted between pages 202 and 203 of Lewis, *The Sinner's Guide*

Domestic Reading and the Presence of the Book

Thomas Connary attaches a particularly rich array of meaning and utility to his books. Books are understood as commodities that can be traded, as gift objects to and from family and friends, as repositories for documentation and miscellaneous reference, as manuals or catechetic instruments for personal and family instruction, and as material containers awaiting extra-illustration, decoration, framing, and annotation. Once enhanced, his books stand as testaments to a life of intensifying devotion; they take the position as mnemonics and miscellanies for personal piety, as props with a form of ceremonial or ritualistic presence, as iconic objects to be revered, and even as vessels of sacrality.

Through the process of enhancement, print and paratext become fused with a pervasive sense of topography and domestic space, in such a way that material, domestic and spiritual values enhance each other. In this process, a new whole is created that one cannot separate and one ought not to think of as separate. When Connary instructs his family to treasure the books, he promotes precisely this notion that a new entity and a new spiritual valence are being forged through the discipline of laboring in books, a discipline that brings together print and "pen mark." By urging his family members to preserve "every Book, word, picture, figure, numeral, and pen mark which I will leave with you," Connary means to assert the deep and meaningful coherence of a book and its added components.

As a form of spiritually motivated deictics, the book enhancements appear both compulsive and compelling to Connary. Laboring across the topography of the page and making his books distinctively his own, he finds precious moments of intimacy and emotional reward in which he can meaningfully bring together the ethical and the aesthetic, the spiritual and the utilitarian. Here print and manuscript exist always in a passionate and meaningful exchange: print, for Connary, is abundant in meaning and it elicits prayer, proclamation, and decorative addition.

It may appear striking that Connary talks of a wide range of books as being not just precious but blessed and sacred. As William Sherman and Peter Stallybrass, among others, have shown, it is common for a family Bible to be enhanced as a treasured tome or a family heirloom: it may preserve traces of historical ownership, genealogical record, and readers' manuscript indices, or it may store precious objects of personal, sentimental value.[1] But for Connary, books on varied secular themes are responded to comprehensively, with notable solemnity, and they elicit pious annotation. Such bibliographic inscription may seem excessive or misguided, a type of fetishization of the common material book that is determined to make it a shrine for worship and prayer. Or we may understand it, as I propose to do here, as a consequence of this devout farmer-bibliophile's prolonged project to explore the phenomenal depth of the book objects with which he surrounds himself.

In his valuable study of the book culture and religious reading habits of early New England, Matthew Brown explores "the phenomenological impress of objects on their devotional subjects" and discusses ways in which the lived religious experience of early Puritans was nurtured by the codex format: "The format of codices, broadsides, and private manuscripts; the visual image of an illustration, or of the page itself; the tactile heft of a duodecimo or folio; the presence of a written record within the scene of reading—all of these factors participate in the imaginative life of spiritual readers."[2] In a similar vein, I argue that Connary's personal, operative involvement with the book centers on the experience of the tangibility of the book object and the reiterated exploration of its material layers. It is through the physical experiences of reading, enhancing, caring for, and in some cases binding books that the owner finds a highly concrete outlet for deep passion and originality.[3]

As indicated in the introduction, the important place for realizing such intimacy with books is in Connary's own study, "the room in which I am busy much of my time." Connary acknowledges location as an important dimension in his rituals of book labor and as part of the complex paratextual layering of the enhanced book. The text housed in the book binding is only one of the several elements in the experience and understanding of the entire book; another is the material and visible embodiment of the book as this is handled and appreciated by Connary in his activity of "Book keeping." With the situational context of Connary's reading in his room, we move into what Gérard Genette has touched on only very briefly as the spatial field of the paratext (or the "epitext"), the complex spatial, topographical circumstances that "surround a work and to a greater or lesser degree clarify or modify its significance."[4] The constituent elements of Connary's private study—its shelves, desk, window, the view through the window, pictures, bindings—give purpose and meaning to the book: they are separate from it, but part of how the text is read and part of the full experience of the book. When Connary looks away temporarily from a book to a picture of a saint on the wall or through the window to the pond in the field outside and to observe the changing seasons, he engages with something external to the book but incorporated meaningfully into the experience of reading it. The important point made by Hester Lees-Jeffries in a study of Renaissance texts applies equally well to Connary's experience of his volumes: "it cannot be assumed that the paratextual is coextensive with the text, the page, or indeed the book; it can also be, on occasion, that which is seen when the reader lifts his or her eyes from the page, the places and spaces where he or she walked in the intervals in between reading and writing."[5]

Connary's experience of using the *Revelations* of Julian of Norwich is documented in particular detail and acknowledges the inevitable physicality that exists between the book and the experience of reading it. The pictures of holy people (he mentions images of John Chrysostom, Julian of Norwich, Thomas Aquinas, and Hugh, bishop of Grenoble, among others) and the window through which Connary is looking northerly are all part of a multidimensional visual frame for the work in books. As he is busy at his desk interleaving notes in *The Council of the Vatican* on the morning of November 24, 1890, he notes that "next to this I have my Blessed and Holy Bibles large, with all of my large and very small Books, including with them Mrs. Herberts two Books for the villagers and The Life and Revelations of Gertrude." A note in *The Sinner's Guide* sets the scene for the activity of reading on Sunday, October 5, 1896, at one o'clock in the afternoon: "my son Joseph T. Connary and His wife go to our North Stratford Church meeting—they say that they have some special business to do there, so they go—me, Lucinda, and the children are at home all day." Connary, who might not have been fit in old age to undertake the trip to North Stratford, withdraws to his room, so he records, to write up a considerable number of pages for insertion in his books.

It is in this private, enclosed location, "the room I am now using for reading and writing purposes," that Connary pursues the discipline which is the important conduit for, and culmination of, lived religious experience. Through the ritualistic discipline of working in books, Connary enhances his volumes as spatiotemporal events, with heightened visual dimensions, imbued with intimacy, spiritual affect, locality, and authenticity. The products of a vigorous mass-publication program of Irish-American writing—titles made affordable through careful management of costs and the utilization of the latest printing techniques, such as stereotyping—are thus made to bear historical witness and manifest unique incidence.[6]

The rest of this chapter looks further at these precious moments of immersing oneself in books and examines how the book object participates crucially for Connary in structuring subjectivity and devotional identity. A distinction will be made between two related processes in this book enhancement project. The first is indicated by Connary's recurring statement "I am here," and suggests the concrete and devout practice of inscribing oneself in books to form a repository for spiritual life and family record. The second is captured in Connary's striking phrase "putting Books to work": books, by being prepared and enhanced in a highly tangible manner, are made to work *for* the owner as intercessory, iconic objects invested with rich phenomenal depth. We may understand both processes as part of a private and withdrawn activity, in which one individual immerses himself in reading and derives considerable emotional and spiritual reward from such dedication. But in fact Connary's "Book keeping" is always imagined as involving social consequences and as instrumental in reinforcing friendships and familial bonds.

The Social Annotator

For Connary, books are domestic objects; they are about home, family ties, and a sense of belonging. There are numerous recorded instances of social transactions in which books—inscribed, personalized books—are presented to or received from others as valued devotional gifts, indicating the social uses of book collecting and enhancement. It is clear that Connary occasionally annotates and enhances a book with a specific recipient in mind, the enhancements thus being incorporated in its transmission and conveying a sense of writing and annotating for an audience—a sense, in other words, of a conscious, pious self-fashioning meant to be read by others. A few handwritten notes record the receipt of religious books from visitors to the household. But much more frequently we find dedications written by Connary himself in books he intended to give to friends and members of his family. At least nominally, the books record an intimate community of readers and a household deeply engaged with books as revered objects.

Exhortations to the family recur in many books. For instance, a marginal note midway through Bishop Camus's *Spirit of St. Francis de Sales* reads, "My Very dear children Simon, Mary, Joseph, John and Anne Connary. Practice the science of the Saints continually always, and you will not ever work for one single moment unjustly against your own parents, against each other, or against any one rational responsible creature under any circumstances during time and Eternity. Your loving Father Thomas Connary." This type of appeal, imploratory of good, deprecatory of evil, occurs throughout the library in almost every book. In Chardon's *Memoirs of a Guardian Angel*, the first page of the translator's preface carries the following directive, which is written in typical spiraling fashion and with part of the writing upside down (fig. 15): "Dearly beloved children Simon P. Mary E. Joseph T. John N and Anne H. Connary Be True continuously to our condescending Creator always and your spiritual Life will be justly Truthful always. Thomas Connary." The moral imperative voiced here is given added weight as the writing and colored border frame a brief newspaper note about the ex-president of a life insurance company convicted of perjury and sentenced to five years at hard labor in the New York state prison—a delicate reminder to adhere to the path of moral virtue, to be sure.

Along with the many inserted notes that stress the urgency of moral action, these appeals to family members demonstrate a genuine concern for the spiritual welfare of those closest to him. The sense of pastoral and paternal care finds a particularly fine expression in the second volume of Balmes's *Fundamental Philosophy* (fig. 16). Connary concludes nineteen inserted handwritten pages of prayers, assertions, transcribed letters, and poetry with the following hopeful appeal, which shows proportionate recognition of the individual and the collective dimensions of salvation:

> You, my own dearly beloved Family Circle of children, grand children and your full offspring of children continually for endless Eternal Life Time under our Divine Condescending Noble Beautiful Creator, may very justly have the full use and benefit incessantly for endless Eternity, with His own endless powerful Help, including all of the real benefit and profit of this, our Stratford Real and Personal Property, in Coös

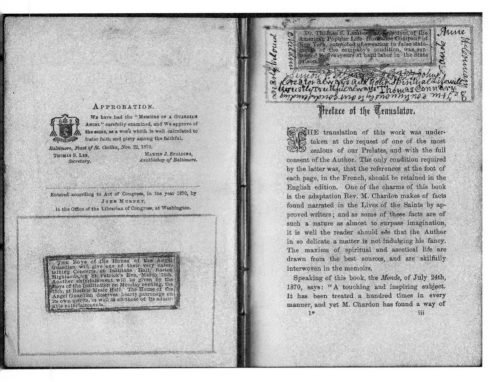

FIG. 15   M. A. G. Chardon, *Memoirs of a Guardian Angel*, page iii

County, New Hampshire,—under the very good safely established general government of the United States of America,—under His own perpetual National Guardianship, if you individually personally and collectively, will incessantly choose to live and to work with Himself Truthfully Justly Peacefully Faithfully for endless Eternity—be good neighbors to all of your neighbors everywhere, good neighborship is God's Goodship—I now speak to every one of you. November 19, 1881. Thomas Connary.

The decision to enhance his library with such appeals to family and friends is motivated in large measure by an understanding that the books are likely to be preserved and appreciated in his family after his death. To borrow words from Billy Collins's exquisite poem "Marginalia," Connary clearly expects to "catch a ride into the future on a vessel more lasting than himself."[7] Thus in Balmes's *Fundamental Philosophy*: "my words are recorded most solemnly

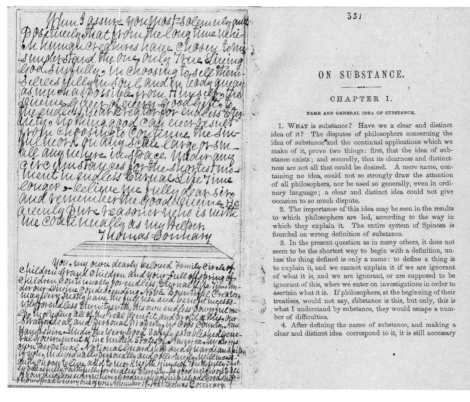

FIG. 16   James Balmes, *Fundamental Philosophy*, volume 2, pages 331–32

and earnestly for every one of you, with all I have written for both Books—keep them and all of my Books safely forever in this, our Old Blessed Family Homestead."[8]

This bring us to an important aspect of Connary's book enhancements, where, by enhancing books, he ensures that they are properly instructive for his family and that they travel with the assertions seen to represent the perennial and timeless truths of the divine plan. Books, as they are imported into the Connary household, are clearly found wanting of a dimension: only when books have become "Books," suffused with desire and didactic guidance, can they serve as edifying requisites to the family. This is when Connary can request, "keep them, and yourselves clean, in harmony with Divine harmony."

We should recognize Connary's reading as a platform for both social activity and for a withdrawal into a silent privacy of spiritual and moral introspection. The social side to his "Book keeping" acquires an additional dimension of passionate directness when he addresses individual family members, as is the case with *The Council of the Vatican*: "Dearly beloved brother Patrick Connary, this little Book is for you and your family from me. Your son Simon Connary and his sister were here Thursday night last, and returned to your home early next day. We are thankful to you and to them for the visit too short for us as you do know."[9] Extending Genette's taxonomy of the paratext, we may see these appeals as part of the "private" or "confidential epitext," where relationship is the important factor in communication and influences the form and content of textual presentation.[10]

The small sixteenmo volume entitled *The Lives of Eminent Saints*, published by Patrick Donahoe in 1853, provides a particularly interesting case in point (fig. 17). At various stages, the book was gifted by Connary to his children Anne and, later, Joseph. An inscription on the front flyleaf notes, "This little Book I marked as a blessed treasure for my dearly beloved daughter Anne H. Connary—

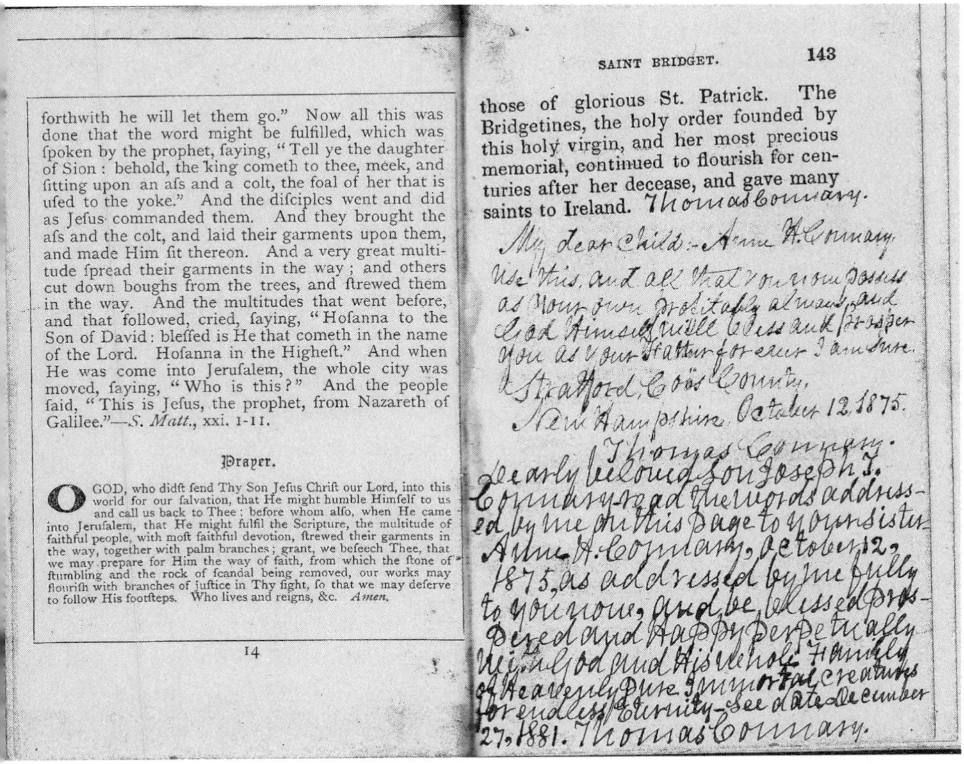

forthwith he will let them go." Now all this was done that the word might be fulfilled, which was ſpoken by the prophet, ſaying, "Tell ye the daughter of Sion: behold, the king cometh to thee, meek, and ſitting upon an aſs and a colt, the foal of her that is uſed to the yoke." And the diſciples went and did as Jeſus commanded them. And they brought the aſs and the colt, and laid their garments upon them, and made Him ſit thereon. And a very great multitude ſpread their garments in the way; and others cut down boughs from the trees, and ſtrewed them in the way. And the multitudes that went before, and that followed, cried, ſaying, "Hoſanna to the Son of David: bleſſed is He that cometh in the name of the Lord. Hoſanna in the Higheſt." And when He was come into Jeruſalem, the whole city was moved, ſaying, "Who is this?" And the people ſaid, "This is Jeſus, the prophet, from Nazareth of Galilee."—*S. Matt.*, xxi. 1-11.

Prayer.

O GOD, who didſt ſend Thy Son Jeſus Chriſt our Lord, into this world for our ſalvation, that He might humble Himſelf to us and call us back to Thee: before whom alſo, when He came into Jeruſalem, that He might fulfil the Scripture, the multitude of faithful people, with moſt faithful devotion, ſtrewed their garments in the way, together with palm branches; grant, we beſeech Thee, that we may prepare for Him the way of faith, from which the ſtone of ſtumbling and the rock of ſcandal being removed, our works may flouriſh with branches of juſtice in Thy ſight, ſo that we may deſerve to follow His footſteps. Who lives and reigns, &c. *Amen.*

14

SAINT BRIDGET. 143

those of glorious St. Patrick. The Bridgetines, the holy order founded by this holy virgin, and her most precious memorial, continued to flourish for centuries after her decease, and gave many saints to Ireland. Thomas Connary.

My dear Child:- Anne H. Connary
Use this, and all that you now possess
as your own profitably always, and
God Himself will bless and prosper
you as your Father forever I am sure.
Stratford, Coös County,
New Hampshire. October 12, 1875.
Thomas Connary.
Dearly beloved Son Joseph J.
Connary read the words addressed by me on this page to your sister
Anne H. Connary, October 12,
1875, as addressed by me fully
to you now, and be blessed prospered and Happy perpetually
with God and His whole Family
of Heavenly pure Immortal creatures
for endless Eternity—See date December
27, 1881. Thomas Connary.

FIG. 17 *The Lives of Eminent Saints*, page 143

I now love it as my own Book—when I can leave it to my family as a Blessed Treasure. I hope my family members will save it and themselves with it individually and collectively unto life everlasting. Thomas Connary." An ownership inscription on the first page (in what seems like Thomas Connary's hand) states, "Anne H. Connary's book, Stratford, Coös County, New Hampshire January first, 1868," and a personalized dedication is found on page 143, signed by Connary in October 1875, when Anne was sixteen years old: "My dear child, Anne H. Connary, use this and all that you now possess as your own profitable always, and God Himself will bless and prosper you as your Father for ever I am sure."

Anne, however, died in 1880, and a later note on the same page re-addresses the religious exhortations: "Dearly beloved son Joseph J. Connary, read the words addressed by me on this page to your sister Anne H. Connary, October 12, 1875, as addressed by me fully to you now and be blessed, prospered and happy perpetually with God and His whole Family of heavenly pure immortal creatures for endless Eternity—see date December 27, 1881. Thomas Connary." Such dedications demonstrate tenderness and concern for the spiritual health of others, and they give the impression of an intimate family circle at the center of whose devotion is the use and circulation of books. They also constitute a passionate declaration of the redemptive value of reading, in which the meticulous dating of the handwritten addresses provides a perspective for recording the writer's certainty of "endless Eternity."

The world of books and the discipline of reading are understood as part of sociability, involving various social transactions such as purchasing, lending, borrowing, gift-giving, and the dedication and annotation of books with specific recipients in mind. A few examples will show how books travel with Connary's markings and are intended by him to become operative in the community and family circle. On the blank leaf opposite the title page of *The Spirit of St. Francis de Sales*, Connary notes, "I can see by my diary page for March 21, 1892, that Miss Theresa McGoldrick was then here. I gave her a small Book then as her own for ever, there are 284 pages of it. The Book is The Devotion to the Heart of Jesus."[11] Connary's annotations are evidently incorporated into the transmission of a book which remains unidentified in a note dated September 28, 1896, and found in the *Spiritual Conferences* of St. Francis of Sales: "I will now speak of my Book, as our postmaster Mr. Riley Brown has it from me, with many of my pure Heavenly words, as all of my Books, and papers have them, very numerously." Here it is clear that Connary intends the books containing his inserted handwritten pamphlets to move beyond the household, as forms of missionary tracts that convey a particular intensity of devotion and a call to reform.

Adding yet more complexity to Connary's use of books, reading also appears to have had the implication of reading aloud in front of others and asserting the public uses of the discipline of "Book keeping" for purposes of religious exhortation. Although I have found no direct mention of any activity of reading aloud to an audience, frequent manuscript punctuation, ruling of paragraphs, and what appear to be acoustic markers constitute likely traces of events of voiced reading, thus pointing to a further dimension in the dynamic of family, reading, and redemption. Markings likely to have guided the vocalization of text occur in only a few of his treasured devotional texts. Manuscript ruling and punctuation such as repeated and enlarged exclamation marks in *The Spirit of St. Francis de Sales* seem to have assisted a somatic and sensory, probably articulated, experience of reading, whether conducted in private or in public (fig. 18).

The many added lines that divide paragraphs in the same volume contain a logic not easily unraveled: they seem to represent attempts to subdivide the

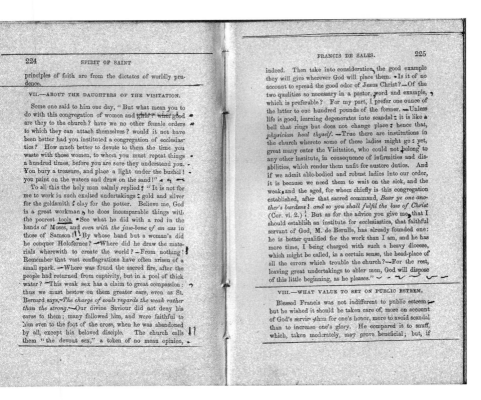

FIG. 18   Jean-Pierre Camus, *The Spirit of St. Francis de Sales*, pages 224–25

text into logical units and to enhance divisions or enumerations in the text, such as the listing on pages 256 and 257 of the ways in which affronts and injuries may be occasions for displaying various virtues, according to St. Francis. The ruling appears consistently throughout a large portion of the text to highlight units of textual meaning, but also potentially as an aid to the vocalization of text and the conveyance of units of moral teaching to an audience.

Also noteworthy are the cases where Connary provides the catchword, that is, the word at the bottom of a page that anticipates the first word on the proceeding page. An example occurs in *The Dove of the Tabernacle*, which also shows sporadic added punctuation (fig. 19). As Charles Lock notes, "the original purpose of catchwords was to help the printer arrange the forme" from which a page may be printed and ensure a correct sequence of text from page to page. But as he observes further, the function "must also have come to serve a quite different purpose: that of helping the reader to sustain the discursive flow in reading aloud."[12] Part of a centuries-old typographical convention, the catchword was phased out in the first decades of the nineteenth century, "redundant when reading had gone silent."[13] That Connary adds this feature on the bottom right- or left-hand corner of a page of some of his devotional books shows him to be alert to the acoustic aspects and potentialities of the text, not just pursuing the silent, solitary form of literacy that we may habitually think of. Thus, a likely context for Connary's reading in his home is an oral and performative reading practice, in which manuscript punctuation, divisions of paragraphs, and catchwords would assist voicing and construing the text. Such manuscript features could potentially help organize what Mark Amsler has termed "somatic literate technologies," such as "coordinating one's eyes and voice when reading aloud, running fingers or hands across the page to note words and lines, articulating phonemes, morphemes, and syllables clearly and expressively with lips, tongue, and voice, and displaying or revealing affect or emotional responses to the text being read."[14]

With these considerations we are, admittedly, in the realm of the speculative. But a possible habit of reading aloud with nuance and expression parallels an interest in elocution evident from several books in Connary's library on various subjects of oratory, including books on homiletics and collections of aphorisms. We find, for instance, the collection of American presidential speeches entitled *The Statesman's Manual* and the anonymous *The Catholic Pulpit: Containing a Sermon for Every Sunday and Holiday in the Year, and for Good Friday.* Also in Connary's library is *The Rhetorical Reader* by the American minister and professor of rhetoric Ebenezer Porter, which has the informative subtitle *Consisting of Instructions for Regulating the Voice with a Rhetorical*

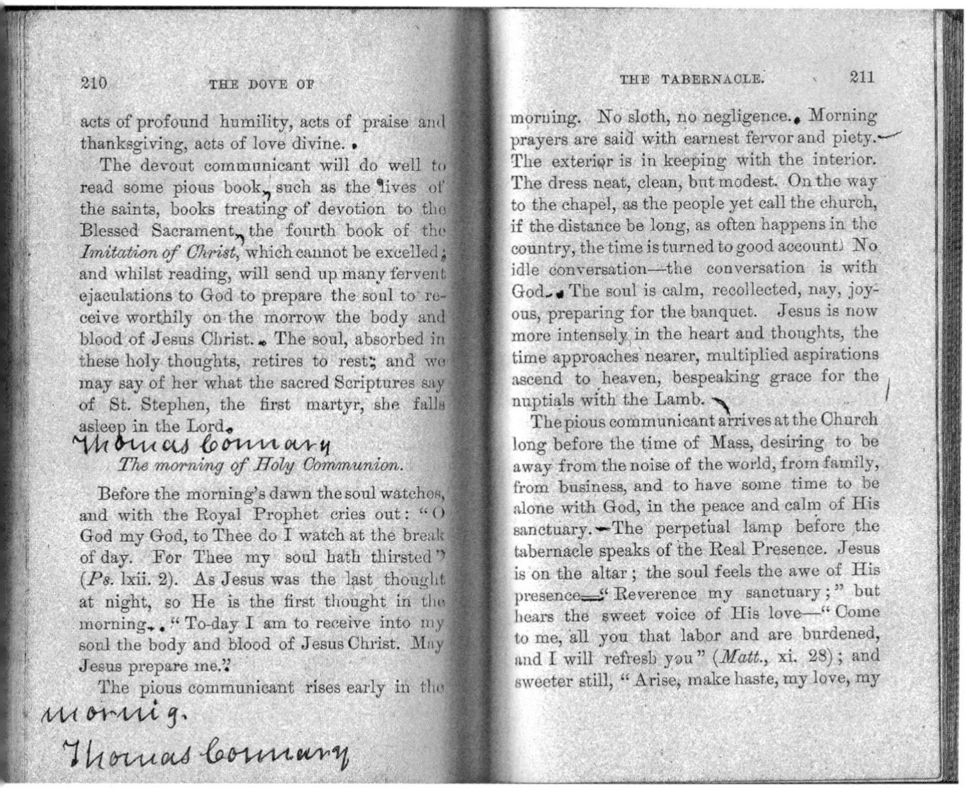

210   THE DOVE OF

acts of profound humility, acts of praise and thanksgiving, acts of love divine. •

The devout communicant will do well to read some pious book, such as the lives of the saints, books treating of devotion to the Blessed Sacrament, the fourth book of the *Imitation of Christ*, which cannot be excelled; and whilst reading, will send up many fervent ejaculations to God to prepare the soul to receive worthily on the morrow the body and blood of Jesus Christ. • The soul, absorbed in these holy thoughts, retires to rest; and we may say of her what the sacred Scriptures say of St. Stephen, the first martyr, she falls asleep in the Lord.

Thomas Connary

The morning of Holy Communion.

Before the morning's dawn the soul watches, and with the Royal Prophet cries out: "O God my God, to Thee do I watch all hours of day. For Thee my soul hath thirsted" (*Ps.* lxii. 2). As Jesus was the last thought at night, so He is the first thought in the morning. • "To-day I am to receive into my soul the body and blood of Jesus Christ. May Jesus prepare me."

The pious communicant rises early in the

morning.

Thomas Connary

THE TABERNACLE.   211

morning. No sloth, no negligence. • Morning prayers are said with earnest fervor and piety. The exterior is in keeping with the interior. The dress neat, clean, but modest. On the way to the chapel, as the people yet call the church, if the distance be long, as often happens in the country, the time is turned to good account. No idle conversation—the conversation is with God. • The soul is calm, recollected, nay, joyous, preparing for the banquet. Jesus is now more intensely in the heart and thoughts, the time approaches nearer, multiplied aspirations ascend to heaven, bespeaking grace for the nuptials with the Lamb.

The pious communicant arrives at the Church long before the time of Mass, desiring to be away from the noise of the world, from family, from business, and to have some time to be alone with God, in the peace and calm of His sanctuary. The perpetual lamp before the tabernacle speaks of the Real Presence. Jesus is on the altar; the soul feels the awe of His presence—"Reverence my sanctuary;" but hears the sweet voice of His love—"Come to me, all you that labor and are burdened, and I will refresh you" (*Matt.*, xi. 28); and sweeter still, "Arise, make haste, my love, my

FIG. 19   Thomas Kinane, *The Dove of the Tabernacle*, pages 210–11

Notation Illustrating Inflection, Emphasis, and Modulation, and a Course of Rhetorical Exercises. The possible acoustic markers that occur in some of Connary's devotional literature may well constitute indicators for the mechanisms of rhetorical, vocal delivery that are described in intricate detail in Porter's manual.

But it is time to offer an important caveat in our efforts to assess Thomas Connary as a social annotator of books, and this pertains to the utter dominance of his voice in the material that I have been able to examine. Connary presents his family with elaborate instructions for reading and claims about the spiritual and moral benefits to issue forth from such reading. Yet where he imagines any such collective book handling, it remains nominal and undocumented: the mention of social transactions that involve books appears invariably univocal, involving the exclusive viewpoint of Connary himself.

Even when we find ownership notations with the names of his children, these seem to have been penned in his own characteristic hand.

What dominates the library is the self-referential character of enhancements and writings, the auto-commentary of the recorded reading plans, and the absence of other voices. The uncertainty, on some level, regards the deictic qualities of Connary's book collecting-cum-enhancement, that is, its reference to contextual circumstances outside of the books and annotations. While there is no reason to doubt that Connary was diligent in communicating his ardent spirituality and rigorous moral perspective to others, that he attended mass when he says he did, or that he received the visitors and gifted the enhanced books when he so states, the material still poses a considerable challenge to anyone investigating the social force of his "Book keeping." The nature of the collection is such that we can examine Connary as a social annotator but not easily move beyond his own portrayal of himself to assess the social implications of reading. "Use this," "treasure this," "have this from me": these are recurring appeals from Connary to addressed recipients of enhanced books, but the actual deictic reference and contextual situation remain obscure. What, for instance, was the nature and degree of involvement of those identified as recipients? What was the experience like for them to sit with an enhanced Connary volume—to experience the voluminous, augmented heft of one of his books, to browse or read through it and discover page after page of inserted writing? Was it a treasured object? Was it regarded as a curiosity, the product of a religious fanatic? Or was it disregarded?

Opposite page 90 of *The Council of the Vatican* is a dedication from Connary to his son, dated October 31, 1885 (fig. 20): "For John Connary and his Family, in Lancaster, Coös County, New Hampshire, as my dearly beloved Faithful Family Relations . . . From me and from my Family in Stratford." Here, generosity and affection are inscribed into books that serve to reinforce relations between members of a family settled independently in the local area. But again, the contextual situation is unclear: when he states that the book is "from me and from my Family," what is the participation of other family members in gifting the volume? Interestingly, a note in the same book suggests that it was given later, in April 1891, to his brother Patrick Connary. Were there routines of book dedication, in which books were received on loan, kept as devotional texts or mnemonics, and then later returned to Connary? Could they have been unwanted gifts, or—a somewhat disturbing possibility, perhaps—do the dedications register nominal actions only, being inserted into books that never left his room? Again, there are no straightforward answers to these questions. The material does not allow us to assert a community of read-

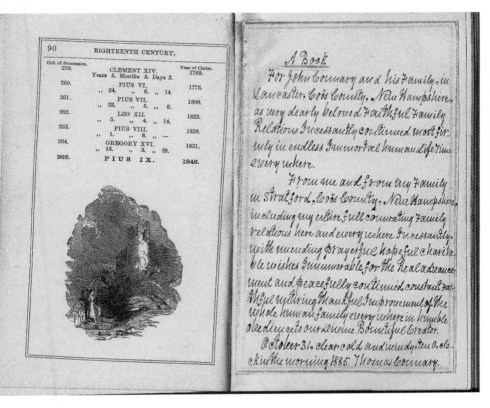

FIG. 20   Thomas Canon Pope, *The Council of the Vatican and the Events of the Time*, page 90

ers or shared patterns of reading, and we cannot assume that other members of the family, who may have seen Catholicism less fervently than Connary, were inspired to pursue similar book enhancement efforts. What is difficult to deny, however, is the understanding of one impassioned book collector that inscribed books have a very special capacity to function as precious iconic artifacts with real spiritual efficacy in the community. It is this association of books and spiritual power that we now need to examine in greater detail.

Heavenly Books

"Books however many, however expensive in price, are not, and can not be heavenly if God will not bless them, make them pure with His own heavenly graces endlessly continually always for ever, so with money, so with the whole of earthly property." Thus writes Connary on January 17, 1890, in the note inserted opposite the title page of Julian of Norwich's *Revelations*. It is this notion of books as potentially sacred objects with generative properties to connect human and divine that motivates their owner's emotional and creative relationship with them. The book—the entire book, inscribed with affect and spiritual experience—is understood to concretize prayer and be imbued with spiritual and salvational power. "Blessed," "holy," and "heavenly" are some of the terms used to describe a variety of books which elicit reverential responses, and titles include John Milner's *End of Religious Controversy* ("all heavenly in Divine words, never to be wrong anywhere"), the *Fables of Aesop*, Leatherman's *Elements of Moral Science* ("the Book is a teaching power under God Himself"), and the didactic tract *The Sinner's Guide* ("it plainly represents divine Truth in every respect").

Connary's religious reflection is always integrated with the rich and symbolically powerful idea of the book. The world of creation, for example, is referred to as "the whole Book of Infinitely perfect eternal everlasting Creation."[15] In *The Lives of the Fathers of the Desert*—a collection of hagiographic biographies presenting moral exemplars—Connary understands human obedience to God and the route to salvation through the metaphor of the book: "We are sure that we cannot be more obedient to God than He requires us to be. Human power we have from God as our Gift: this Gift is everlasting, every moment of it is the Book of everlasting heavenly pure life time for every one of us all." Similarly, on a note in the *Spiritual Conferences* of St. Francis of Sales, we see Connary's very own usage of the metaphor of the divine book or the Christ-book, an image popular from the early Middle Ages and subject to creative development through the ages: "Now God Himself as our blessed and holy Book never to be bound as a Book anywhere, we have Him here and everywhere in choosing to be heavenly immortal creatures with Him endlessly, all who go the other way are lost forever. Thomas Connary."[16] Unlike the material book commodities available in affordable cloth-bound editions, God is a book "never to be bound as a Book anywhere." Ultimately, Connary has to assert the transcendence of God in relation to familiar concrete images, and it is the book object that continues to determine his understanding, even if the inadequacy of this image is recognized: "Now I have Books thank God, I have Him as my director, and everlasting good Teaching power. . . . He is for me much more than Books—much more than earthly treasures can ever be in Books—in everything—in all things."[17]

When talking about God and his law in terms of the "Book," Connary is indeed resorting to metaphor, but he never intends such usage entirely metaphorically, and he never understands notions of divinity and transcendence apart from material books. In the second volume of *Mrs. Herbert and the Villagers* (referred to as "Mrs. Herbert's beautiful language to the villagers"), Connary notes that "every word—in both of the Books, and in all of them together, are blessed holy and heavenly." Another page in the same volume, dated May 22, 1891, combines observations about the materiality of the book and Connary's own reading history, with an assertion about the blessed nature of the work: "The little Book in binding is six inches long and four inches wide of volume second of Mrs. Herbert and the Villagers,—I read that work with much satisfaction as a pure heavenly work in my native home Old Ireland. Now every word in the two volumes of that work are blessed holy and heavenly everywhere."

These treasured didactic dialogues were thus read by Connary in Ireland when in his teenage years and reexperienced in his New Hampshire setting, within a new context of family supervision and instruction. The same may well be true of his copy of *Fables of Aesop and Others*, which Connary, who is invariably drawn to the didactic genres, esteems and even reveres as an expression of God's moral law. Fables are considered by him as "reliable" conveyors of divine teaching, and they are directly associated with righteous living. As an inserted statement in the *Fables of Aesop* indicates somewhat cryptically, the reading of this genre is a beneficial discipline, part of the harmonizing of human and divine wills: "I love Fables as beautiful and pure heavenly parables. . . . I love them dearly only for the good reason that the words in such Books are amusing and instructive when they are amusing and instructive, as we are required by God Himself to love as He loves, and to instruct as He chooses to instruct the whole human family everywhere into heavenly felicity."

"God's Law we have everywhere, as He is everywhere in Creation Himself," states Connary, and clearly this is felt nowhere more vibrantly than in the numerous printed and enhanced volumes that surround him in his room. This is a place (and an individual) deeply enriched by the presence of blessed "Books": books are enhanced as physical objects that have the power to materialize domestic intimacy, religious belief, and divine truth. For a process of book enhancement that proceeds from such conviction and sentiment, what appears messy, complex, and ad hoc generates its own logic, and the process simultaneously asserts the heavenly nature of books while being very strongly attuned to the material embodiment of the book, to its visible, tactile constitution. In fact, Connary never tires of recording details about printers, prices paid, book bindings, book and paper formats, numbers of pages, dates and places of publication, images, and typefaces, along with observations about the movements of books, including procurement, shelving, and exchange. Indeed, he reiterates such paratextual details tirelessly, in such a way that it can sound like a mantra asserting the extraordinarily powerful iconic and associational value of the material book. Of Joseph Story's *Commentaries on the Constitution of the United States* he remarks, "I have Judge Story's work in 2 volumes. Volume First 574 pages. Volume Second 676 pages. Both volumes have 1250 pages. In volume second next to page 548 Judge Story dies aged 66 years. Both Books are 9¼ inches long and 6 inches wide bound well in cloth as good Books. Good Books, cannot be bad."[18]

Quantifiable observations akin to this abound. Often, this interest extends to the factual or situational paratext, notable when Connary displays interest in the life and age of authors. For example, Connary imports into his volumes of Balmes's *Fundamental Philosophy* several short printed items on the author's biography, and he notes the following: "James Balmes was born on the 28th of August 1810, died on the 9th of July, 1848, see page xii—1848/1810—38 years of life in this world, less a few days only." In a peculiar extension of this biographical detail, he continues: "I was born on the first day of May 1814, May first 1886, now passed and gone forever—I now take from the year above 1886/1814, and have 72 years of life time credited to me by our Divine Creator." The precise significance to Connary of such recording may elude a reader of his annotations today, but it appears that the lives of esteemed authors—his spiritual allies, in all their quantifiable biographical detail—put his own life in valuable perspective and bear directly on his understanding and appreciation of the text. And to establish such biographical perspective, Connary draws on a rich factual paratext, whether internal to the book object or pointing to reading or situations external to it. (In his *Spirit of St. Francis de Sales*, for instance, Connary refers to volume 7 of "My New American Cyclopedia in 16 volumes" for more information about the saint.)

At all stages, Connary is intently engaged in a collaboration with his blessed books—enhancing and experiencing them, mapping them as proper reflections of the vast ideality of God's law. Text, book, and enhancement become a unified whole that serves as a testimony to a life of dedicated Catholicism—even a proof of life everlasting: "My Books, with the whole Book of my Life, proves to the full satisfaction of God, that my endless home is with Him in Heavenly felicity." The following carefully composed statement shows the capacity of a lexicon of the material book to structure Connary's views on salvation and righteous living: "Please read a few of my old English words on this paper, exactly as the one only True Living God will incessantly read my truthful faithful peaceful dutiful words in the Book of my Own Living Immortal Soul for the full endless Eternity of His own Divine Life Time, and know positively perpetually that He, Himself, and His whole family of human creatures everywhere in space, cheerfully feel firmly bound together individually personally and collectively, unlimited in power as one Happy Immortal family of peacemakers for endless Eternity."[19]

Here it becomes clear that the idea of the "Book" is ripe with salvific implication, signifying his own eternal life and the community of the elect "firmly bound together individually personally and collectively." This image of a dutiful, obedient community bound together and to God (himself an "unbound, unsealed unclosed Book") is contained comprehensively in that of the enhanced book and those of his books "bound firmly by myself." In the enhanced book, we find "Book, word, picture, figure, numeral, and pen mark" bound together individually and collectively as one inseparable unity. They are powerful, and powerfully felt, images of incorporation and binding that guide Connary's labors of prayerful "Book keeping."

"Putting Books to Work": A Culture of Redemptive Reading

"My words, dearly beloved, addressed to you my own family members, help you more with Divine Heavenly strength, in being fully designed by God Himself for the purely just impartial benefit of the whole family of immortal creatures continually for endless Eternity—faithful purely just work in harmony with Divine Order must be unlimited in value as long as God will be unlimited in power." This statement, which is found on an undated note inserted in the first volume of Balmes's *Fundamental Philosophy*, is an expression both of paternal care and of the unswerving confidence with which Connary provides spiritual advice. "I am not a clergyman," he remarks elsewhere in the same volume, but he proceeds to present himself in a pastoral role, as someone attending to the spiritual health of his dependents. The above statement also begins to convey what Connary regards as one of the primary functions of his enhanced books, which is to serve as objects of invocation and intercession in the relationship between man and God.

Connary's book collecting represents years of laborious accumulation and investment on his part, but books are also understood to work *for* him, as intercessory, iconic objects that function as instruments with real salvational power. Several notes associate books with the metaphysical category of re-demption in very direct terms. A statement in the *Revelations* by Julian of Norwich claims the empowering and redemptive nature of the discipline of "Book keeping": "I have loved my Books well only for the power which they give to me to have a heavenly home with our divine Creator continually for unending eternity. This way alone of Book keeping is God's way to prosperity and heavenly happiness unending." When Connary urges his family to pre-serve and esteem his book *The Lives of Eminent Saints*, he asks them to "save it and themselves with it individually and collectively unto life everlasting." This volume (a sixteenmo format and one of the smallest in his library) signifies through a rich metonymy: "This small Book, tells the whole story, in a few words, read the small Book, and read all of your powers right, and your home is heavenly with God." Assertions such as this point to a reciprocity—a col-laboration—of the individual and the material book in the scheme of eternal salvation. The striking formulation "putting Books to work" (found in notes in St. Francis of Sales's *Spiritual Conferences* and the *Revelations* of Julian of Norwich) captures best the perceived exchange between books and the reader hopeful for salvation. By inserting what he terms "my theological work" into his books, by inscribing himself into books and testifying to their veracity, he imbues them with spiritual meaning and agency. Books are waiting to be inscribed and activated in order for them to release their full efficacy in a pro-cess of redemptive reading.

Being habituated to the manual labor of cultivating the fields, Connary rejoices in old age that his books provide him with ample space to cultivate for the inception of grace: "Now as we have room enough to write without crowd-ing we will in this be more clearly plain in our wording power . . . here we have unlimited millions of acres in Book room."[20] As Connary the farmer tills the pages of his "Book room," he carries out what he sees as urgent intercessory work to secure the spiritual health of others, and here I use "till" in the sense of "to labor" and "to exert oneself," but also in the earlier, now largely obsolete, senses recorded by the *Oxford English Dictionary*, "to earn or obtain something through labour" and "to attend to" or "treat" (with medical implications). His understanding of such a mission of manual cultivation inside books for the health of himself and others leads him to compose some of his most remark-able writing, including recurring performative statements about books glossed as conduits for grace: "Profit fully by my pen work," "I work in this paper with a view of doing as much good as possible for all who can ever see it," and "this paper of my words with His Endless Help will I hope, remove much trouble from this world."[21] These are declarations with some illocutionary force about the power of writing in books to secure future salvation, and they show a firm commitment on Connary's part to labor as hard as he can.[22] The remainder of this section will discuss two examples of the carefully crafted statements through which he describes his own work of invocation and intercession in enhanced books.

Concluding a cluster of inserted pages in Peter Fredet's *Modern History*, we find a transcribed religious poem entitled "Sunshine" by Ellis Gray, a lyrical poem in four stanzas, ending "No longer I now am sighing; / The reason canst thou divine / The birdling with me abideth / And sunshine and song are mine." The inclusion of this item amid Connary's discourse on salvation and moral virtue suggests that he valued the poem, not merely as a source of spiritual consolation, but as an expression of God's salvific work.[23] Immediately following Gray's composition is a declaration about the book enhancements, and again we notice Connary's distinct vocabulary for the discipline of redemptive "Book keeping" and a sentence as enhanced as the book in which it is inscribed:

> I have used a pen in this way much and long in conforming all of my power fully strictly entirely to my paper surface room, as a last word on every subject written must be written in full harmony with the first word and all of the words of the subject to be exactly right anywhere under any circumstances, and as long as our Divine Creator Is the Best business schoolmaster in space, that one Grammar Rule must be alone exactly Right everywhere in all Languages I am positively certain. "Give no place to the devil."—Ephesians Chapter iv, 27. Thomas Connary.

Here, as elsewhere, the laborious proclamation of the harmony and universality of the divine law, "that one Grammar Rule," leads to a page filled to the point of overflowing, with tightly packed writing extending along the margins to accommodate all. Indeed, the saturated page becomes metonymic for the totality of Connary's commitment and what he understands as the fullness of the divine law.

A handwritten quotation at the end of Balmes's *Fundamental Philosophy* suggests how the activity of extending books implies hortatory zeal and transcendence, as the working of God is made manifest on the page. As is so often the case with Connary's high-minded exhortation, this reads as a brief sermon-like appeal, motivated by a sense of pastoral responsibility:

Monday February 6th, 1893, cloudy, and 12 degrees below zero early in the morning—moderate snow in the afternoon, speaking with my pen in this paper, words strictly Just, Faithful, Peaceful . . . I say in this silent slow way, God knows Infinitely more than all of His creatures can ever know. He knows all of my thoughts in Books and in papers, they are not heavy, they are now faithfully extending with God's Divine everlasting help everywhere in the whole of Creation into Heaven, and His work alone is never to fail, we never can love God and obey Him too faithfully like the Sun. I must now speak slowly, and say to all who are now living as human creatures everywhere in this world, and to all who will ever choose to live in it,—never choose to be wrong anywhere, and your home is heavenly with God for endless Eternity. To have a heavenly home with God everywhere in the whole of Creation, we must be endless peacemakers: endless peacemakers are all heavenly in conversation, in thought, in every respect, to be so, we must be as free from pride as the rocks and the stones covered miles deep in the earth are free from pride. In this way alone we can be heavenly pure Immortal Creatures.

We can wonder about the inspiration for such a proclamation. One likely source could be the sermons Connary heard from the pulpits of the Catholic churches he attended regularly in North Stratford and in neighboring Bloomfield, Vermont. The above passage certainly retains elements from the fixed sermon structure, including introduction, proclamation of theme (sometimes with scriptural quotation and some exposition thereof), invocation, and, finally, the exhortation, which counsels the abandonment of dissension and pride and holds out the promise of salvation. An element of pulpit oratory clearly feeds into Connary's statements, and as we have already noted, the likely context for many of his announcements is a performance of vocal instruction within the household. But as Connary is keen to point out, it is book enhancement that constitutes his main mode of preaching: in the devoted cultivation of the book page, he preaches "in this silent slow way," "speaking with my pen in this paper."

Book Signing

Connary's thinking about books revolves around the capacity of small objects for containing large messages. He appears to think in metonymic structures almost effortlessly and unconsciously, and occasionally, as we have just seen, he pauses to make explicit the association between a small sixteenmo volume (*The Lives of the Fathers of the Desert*) and the larger scheme of salvation: "The Book is small, very small, as a beautiful picture of all, who never will choose to disobey our Divine beautiful Creator anywhere." For Connary, metonymy is a particularly creative principle that makes of books the signifiers of personal devotion and epiphanic experience. Also, the principle of metonymy directly affects interpersonal relationships as books are being deployed in the community as the tokens both of large-scale social incorporation and of the call to the moral life. The metonymic consciousness is reflected also in the many signatures scattered throughout the enhanced books: these are part of an exploration of how a name can signify comprehensively, an exploration of what it means—of what it can mean—to write one's name in a book.

As Connary enhances his books with his highly personal, heartfelt creed, the signature assumes a crucial position as that which transforms the book into a signed memorial and personal testimony. Each single page of handwritten prayer inserted into a book is carefully signed, testified, and almost invariably dated. More than that, a sprinkling of signatures occurs in the margins of the print in several books, and in some of the devotional literature nearly on every single page, sometimes with as many as five signatures per page. With such meticulous, even obsessive, signing of books we have far transcended the ownership inscription: the repeated act of signing a page shows a reader determined to insert himself into the religious experiences recounted and to assert the fervor of his devotion with its concomitant rigor of moral perspective and linguistic choice.

But some of the earliest signatures are in fact ownership markings and date back to the early 1860s. These markings are usually found on a book's first page and do not always record the time of acquisition. They use the two forms "Thomas Connary's Book" or "Thomas Connary's Property," followed by date and place, and assert ownership in a community where books are gifted and exchanged—possibly in order that a book gone astray might be returned to its owner. On the page that announces the first book of Balmes's *Fundamental Philosophy*, on the subject of philosophical certainty, we find a collaboration of no less than three signatures, each functioning in different ways (fig. 21). Dividing the page into two compartments, each ruled with yellow and blue crayons, the topmost asserts ownership of "Thomas Connary's Book." In the compartment below, Connary signs his name to an elaborate one-sentence declaration of his religious conviction, which has obviously been composed in response to the chapter title "Certainty." The sentence begins, "Positive Certainty flows freely from God the giver of every good gift—the fountain head

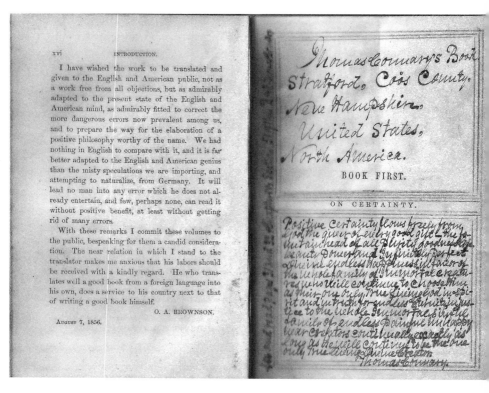

FIG. 21   James Balmes, *Fundamental Philosophy*, volume 1, pages xvi–1

of all purity goodness life beauty power and Infinitely Perfect Divine endless Happiness." Outside the two compartments, and along the left-hand margin of the page, is the following reading directive, similarly with a signature at the end: "See and read page 31 and 32 Chapter IV, Section 51 of this Book. Thomas Connary." The three signatures on the page work together to establish affinity between the object of the book on the one hand, and a person, a conviction, and a location, on the other. The record of ownership, with its "Thomas Connary's Book. Stratford, Coös County, New Hampshire, United States, North America," exceeds any reasonable thoroughness: surely "Stratford" and maybe "Coös County, New Hampshire" would suffice to identify an owner in the area where the book was likely to travel and make possible the book's safe return. However, ensuring the book's return seems much less a concern here than does the intention to combine statements about salvation with a fully and meticulously recorded location—that is, a location and a household enriched through the presence of books and partaking in the scheme of universal salvation.

Signing a name is the act of claiming affinity with a text and an author, as well as of testifying, subscribing to the veracity of the text that accommodates the signature. In the example of Balmes's *Fundamental Philosophy*, Connary's name is found opposite another signature, and another testimony to the validity of Balmes's philosophical positivism, which is that of O. A. Brownson at the end of his introduction to the text. Connary and Brownson agree in their different ways on the capacity of Balmes's text for providing reliable guidance. For Connary, "certainty" involves the right moral choice, which allows incorporation into "the whole family of immortal creatures"; for Brownson, the intellectual certainties of the Spaniard's system ("far better adapted to the English and American genius than the misty speculations we are importing, and attempting to naturalize from Germany") will reliably guide readers and eliminate errors.

As noted, Connary points forward in Balmes's text to "page 31 and 32 Chapter IV, Section 51." This is one of his innumerable efforts to structure the activity of reading printed text and annotation. But in this particular case, we cannot underestimate the significance of this reference to Connary. On these pages, Balmes characterizes what he terms "the character of true genius," concluding that "men of true genius are distinguished by the unity and extent of their conceptions": "If they treat a difficult and complicated question, they simplify it, consider it from a high point of view, and determine one general idea which sheds light upon all the others. . . . If there is question of a discovery, while others are seeking here and there, they strike the ground with their foot, and exclaim, 'the treasure is here.' They make no long arguments, nor evasions; their thoughts are few but pregnant; their words are not many, but in each of them is set a pearl of inestimable value."

We could choose to see in this—as Connary undoubtedly did—a validation of the theological and moral perspectives that besieged his mind and are constantly rehearsed in his book enhancements. Connary in fact employs the phrase "the nature of true genius" a number of times in his writings, and the reiterated declaration throughout his notes of a few key religious and moral ideas connects particularly well with Balmes's notion of thoughts few but pregnant (though Connary's words are more abundant than Balmes ever had in mind). Often, very brief but pregnant statements that appear to occur spontaneously in the margin of a page are signed as declarations of religious truth: "I am for Heavenly pure endless Peace. Thomas Connary"; "We will now thank God for His endless Divine Goodness mercy and endless Infinitely

Perfect Power. We never can obey God too faithfully. Thomas Connary." Connary is able to sign as someone who bears witness by choosing rightly and who believes that he has a divine mission.

The signature functions as a trace of the reader—a trace of a particular act of reading, of being in the book, and of consolidating its teaching. On pages 120 and 121 of *The Dove of the Tabernacle*, Connary's signature is found at the end of a chapter about the teaching of Irish saints on the nature of the Real Presence in the sacrament of the Eucharist. The "Resolution" of devotion to the Eucharist has similarly been signed, and an instruction notes, "Read often words from page 203 to page 234" (a chapter on preparation for the sacrament of the Eucharist). The directive may be intended for himself or for his family members, and probably for both. Signing his name here asserts proximity with elements central to his own spirituality, such as Irish saints and the Holy Eucharist. It also works to establish the homely, intimate feel of books in which Connary's children, who are envisaged as readers and addressed affectionately throughout the volume, can see their father in the book, constantly discovering traces of his management of books and his fervent devotion. Thus the signature deployed in the book can function like the "memento mei" that is sometimes written in the margins; it is inscribed into durable vessels and stands as a memorial for future users to facilitate remembrance and prayer.

The signature can come to contain a statement within it. It can signify abundantly to a family member who is already familiar with the rigor of Connary's moral and religious outlook. The signature thus becomes one of the metonymies of the text, regardless of whether it stands on its own, at the end of a short assertion, or as the conclusion to a long statement that stretches over pages. Connary can intend with his signature what he intends with one page in his much-enhanced *The Six Hundred Thousand Combatants*: "This one page is my evidence of the whole." Part of the metonymic operation of the signature can be to register surety of life everlasting, to mark the culmination of desire and sincerity. It can contain an entire creed, testify to the veracity of the text, and function as an exhortation to moral virtue.

We cannot know for certain if the emphatic and reiterated signing of a book, as we see it on pages 316 and 317 of *The Dove of the Tabernacle* (and on more than a hundred other pages in the same book), occurs more or less spontaneously in a book that advocates affective devotion to the sacred body of Christ (fig. 22). Probably the signature is added at the actual time of reading, next to those prayers and invocations used regularly by Connary, and perhaps it is intended also for the viewing and guidance of others. Connary does not comment in any direct way on the concrete practice of inserting and repeating

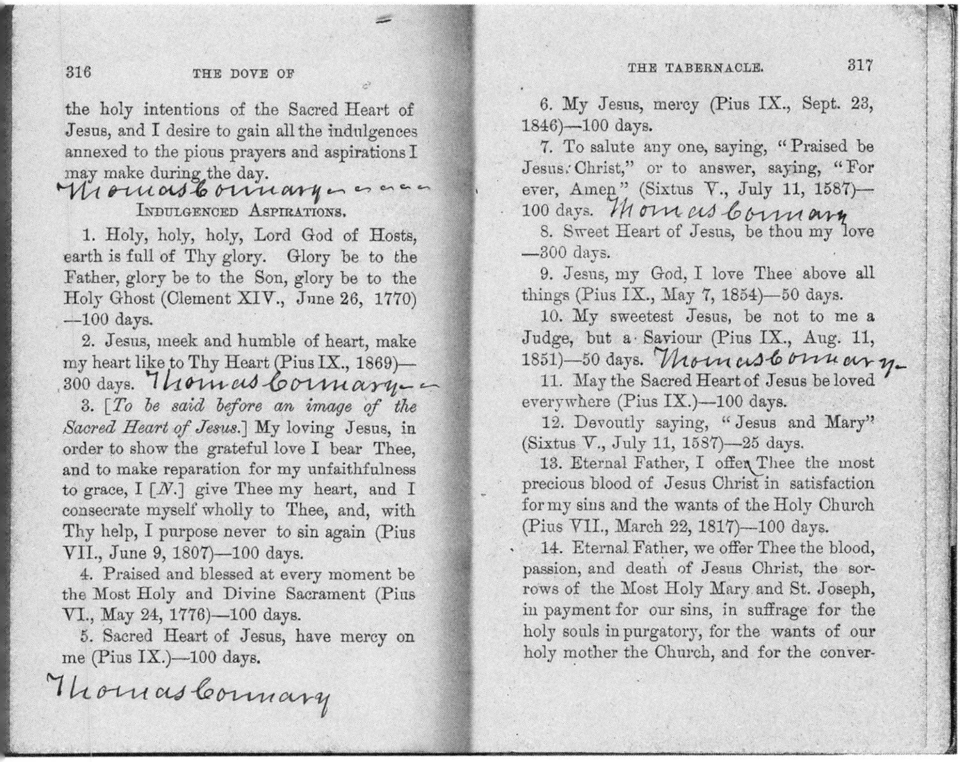

316 THE DOVE OF

the holy intentions of the Sacred Heart of Jesus, and I desire to gain all the indulgences annexed to the pious prayers and aspirations I may make during the day.
Thomas Connary

INDULGENCED ASPIRATIONS.

1. Holy, holy, holy, Lord God of Hosts, earth is full of Thy glory. Glory be to the Father, glory be to the Son, glory be to the Holy Ghost (Clement XIV., June 26, 1770) —100 days.

2. Jesus, meek and humble of heart, make my heart like to Thy Heart (Pius IX., 1869)—300 days. Thomas Connary

3. [*To be said before an image of the Sacred Heart of Jesus.*] My loving Jesus, in order to show the grateful love I bear Thee, and to make reparation for my unfaithfulness to grace, I [*N.*] give Thee my heart, and I consecrate myself wholly to Thee, and, with Thy help, I purpose never to sin again (Pius VII., June 9, 1807)—100 days.

4. Praised and blessed at every moment be the Most Holy and Divine Sacrament (Pius VI., May 24, 1776)—100 days.

5. Sacred Heart of Jesus, have mercy on me (Pius IX.)—100 days.

Thomas Connary

THE TABERNACLE. 317

6. My Jesus, mercy (Pius IX., Sept. 23, 1846)—100 days.

7. To salute any one, saying, "Praised be Jesus Christ," or to answer, saying, "For ever, Amen" (Sixtus V., July 11, 1587)—100 days. Thomas Connary

8. Sweet Heart of Jesus, be thou my love —300 days.

9. Jesus, my God, I love Thee above all things (Pius IX., May 7, 1854)—50 days.

10. My sweetest Jesus, be not to me a Judge, but a Saviour (Pius IX., Aug. 11, 1851)—50 days. Thomas Connary

11. May the Sacred Heart of Jesus be loved everywhere (Pius IX.)—100 days.

12. Devoutly saying, "Jesus and Mary" (Sixtus V., July 11, 1587)—25 days.

13. Eternal Father, I offer Thee the most precious blood of Jesus Christ in satisfaction for my sins and the wants of the Holy Church (Pius VII., March 22, 1817)—100 days.

14. Eternal Father, we offer Thee the blood, passion, and death of Jesus Christ, the sorrows of the Most Holy Mary and St. Joseph, in payment for our sins, in suffrage for the holy souls in purgatory, for the wants of our holy mother the Church, and for the conver-

FIG. 22 Thomas Kinane, *The Dove of the Tabernacle*, pages 316–17

his signature. But what we can say is that the signature shows a reader determined to be in the text. It contains an identity and a creed already established in the many book enhancements, and it is housed inside those precious material objects that bring the signer closer to the divine eternal law.

"The Pen and the Press—Blest Alliance Combined!": Thomas Connary in Print

A newspaper cutting of a poem entitled "The Pen and the Press" is pasted on page 74 of Connary's *Six Hundred Thousand Combatants* (fig. 23). The source of the cutting is unknown: judging from the paper and typography, it probably came from the *Pilot*, along with hundreds of other items in Connary's books also from this paper, including much poetry. The poem is by the British

Victorian poet John Critchley Prince (1808–1866) and was included in his poetry collection *Hours with the Muses*, published in Manchester in 1841.[24] Being appreciated in his own time chiefly as a local Lancashire poet, and now largely unknown, Prince is yet another of those forgotten voices that have been preserved in anthology form on the pages of Connary's enhanced volumes. The poem has been carefully cut out by Connary and framed in blue, and I quote it here in full:

The Pen and the Press

Young Genius walked out by the mountains and streams,
Entranced by the power of his own pleasant dreams,
Till the silent, the wayward, the wandering thing
Found a plume that had fallen from a passing bird's wing;
Exulting and proud, like a boy at his play,
He bore the new prize to his dwelling away;
He gazed for awhile on its beauties, and then
He cut it, and shaped it, and called it a Pen.

But its magical use he discovered not yet,
Till he dipped its bright lips in a fountain of jet;
And, oh! what a glorious thing it became!
For it spoke to the world in a language of flame;
While its master wrote on, like a being inspired,
Till the hearts of the millions were melted or fired;
It came as a boon and a blessing to men,—
The peaceful, the pure, the victorious Pen!

Young Genius went forth on his rambles once more,
The vast sunless caverns of earth to explore;
He searched the rude rocks, and with rapture he found
A substance unknown, which he brought from the ground;
He fused it with fire, and rejoiced at the change,
As he moulded the ore into characters strange,
Till his thoughts and his efforts were crowned with success,
For an engine uprose, and he called it the Press.

The Pen and the Press—blest alliance combined!
To soften the heart, and enlighten the mind;
For that to the treasures of knowledge gave birth,
And this sent them forth to the ends of the earth.

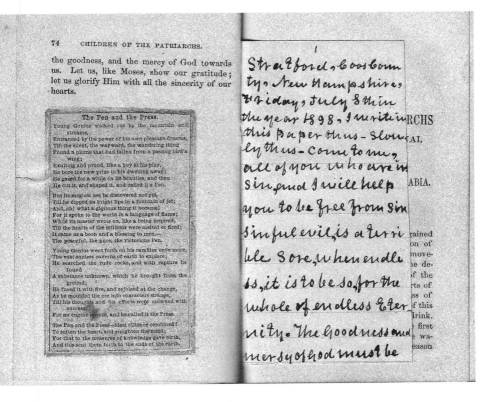

FIG. 23   Philippe, *The Six Hundred Thousand Combatants*, page 74

The poem as excised by Connary (or possibly as printed in the *Pilot*) omits the four concluding lines of Prince's poem:

> Their battles for truth were triumphant indeed,
> And the rod of the tyrant was snapped like a reed;
> They were made to exalt us, to teach us, to bless,
> Those invincible brothers, the Pen and the Press!

It is not difficult to see how this poem would appeal to Thomas Connary, for whom the enhanced book that fuses print and "pen mark" is indeed the "blest alliance combined." To him the exchange between print and manuscript is always imbued with meaning and passion, and print is seen as inherently rich and meaningful, as something with the power to elicit prayer, impassioned proclamations, and creative participation. As in Prince's poem, Connary never intends an opposition between, on the one hand, a manuscript text, regarded as a particularly intimate, sincere mode of communication with God, and, on the other hand, the facile, mechanical, impersonal reproducibility of printed editions (often stereotyped reprints). Instead of such simplistic antithesis, Prince and Connary understand a shared purpose and collaboration of print and manuscript: "They were made to exalt us, to teach us, to bless." With its focus on passionate communication (speaking "to the world in a language of flame") and on dissemination ("And this sent them forth to the ends of the earth"), Prince's "The Pen and the Press" must have signified profoundly to Connary, who inserts next to it one of his handwritten notes on the subject of salvation and righteous living. Here, the trinity of print, pious proclamation, and soteriology is established very directly.

The idea of print is immensely powerful to Connary, not least for its capacity to assert and disseminate. It is perhaps inevitable, then, that Connary himself strives toward, and acquires, the status of print. His act of self-publication consists of a printed text of one page, long enough to declare all that is needed, and it is inserted into a number of his books, all on religious subjects (fig. 24). Dated February 11, 1888, Connary's printed text is a letter addressed to his family with this instruction: "When you can have this from me, please have it well printed, that the whole human family everywhere may have the full benefit of it endlessly. Keep this original paper as your own forever." The substance of the letter is his routine moral assertions: "We are in every respect well, very much better, and more free from real troublesome, laborious, oppressive annoyance, than we ever had power to be free from discouragement anywhere in this world, before Saturday, February eleventh, 1888. So exactly for all of you, and for the whole human family living everywhere in this world to-day, who will never choose to be unhappy, unheavenly, human immortal creatures anywhere, with the whole immortal, unhappy, infernal, evil family of creatures."

His desire to partake in a print program leads to the production of his one-page text rich in implication and sincerity. In a way it is the embodiment of Balmes's notion of the treasure of thought: no long arguments, nor evasions, but instead "thoughts few but pregnant." The printed letter has been inserted in O'Leary's *History of the Bible* opposite the approbation from John Cardinal McCloskey, archbishop of New York. In this case, two forms of proclamation lean on each other—one being ecclesiastical, guaranteeing archiepiscopal sanction and doctrinal orthodoxy, and the other declaring personal faith and the certainty of salvation. Both are signed proclamations of spiritual authenticity.

Connary's act of self-printing constitutes, in a sense, the boldest of paratextual moves. His self-styled paratext is in plain sight, inserted at the front of books as a devout preface before the title pages. But it is also an insertion of a

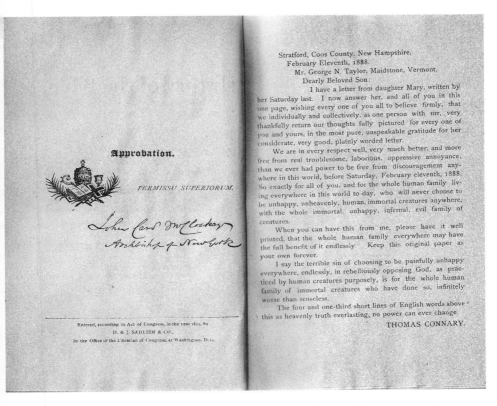

Stratford, Coos County, New Hampshire,
February Eleventh, 1888.
Mr. George N. Taylor, Maidstone, Vermont,
Dearly Beloved Son:
I have a letter from daughter Mary, written by her Saturday last. I now answer her, and all of you in this one page, wishing every one of you all to believe firmly, that we individually and collectively, as one person with me, very thankfully return our thoughts fully pictured for every one of you and yours, in the most pure, unspeakable gratitude for her considerate, very good, plainly worded letter.

We are in every respect well, very much better; and more free from real troublesome, laborious, oppressive annoyance, than we ever had power to be free from discouragement anywhere in this world, before Saturday, February eleventh, 1888. So exactly for all of you, and for the whole human family living everywhere in this world to-day, who will never choose to be unhappy, unheavenly, human, immortal creatures anywhere, with the whole immortal, unhappy, infernal, evil family of creatures.

When you can have this from me, please have it well printed, that the whole human family everywhere may have the full benefit of it endlessly. Keep this original paper as your own forever.

I say the terrible sin of choosing to be painfully unhappy everywhere, endlessly, in rebelliously opposing God, as practiced by human creatures purposely, is for the whole human family of immortal creatures who have done so, infinitely worse than senseless.

The four and one-third short lines of English words above this as heavenly truth everlasting, no power can ever change.

THOMAS CONNARY.

Approbation.

PERMISSU SUPERIORUM.

John Card McCloskey
Archbishop of New York

Entered, according to Act of Congress, in the year 1873, by
D. & J. SADLIER & CO.,
In the Office of the Librarian of Congress, at Washington, D. C.

FIG. 24   James O'Leary, *A History of the Bible, its Origin, Object, and Structure*, verso of title page

new primary text that other readers can access in its own right and that may make of the main text, such as O'Leary's *History of the Bible*, a paratext, a frame for the reading and appreciation of Connary's own writing. Books can be accessed in ways that unsettle the distinction between text and paratext, primary and subordinate. Connary's inserted self-publications, prefaces, dedications, and indices become part of the medium of the book, but their status need not always be paratextual and their function not chiefly, as Genette would have it, to aid the reception of the main text.

Connary concludes his letter to his family with a brief admonishment and declaration of just over four lines.

> I say the terrible sin of choosing to be painfully unhappy
> everywhere, endlessly, in rebelliously opposing God, as prac-
> ticed by human creatures purposely, is for the whole human

family of immortal creatures who have done so, infinitely
worse than senseless.

The four and one-third short lines of English words above
this as heavenly truth everlasting, no power can ever change.

THOMAS CONNARY.

We do not know if Connary's children had the statement printed as per his
instructions, or if he in fact arranged it himself. In any case, his family members would have been aware of Connary's drawing attention to himself as a
composer and as a pastor, disseminating his message through both the pen
and the press. Ultimately drawn to the durability, fixity, and dissemination
that print can signify, he enhances his books as conveyors of prayer across
space and time and as intercessory objects instrumental in human salvation.

There are interesting echoes here of a considerably older initiative for the
circulation of devotional material, namely, the "common-profit" book scheme
as this was practiced in England in the later Middle Ages, most notably in
fifteenth-century London.[25] As a way of securing the provision of books
among laypeople and secular clergy of lesser means, books of common profit
were sponsored through bequests and testamentary charity, with the donor
requesting that books be passed on to those in need of edifying literature. Such
books—mostly devotional miscellany volumes—would often travel within
small devout reading circles as carriers of relationship that reinforced social
and familial bonds. Often they carried manuscript injunctions that the new
readers pray frequently for the soul of the deceased donor, whose spiritual
capital was understood to increase through the donation and circulation of
wholesome reading material.

Though he was not a member of a secular clergy, we are familiar with Connary's own self-fashioning as a pastor laboring inside books, practicing charity
and fulfilling his responsibility for the cure of souls through his common-
profit library of personalized devotional compilations. As the common-profit
miscellany of the pre-print era stipulates that it be "delyuered and committed
fro persoone to persoone man or woman as longe as the booke endureth," so
Connary regards books as durable entities with life and circulation after the
owner's death: he can even request that his books be consulted by his family
"in all coming endless Life Time."[26] Each time a book is used, it fulfils its
purpose and functions as a form of social exchange, facilitating new relationships between people. When Connary scribbles in the margin his "memento
mei" and "see and read this most profitably," he assumes a role not unlike the

donor of a late medieval devotional compilation keen to see the book loaned out to souls in need of religious guidance. For both, books are understood to function as social instruments of exhortation and intercession. The next chapter examines Connary's reading and enhancement of classic spiritual texts to provide a more developed discussion of how particular texts shaped his own thinking about the all-important subjects of reading, virtue, and common profit.

EPIPHANY

The Road to Lancaster

The following account is dated May 16, 1883, and it is part of an eight-page cluster of notes inserted in *The Sinner's Guide* between pages 202 and 203; Connary suggests elsewhere that the event referred to occurred in the mid-1860s.

> I had full power to know positively continually what our Divine Creator really required me to do—I had no power to disobey Him—no inclination to disobey Him. . . . He required me in the night to accompany Him to Lancaster village, indicated the exact very narrow pathway for me all of the time—did not permit me to take time enough to put my slippers from my feet that I might have my boots to walk in to that village I had often visited—no time permitted to change clothing, no money property outside of myself permitted—He very plainly traced the one narrow path for me to walk the whole distance—when clouds full of darkness often prevented me from seeing the way, His very musical Bell directed me first on one side, then on the other—my only safe way was the centre traced by Himself—when I plainly saw my way, no bell music filled my ears—no weak sleepy hungry painful wet or dry feeling had power to live in me—His musical worded Heavenly Divine instructions for me continued the whole time in walking that whole distance—He, during the whole of time read my thoughts fully—did not touch any part of my body, though closely very near my body really, every word was plainly expressed for me outside of my own body as He alone can do—on the way down in crossing the Northumberland Ammonoosuc Bridge He pictured in a beautiful cloud a large bottle of wrath which must come everywhere in this world as punishment for incessant disobedience to Him in this world and in eternity. My Lancaster friends say they believe me.

"My Lancaster friends say they believe me": verification and the approval of others do matter to Connary, who otherwise expresses himself in terms of the confident assertion. Again, we are in the realm of concrete visual and auditory sensation. This is, in other words, an account of topographical familiarity and of hermeneutic repertoires that remain strikingly literal, centering on the corporeal impression of seeing and hearing "very plainly."

But the account does not remain simply literal, because, for Connary, familiar topography vibrates with symbolic possibility. And so bodily vision and audition become interspersed with abstract images and visionary metaphor, and striking use is made of literary and rhetorical topoi. Most notable is the image of the large bottle of wrath pictured in a beautiful cloud. Connary glosses this as a sign of the punishment that must follow the sin of disobedience, and this tells us that his account of the journey to Lancaster is to be read as a moral *exemplum*, and indeed as a metaphor for righteous living. A handwritten note in St. Francis of Sales's *Spiritual Conferences* uses the same idea of centering about the virtuous, devout life, stating that "the Line of Right is firmly centred for me in God Himself. There I am perfectly safe thank God for endless Eternity."

Preceding the epiphanic narrative in *The Sinner's Guide* are Connary's cautionary admonitions to those who choose to work against God and who multiply "their own unjust, unpeaceful, unlawful, ungrateful, unthankful, unfaithful, contradictory, ungodly, unnecessary, rebellious powers at their own endless Eternal expense." Directly following the narrative is his transcription of the words of John 8:44, "You are of your father the devil and the desires of your father you will do." The context for Connary's story is thus the pervasive theme of contradiction and disobedience, and it becomes clear that the relation between the text of *The Sinner's Guide*, Connary's notes, and his visionary account is one of tight thematic coherence. His experiential testimony and the sobering didacticism of Lewis's treatise thus face each other and annotate each other—both are equally primary texts, but the meaning of one is enhanced and glossed through the presence of the other in a productive intertextual relationship.

We find the same account preserved in a very late note dated July 31, 1897, in the copy of *In Heaven We Know Our Own*. The details here are nearly identical: on the road to Lancaster, "I was directed by Him in bell ringing beautiful in sound to take the best way." But what is revealed to Connary as he nears the village of Groveton is not precisely a large bottle of wrath pictured in a beautiful cloud: "I saw in the east a very large square star much larger than the sun or the moon—then immediately the star moved in a southerly direction, in rain moving buildings from their foundations, I was not hurried of time on my way to Lancaster." In both accounts, Connary produces a moral-aesthetic transfiguration of an experience whose exact truth-value should not concern us much here. But it is fair to conclude that his nocturnal expedition would be a remarkable feat for anyone. The journey would have taken him from his home in Stratford Hollow the approximately five and a half miles along the Connecticut River to Groveton, and an additional three miles toward the village of Northumberland to cross the bridge across the Ammonoosuc River (a tributary of the Connecticut River). At that point he faced the remaining nearly five miles into Lancaster—a total of about thirteen miles—all this at night and in slippers, along the meandering Connecticut River, when "the ground at that time was wet."

For Connary there was no inclination ever to disobey Him. He walks the road "firmly centred for me in God Himself," and on the way is granted sensory impressions revealed to him as a profound didactic vision which provides further affirmation of his spiritual and moral perspective.

4

THE FARMER'S TREASURE: THOMAS CONNARY READING
ST. FRANCIS OF SALES AND JULIAN OF NORWICH

Good Books, cannot be bad. Thomas Connary.

**—Note dated June 29, 1881, inserted between
pages 328 and 329 of the second volume of Balmes,
*Fundamental Philosophy***

Reading the Classics

The library of Thomas Connary reflects the continuity of a centuries-long tradition of Catholic spiritual writing. This chapter examines Connary's attentive reading and enhancement of two classic texts, the *Revelations* of Julian of Norwich and St. Francis of Sales's *Spiritual Conferences*, which form part of a spectrum of readings of medieval and early modern devotional and mystical writing. Connary makes reference, for instance, to a book entitled "The Glories of the Virgin Mother, and Channel of Divine Grace," almost certainly the text printed by Patrick Donahoe in 1867 with English translations of sermons by St. Bernard of Clairvaux (1090–1153), including *Sermones super Missus est Angelus Gabriel, Sermo de Virgine Deipari*, and the *Sermones de Tempore et de Sanctis*. We find also one of the most famous and widely copied devotional works of the later Middle Ages, *The Following of Christ (Imitatio Christi)*, assumed to have been written by Thomas à Kempis (ca. 1379–1471). Consisting of a number of devotional booklets of admonitions and proverb-like statements, this spiritual classic was associated with the spiritual movement of the Modern Devout in the fourteenth- and fifteenth-century Netherlands—a movement centered on conversion, a probing spiritual interiority, and fervent Christocentric devotion. Connary also had a copy of Thomas à Kempis's lesser-known *The Little Garden of Roses and Valley of Lilies*. Other elements of medieval spirituality are represented by a large gathering of saints' lives, including, of course, a book referred to as "my Life of St. Patrick." Besides the *Revelations* of Julian of Norwich (ca. 1342–ca. 1416), female spiritual and mystical writing is represented by Mary Francis Cusack's biography from 1871 of

St. Gertrude of Helfta (1256–1302) entitled *The Life and Revelations of Saint Gertrude, Virgin and Abbess of the Order of St. Benedict*. Moving into the early modern period, we find comprehensive texts of practical spiritual guidance, including *The Practice of Christian and Religious Perfection* by the Spanish Jesuit Alphonsus Rodriguez (1526–1616), and no fewer than four titles by St. Francis of Sales (1567–1622), author of several popular and influential treatises of spiritual direction: *The Spirit of St. Francis de Sales*, the *Spiritual Conferences*, the *Introduction to the Devout Life*, and the *Treatise on the Love of God*.[1]

This chapter examines the range of Connary's interactions with the works of Julian of Norwich, the English medieval anchoress and visionary, and St. Francis, the French-born bishop of Geneva, in order to show how he systematically inserts his own voice alongside the theological reflections of these early voices. The volumes of Julian's *Revelations* and Francis of Sales's *Spiritual Conferences* are augmented by Connary as precious composite books. In them we see not just facts or records of ownership, and even readership, but also the material residues of past religious thinking and lived spirituality. I want to argue further in this chapter that these two books occupy a very special position in the library. They are some of the most thoroughly enhanced and annotated volumes, and laboring inside these books constitutes for Connary an experience of the strongest engagement and focus. I will venture the claim here that these two books help Connary experience moments of particular intensity, and that it is through them, more so than with other books in his library, that he feels closest to the holy and to divine truth.

It is useful first to look at the material makeup of Connary's copies of the *Revelations* and the *Spiritual Conferences* and to make observations about the contents and printing history of the two books. We will then examine Connary's writing in the *Spiritual Conferences* to give an impression of how the experience of intensity and absorbed engagement in the discipline of book enhancement is manifested in writing with an almost tangible desire for union with God, but also with a pastoral drive toward moral exhortation and conversion. The final part will comment on the special affinity that Connary perceives between himself and the writing and spirituality of Julian of Norwich. This section enters more speculative terrain by considering shared theological emphases between Connary and Julian: the focus will be on how Julian's probing theological discourse on salvation and divine love and grace inspires in Connary a series of thoughts and declarations on similar themes.

Connary's voice is evidently enabled by medieval and early modern texts—enabled, of course, by the material book, which invites, with its ample blank margins, elaborate self-expression and fervent proclamation. But Connary is also enabled by early spiritual guidance and a rich and articulate medieval visionary tradition, which invites a dialogue he finds irresistible. The annotations inserted by the New Hampshire farmer into his copy of the *Revelations* (and other medieval and early modern devotional texts in his possession) constitute an intellectually and culturally important record that bears witness to the appeal and cultural mobility of past spiritual and visionary writing. We find in this material a striking example of how medieval mysticism and visionary autobiography can lend themselves to the appropriation and reorientation in a new location, and within a different set of cultural dynamics and tensions, when in the hands of a particularly creative and opinionated reader-cum-annotator.

The Books of "Mother Juliana" and "Our Saint Francis"

The title pages and preceding flyleaves provide a good starting point for examining Connary's work in his Julian and St. Francis texts. In the *Spiritual Conferences*, a full nineteen pages of inserted leaves and enhanced flyleaves precede the title page, including an inserted factual paratext in the form of a three-page newspaper clipping with an article entitled "St. Francis of Sales Proclaimed a Doctor of the Church" that provides some background on the author. Part of Connary's writing inserted at the front of the volume reflects on the theological virtues of faith, hope, and charity, before rehearsing his routine declarations about the virtuous life (fig. 25). Opposite the title page, Connary remarks: "I am doing my best in humble obedience to God in working with Him for endless Divine Heavenly pure reward, so that all may see now, that no one of the human parties can ever be justified in rebelliously fighting against God for endless Eternity. God is exactly Right, the opposite is exactly wrong."

Taking the characteristic kind of diptych form, the title page and the facing inserted page proclaim and convey authority: the informative printed title announces author, title, date, and place of publication, together with aspects of biography ("Bishop and Prince of Geneva, Institutor and Founder of the Order of the Visitation of Holy Mary"), translation ("faithfully translated from the French"), and authorization ("with a preface by His Eminence Cardinal Wiseman"). Connary's insertions, too, identify author along with time and place of publication ("Wednesday, January 31, 1883, cloudy windy and mild, eleven O,clock in the forenoon, Stratford, Coös County, New Hampshire"), and its style is that of the authoritative proclamation ("I will now say

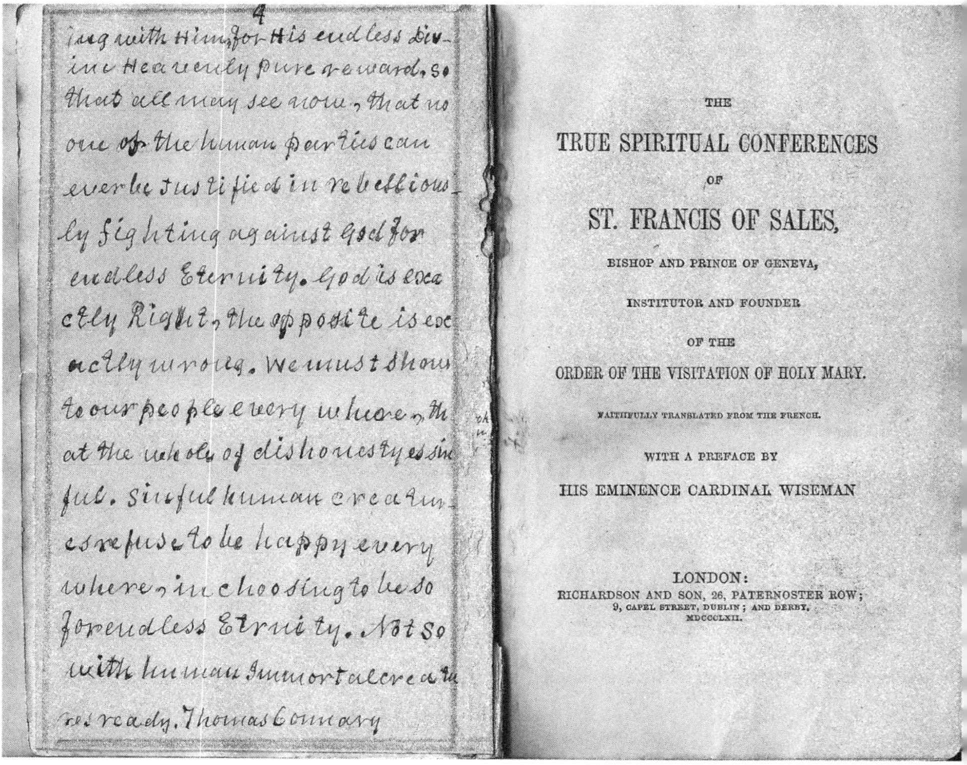

ing with Him, for His endless Divine Heavenly pure reward, so
that all may see now, that no
one of the human parties can
ever be justified in rebelliously fighting against God for
endless Eternity. God is exactly Right, the opposite is exactly wrong. We must show
to our people every where, that the whole of dishonesty is sinful. sinful human creatu-
res refuse to be happy every
where, in choosing to be so
for endless Eternity. Not so
with human Immortal creatures ready. Thomas Connary

THE

TRUE SPIRITUAL CONFERENCES

OF

ST. FRANCIS OF SALES,

BISHOP AND PRINCE OF GENEVA,

INSTITUTOR AND FOUNDER

OF THE

ORDER OF THE VISITATION OF HOLY MARY.

FAITHFULLY TRANSLATED FROM THE FRENCH.

WITH A PREFACE BY

HIS EMINENCE CARDINAL WISEMAN

LONDON:
RICHARDSON AND SON, 26, PATERNOSTER ROW;
9, CAPEL STREET, DUBLIN; AND DERBY.
MDCCCLXII.

FIG. 25   St. Francis of Sales, *Spiritual Conferences*, title page

very truly to all everywhere . . ."). Just as the title page of the *Spiritual Confer-ences* provides the year of publication in archaic Roman numerals, we often find Connary writing his years in Arabic numerals together with the Latin "Anno Domini."

The *Spiritual Conferences* is unusual as one of the very few books in Con-nary's library that are not printed in the United States. Published in London in 1862, the book was available from Thomas Richardson and Son, with offices in London, Dublin, and Derby, the provider of many Catholic works of piety and instruction.[2] We know how Connary procured the title, for he notes the following on the pastedown endpaper: "Thomas Connary's book, Stratford, Coös County New Hampshire, March 12th 1864. Bought of Patrick Donahoe, Boston, Massachusetts, Price $1.65 including postage."

With forty leaves inserted into the *Spiritual Conferences*, making eighty pages of Connary's religious ruminations and declarations, this is the most thoroughly enhanced of all the books in the collection. In addition to the interleaved pages, we find in the volume fragments of colored textile attached to the top of some pages, a postcard addressed to "very Reverend Father George F. Marshall, Saint Patrick's Church, Milford, New Hampshire" (obviously never posted), and thirteen newspaper cuttings of poems (with titles such as "The Rosary of My Years," "The Penitent at Prayer," and "God Bless Our Patriot Soldiers"). It is clear that Connary regularly experienced the feel and volume of this much-enhanced book, whose blue cloth binding has come apart, the pages worn and thumbed into a state of dirty softness, and the top of the spine damaged as it must have been regularly pulled from the shelf.

Like the *Spiritual Conferences*, the now-missing copy of the *Introduction to the Devout Life* must also have held special significance to Connary. It certainly engages with a theme of particular relevance to him, namely, how best to reconcile a desire for deep and sustained devout meditation with the active, day-to-day responsibility for the spiritual welfare of others. St. Francis's work provides both a practical guide to the lived religious life (with counsels on prayer, sacramental participation, the exercise of virtue, social participation, and so on) as well as a more profound rationale for the integration of secular and spiritual. The following statement from the preface of the *Introduction to the Devout Life* must have caught the interest of a devout Irish immigrant with responsibility for the practical affairs of family and household:

> Almost all those who have written concerning the devout life have had chiefly in view persons who have altogether quitted the world; or at any rate they have taught a manner of devotion which would lead to such total retirement. But my object is to teach those who are living in towns, at court, in their own households, and whose calling obliges them to a social life, so far as externals are concerned. Such persons are apt to reject all attempt to lead a devout life under the plea of impossibility. . . . Everybody fulfills his special calling better when subject to the influence of devotion: family duties are lighter, married love truer, service to our King more faithful, every kind of occupation more acceptable and better performed where that is the guide.[3]

The writings of St. Francis form a small corpus within the Connary library that could provide practical and multifaceted religious instruction. In the *Introduction to the Devout Life*, Connary would find validation of his own spiritual yearning and be motivated (if motivation he needed) by a model for religious practice firmly grounded in the world, a model of inward spirituality compatible with, and even enriched by, different configurations of secular obligation. In the *Spiritual Conferences* (originally conversations addressed to the convent of the Visitation of the Blessed Virgin) was found a sweet taste of the higher rungs of spiritual contemplation: here Connary could partake in the experiences and religious direction of a saint of the Catholic Church addressed to a congregation of committed, enclosed religious.

On a note from 1893 inserted in the *Spiritual Conferences*, Connary associates St. Francis's work with the book of Julian of Norwich in his program of religious reading: "Read next 16 Revelations of Divine Love By Mother Juliana. Purely Roman Catholic. Published by the Protestant publishers Ticknor and Fields in 1864. She was not expensively educated but purely faithful and heavenly." Julian's *Revelations* was published by the Boston-based Ticknor and Fields, an important publishing house which, by the middle of the nineteenth century, had become one of the foremost publishers of literature and belles lettres in the United States. As Michael Winship has documented in his examination of the company's records of 1840 to 1859, Ticknor and Fields published nearly equal numbers of American and British authors.[4] Alfred Tennyson, Walter Scott, and Thomas De Quincey are some of the names that top the list of the firm's most popular authors, alongside American writers like Henry Wadsworth Longfellow and Nathaniel Hawthorne.[5] (As is well known, it was James T. Fields who persuaded Hawthorne to revise and expand a draft short story that was published in 1850, by what was then Ticknor, Reed, and Fields, as *The Scarlet Letter*.[6]) The Boston company also published works on religion, science, and medicine. Their edition of Julian's *Revelations* appeared in 1864 and became neither a steady seller nor a best seller. Ticknor and Fields must have incurred all costs of manufacture and distribution for this publication, but they had the book printed with Welch, Bigelow & Company, university publishers in Cambridge, Massachusetts, who are acknowledged on the verso of the title page.[7]

The edition of Julian's text that appeared with Ticknor and Fields is the same as that published first in 1670 by the Benedictine Serenus Cressy (1605–1674), who for many years was chaplain with the English Benedictine Congregation in Douai and later served as cathedral prior of Rochester (fig. 26).[8] The text retains the flavor of Julian's Middle English (even with the occasional invented archaism), and an eleven-page glossary at the rear of the volume clarifies obscure or obsolete meanings. In addition to Cressy's seventeenth-century dedication (to Lady Mary Blount of Sodington) and preface, Connary's edition includes a preface by Isaac T. Hecker (1819–1888), the American Catholic priest of indomitable missionary zeal who was acknowledged as a

Servant of God by the Catholic Church and initiated several print programs, including the Catholic Publication Society, now the Paulist Press. Hecker's preface praises Julian, "our nun," for her "rare thought, warmth of piety, and charming simplicity . . . showing what hearts beat in English cloisters in the olden time, and how sweetly the voice of piety sounded in our good old Saxon tongue." Connary shows similar appreciation for Julian, and he remarks several times that he does not require the aid of the glossary to understand her words. He notes in 1884 that "I think I bought this Book soon after it was printed," and twenty-eight leaves (fifty-six full pages of writing) have been added to the volume in the period 1884–97, including an amount of transcribed correspondence to various publishers, such as the proprietors of the *Coös County Democrat*, the *New England Homestead*, and the Pilot Publishing Company.

To enter into exchange with the medieval anchoress and visionary—to interpolate his "theological work" into her exercises of theological contemplation—is

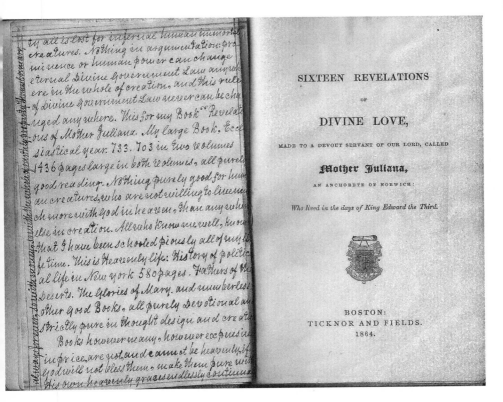

FIG. 26   Julian of Norwich, *Sixteen Revelations of Divine Love*, title page

inherently attractive for Connary, not least for the way in which such interpola-tion works reciprocally by way of mutual validation. Julian's writing and theol-ogy prove profoundly enabling and motivating to Connary, while he, in turn, can assert of it in an annotation on page v dated April 30, 1895, "I prove it to be exactly right in every respect. She lived in perpetual practice heavenly pure Law. God blessed her in all of her work fully. We see that in her. Thomas Connary."

When Julian composed her text around the year 1400, she frequently affirmed her obedience to the doctrine of what she refers to as "Holy Church," the institution of the one unified Roman Catholic Church. However much the medieval Catholic Church was the site of dynamic pluralism and reform-minded thinking, the idea of a division into different distinct churches was to most in Julian's time, if not to all, an utterly alien one. By contrast, when her *Revelations* were published by Cressy nearly three centuries later, this occurred against a backdrop of religious controversy and clearly separated churches. As Cressy notes in his preface, the book was published by the "order and liberality" of the Abbot Guscoyn of Lambspring, a Benedictine abbey near Hildesheim in Germany, one of the centers for English Catholics in exile on the Continent in the seventeenth and eighteenth centuries. Cressy's edition was thus part of the seventeenth-century Catholic mission and of the justification for the exiled recusant community at a time when Catholicism had been identified with trea-son in England for decades.[9]

Another two centuries were to pass before the *Revelations* appeared in print from the house of Ticknor and Fields in Boston. By this time, the background for the reception of the work, as Connary would experience it, is once again that of expatriation and a sectarian divide of clearly separated churches and, to some extent, of demarcated institutional systems. Thus we may say that the polemical thrust of the edition is reawakened in his New England setting. Certainly, what he sees as the rather surprising fact that it appears from Prot-estant publishers receives repeated mention: it indicates that the book, which is first and foremost a devotional work to assist a life of prayer and religious meditation, is perceived by Connary as part of that large body of his literature that is Catholic apologetics and polemic.

Both Julian of Norwich and St. Francis of Sales were read by seventeenth-century exiled Catholics in recusant communities in Continental Europe, and both were printed in nineteenth-century New England predominantly—but not exclusively, as we see with Julian—by American Catholic publishers. Fran-cis of Sales clearly found the wider circulation, being printed by key names in Irish American publishing such as Fielding Lucas Jr. in Baltimore, Patrick Donahoe in Boston, and D. & J. Sadlier, P. O'Shea, and P. J. Kennedy, all in

New York. A very early printing of the *Introduction to a Devout Life* appeared in 1816 from Bernard Dornin in Baltimore, "for sale at his Catholick bookstore, no. 5, Saratoga Street, within a few yards of the Arch-bishop's."[10]

Contemporary religious controversy aside, it is clear that Connary treasures Julian of Norwich and St. Francis of Sales as exemplars of the pure spiritual life dedicated to God. He finds in their writings real spiritual consolation and models for theological reflection.[11] In the *Spiritual Conferences*, to which we now turn, Connary reads the words of St. Francis, whose "every word—every movement of his soul was blessed, holy, and heavenly," and he discovers teaching with profound implications for the life of the ordinary Christian.[12]

On Being Elsewhere: Inscribing Longing and Transcendence in the *Spiritual Conferences* of St. Francis of Sales

Connary's thinking about intercession and redemptive reading culminates in his copy of *Spiritual Conferences* of St. Francis of Sales, which is enhanced in a way that reveals key aspects about the affective and quasi-mystical nature of his Catholic devotion. Although I will argue that Connary is engaged at a deeper level with the theology of Julian of Norwich than with that of St. Francis, there are a few instances where he gives some indication of the aspects of the saint's teaching that resonate most strongly with him.

One of the chapters that Connary singles out for special attention is entitled "On the Rules and the Spirit of the Visitation." Being an examination of the spirit of religious orders in general, and of the Congregation of the Visitation in particular, the chapter treats of the central virtues to be fostered in the congregation, such as observance, stability, obedience, and humility, while also formulating a rationale for the avoidance of asceticism and corporeal austerity. Such teaching would help establish the relevance of the text to an individual like Connary, for whom withdrawal and the ascetic life were not possible. Connary occasionally highlights the words "obedience," "humility," and "obligation," indicating his interest in religious virtues that pertain not only to the devotional practice of the cloistered religious life. Where the work read translates religious guidance from the seventeenth-century French of St. Francis into nineteenth-century English, it also translates a tradition of conventual regulation and stability into the ritual discipline and self-improvement that are central to Connary's lay spiritual context.

Also of considerable interest to Connary is a chapter on the virtue of "cordiality," which St. Francis defines as "the essence of true and sincere friendship."

The focus of the chapter is primarily on directing sisters of a religious house and encouraging cordial love between them ("yet without too much familiarity"), but Connary marks the following passage regarding friendship and filial love within the family: "The love which fathers have for their children is not called friendship, nor that of children for their fathers, because it has not that correspondence we are speaking of, but is of a different nature; the love of fathers being majestic and full of authority, and that of children a love of respect and submission; but between brothers, on account of the resemblance of their condition, the correspondence of their love produces a firm, strong, and solid friendship."[13]

Generally, it is the applicability of St. Francis's teaching to family life and filial relationship that interests Connary, and this is evident also in the many book enhancements that explore themes of intercession and common profit. The long eight-page booklet of religious reflections inserted before the title page concludes by incorporating words from one of his children: "I now connect with my work, Mottoes worked by my loving daughter Anne H. Connary—1. Pray without ceasing. 2. Hallowed be thy name. 3. Charity never faileth. 4. Remember me." The injunction "remember me" from Anne Connary (who had died a long time before Connary completed this note in 1883) points once again to the theme of common profit and to the understanding that books "safely retained in my Family continually forever" function as memorial objects with reminders to pray for the soul of deceased family members. As this illustrates, Connary explores the ways in which books can preserve emotional ties and the memory of a loved one, and he very meaningfully ensures that the booklet inserted at the front of his St. Francis consists of the precious paper left behind by his daughter: "This very small piece of white paper was left by my now dearly beloved daughter Anne H. Connary, deceased, I now use it full size as a paper sheet, I have a few more sheets of it, and will indicate it in my Books full size, never to waste any of it under any circumstances."[14]

One single paragraph from the chapter "Remember the Departed" in Bishop Camus's *Spirit of St. Francis de Sales* has been circled by Connary, and the succinct note "Chapter remember" is written beside it. In the passage, St. Francis asks, "why can't we compare the merit of working in behalf of departed souls with that of the works of spiritual mercy, giving counsel to the simple, correcting the erring, teaching the ignorant, pardoning offences, patiently bearing injuries?"[15] Indeed, enhancing the book with injunctions to remember and pray with others in mind becomes for Connary a virtuous devotional exercise and one of the most important spiritual works of mercy.

Occurring sporadically in the blank spaces of the *Spiritual Conferences* are short didactic appeals to his children, such as the one at the bottom of page 180 from February 1877 with the instruction, "Obey God justly always and you will never really die." These brief injunctions are imbued with the drive toward conversion and moral didacticism that characterizes each of the many handwritten notes inserted into the volume. Found in the book mostly in small, interleaved four-page "booklets," these notes operate as mini-sermons, in which the carefully crafted devices of reiteration, invocation, and personification suggest the cadences, and certainly the admonitions, of the pulpit. A note can start out by declaring a theme or concept (e.g., cordiality, humility, sin, eternal life), and occasionally a biblical quotation or story is invoked in support of the theme. Then a longer disquisition or assertion on the theological or moral topic follows, and the conclusion is in the form of an address and exhortation to the family. Of course, the notes are not always structured in such systematic fashion, but the movement from a theme toward exhortation and application is a stable feature, suggesting that Connary found this book of St. Francis a particularly fertile ground for experimenting with an appeal that resembles the sermon form.

Noting that common profit, religious direction, and paternal affection are preeminent themes in Connary's enhancements of his St. Francis, it can come as no surprise that Connary's printed letter to his family, discussed in the previous chapter, is inserted in the front of *The Spirit of St. Francis de Sales*. (The printed page, at 11 × 18 cm, is too large to fit in the small-size octavo that is the *Spiritual Conferences* [fig. 27]). On the page facing the letter is pasted a composition entitled "A Spanish Poem," on the theme of the imminence of death and the transience of the created order. Encircling the poem in two layers is Connary's confident remark about the spiritual efficacy of the enhanced "Book," and again we note the self-reference and the performative nature of his assertion: "By justice to the beautiful spirit of pure harmony which lived in Old Spain I cheerfully paste the words inclosed in this border as a page of this valuable Book, on Tuesday dark mild and snowy, December 12, in the year Anno Domini 1876, and if the members of my small family circle will choose to be wise unto Salvation they will profit by my good Books. Thomas Connary." We can conclude that such appeals to Connary's family are considerably more dominant in the *Spiritual Conferences* and *The Spirit of St. Francis de Sales* than in any of the other books that have been examined for this study. Clearly Connary's concern with the welfare of his family is found to resonate strikingly with the main themes of St. Francis's text, which are cordiality, the incorporation into a spiritual community, and the love of one's neighbor or the religious brother or sister.

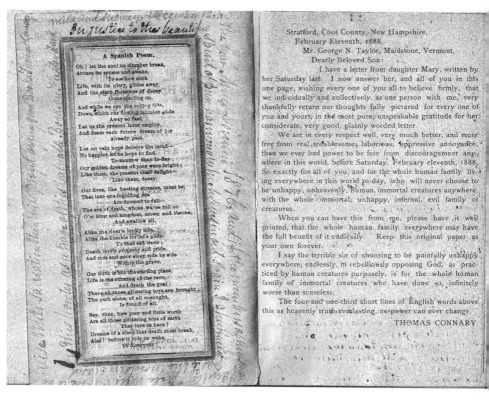

FIG. 27   Jean-Pierre Camus, *The Spirit of St. Francis de Sales*, front flyleaf

So far, I have examined Connary's copy of the *Spiritual Conferences*, "this valuable book," in terms of now-familiar themes: paternal affection and guidance, common profit, and redemptive reading. However, there is a sense in which the enhanced books of St. Francis move beyond such concerns to manifest a passion and a desire of a different category. Through the conduit of the material book, Connary is transported beyond it: he is emphatically *in* the book, enhancing its material and aesthetic components, and at the same time looking beyond it, with his attention directed toward the divinity. Thus on the verso of the title page of *The Spirit of St. Francis de Sales*: "Our only business is to fit and prepare ourselves fully for that Heavenly Home— I am now there thank God, much more in pure living power, than I am in my body through which I see my work in this Book, bordering on page 211. Thomas Connary."

The material book continues to furnish the larger context of meaning and expression, as when Connary describes God in the *Spiritual Conferences* as a "blessed and holy Book never to be bound as a Book anywhere," but his gaze is directed, via the book, toward the transcendent. On an inserted note bordering on page 211 is found the following statement, which shows how the books of St. Francis prompt Connary to look beyond their material components to affirm the ultimate efficacy of his own book enhancement efforts: "I see incessantly that every material Book of words in this world must be like this world limited and as nothing comparable to our Heavenly Father's Unlimited Divine Infinitely Perfect Eternal endless powerful living government unbound unsealed unclosed Book of pure necessary incessant sciences here and everywhere, and this paper of my words with His endless Help will I hope, remove much trouble from this world everywhere peacefully."

Through the enhancement of the books of St. Francis, Connary releases his most pious self and is brought to an experience of spiritual intensity and connection. Two poems expressing Connary's deep spiritual desire have been transcribed in his own hand into the *Spiritual Conferences* and *The Spirit of St. Francis de Sales*. One is entitled "Sunshine" and is found in several of his books; the other is the poem "Sometime" by May Riley Smith, "copied by me from 'Massachussets Plowman' Boston, for October 28, 1876." As a poetic echo of Connary's longing and assured hope, the final stanza of "Sometime" ends with the words, "And if through patient toil we reach the land where tired feet, with sandals loose, may rest, When we shall clearly know and understand, I think that we will say, God knows the best."

Besides some repeated affirmations about sin and salvation, the annotations in the books of St. Francis of Sales are not in any strict sense concerned with theological or doctrinal questions. They seem first and foremost designed to forge an expression of spiritual authenticity, and they provide some of the best illustrations of how lived religious experience finds its elaborate and impassioned manifestation in the discipline of "Book keeping." This finds a particularly striking expression when books are enhanced to contain the owner's spiritual epiphanic experiences, in what is a directly felt confrontation with the dimensions of salvation, transcendence, and union.

The Spiritual Epiphany

Writing in the mid-seventeenth century, Serenus Cressy notes the following about Julian of Norwich's visionary activity in his preface to her *Revelations*:

As for the manner of these Revelations, it was the same of which we read innumerable examples, both among ancient and modern saints. The objects of some of them were represented to the imagination and perhaps also to the outward sight; sometimes they were represented in sleep, but most frequently when she was awake. But those which were more pure, intime and withall more certain, were wrought by a divine illapse into the spiritual part of the soul, the mind and understanding, which the devil cannot counterfeit, nor the patient comprehend, though withal it excluded all doubt or suspicion of illusion. (xvi–xvii)

These lines formulate a classical Augustinian division between, on the one hand, the purely supernatural intellectual vision manifested in the understanding and, on the other, the imaginative or corporeal visions, usually of short duration, that take the form of sensible (typically visual and aural) representations. Connary may well have read these lines attentively. He claims on several occasions to have experienced a supernatural reality from which he derives simple and overwhelming certainty about God and the good life. And these profound moments of *claritas* and *veritas* were themselves granted him in the form of sensible apparitions, whether in the form of the Virgin and her company appearing to him in his own home, or a vision of a burning lamp experienced while he was half-asleep in bed.

In the annotations found in the books of St. Francis of Sales, Connary records a sense of residing elsewhere, of being "much more with Him than I am living in my own human body outside of His Celestial City," and the visionary accounts capture best this sense of transport. Writing down his spiritual experiences and inserting them into important books becomes a way of holding on to them—a way of reliving and communicating them, sometimes interpreting them, and always asserting their momentous significance to him in the present moment. These inserted accounts are likely very closely associated with the experience of reading a particular text: we may see them as a form of direct reader response and a feature of Connary's reading activity, in which he is moved at one moment of reading to inscribe his own record of an experience. In this case, the process is that of a transport beyond the printed text into a mode of creative self-narration.

As the short interludes in this study make clear, Connary's epiphanic accounts are conveyed in a carefully crafted language that makes rich use of metaphorical and quasi-mystical registers but also draws on the resources of familiar local topography and the domestic environment. Visions are granted him "very plainly, in this, my own house," such as the moment when two "beautiful Angels dressed and blessed in robes of celestial bright sunlight" appear to him in his Stratford house on a rainy autumn day in 1884. Connary's is a receptive mind stimulated by the fervent piety and mystical yearnings of Catholicism—a mind of desirous imaginings, stirred by graphic, corporeal images of angels and saints that beckon imaginative participation. And when Connary participates and experiences, he does so not in a way that transcends language, familiar setting, or the realm of mundane pursuits, but in a way that enriches and suffuses the familiar with the perceived presence of the holy.

Interpolating his experiences into the works of an established visionary tradition gives him an opportunity to associate with powerful and authoritative spiritual experience. Thus, we may discern an imitative dimension to Connary's annotations, as he merges elements of his own spirituality with those depicted in the works of Julian of Norwich and St. Francis as well as St. Gertrude, works that were instrumental in shaping his own desires. Clearly Connary is influenced by what he perceives others as desiring or achieving; when he produces a complementarity of printed text and his own manuscript, he also establishes a form of intertextual association between his own spirituality and that of past voices.[16]

"What is the relationship between annotation and intertextuality?" asks the French philosopher Jacques Derrida, who has offered penetrating analyses of the writings of mystics as powerful annotations to the ineffable mystical experience. Annotation "is intertextual through and through," he suggests, "from the moment we understand 'text' in the classical sense as a notation representing one discourse propped on another. It consists, in effect, of a text related to another text that has meaning only within that relationship."[17] Whether meaning exists *only* within such relationship, or is enriched or complicated by it, Connary seems to find the opportunity of inscribing himself into texts—of subscribing to the experiences in them in a form of intertextual exchange—compelling and irresistible. Most notably, we find heightened experiential accounts veering toward the mystical in the works of St. Francis of Sales and in *The Sinner's Guide*. The lapidary inscription "I am here"—as we find it on page 205 of *The Spirit of St. Francis de Sales*, along with Connary's abundant signatures—suggests a spiritual deictics of dedicated and reiterated acts of inscription and subscription. This is the written assertion that is simultaneously inside the book and pointing beyond it to the lived and felt religious experience.

The experiential thus occupies an important place in Connary's Catholicism and spiritual self-articulation, and it never exists apart from his didacticism. "Seeing very plainly" always leads to what he terms "showing very plainly," inasmuch as the accounts of emotionally charged spiritual impressions invariably develop into moral and religious assertions. Or, conversely, is it the case that the constantly rehearsed didactic assertions develop into corporeal sensations? Does the imperative to instruct and proclaim look for a culminating experiential and somatic manifestation that can verify it? Inserted into the chapter on the virtue of cordiality in the *Spiritual Conferences* is Connary's record of his vision of the Virgin in his home, and it shows the coherent whole that is forged of affirmation in the intellectual power and somatic experience (fig. 28). The vision he has been granted is viewed as a sign of the sovereign cordiality of God, and he now sees it as his task to gloss it in words that are "cordially and most Faithfully Truthful": "God is fully Right with all of His Blessed and Holy Angels and Saints: Now God is King and Judge of all everywhere in this world as well as everywhere in Eternity, and cordiality where

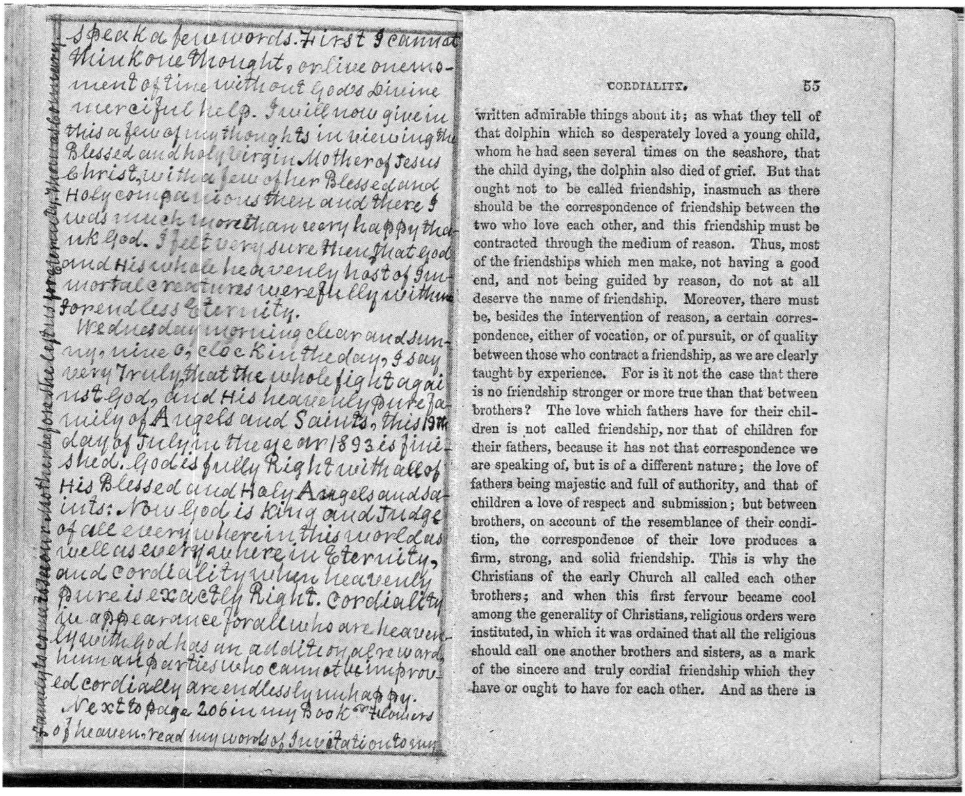

FIG. 28   St. Francis of Sales, *Spiritual Conferences*, page 55

heavenly pure is exactly Right." Here the corporeal showing leads to an intellectual realization, precisely as Serenus Cressy said of Julian's revelations granted
in the understanding that they are to be regarded as "certain" and "exclude all
doubt and suspicion of illusion." For Connary, certainty concerns the notion of
"cordiality," which for him becomes a theological notion about a reciprocal
cordiality between human and divine in the larger scheme of salvation.

The many didactic declarations that crowd the blank spaces in St. Francis
of Sales may seem like routine assertions, marked by frequent reiteration and
Connary's peculiar linguistic fixity. But they find verification in perceived spiritual impressions that consume heart and mind and impart a moral perspective directly applicable in the world. It is not unusual for his handwriting to
become increasingly engaged in the process of describing such epiphanic sensations; the writing is more widely spaced and charged with affect, strings of
capitalized adjectives abound, and full stops become absent, while elongated
hyphens are used to tie sentences or elements of sentences together. In these
instances, Connary appears as a moved respondent to his spiritual literature
and as a book enhancer of prodigious enthusiasm. We may indeed recognize
an imitative component in his recordings, and when Julian, St. Francis, and
St. Gertrude set the example, he cannot *not* speak. But he speaks with the
utmost sincerity and certainty, recording the cherished sensations that are so
closely associated with the intense and somatic experience of inscribing himself into books.

Reading Julian

The enhanced book of Julian of Norwich's *Revelations* contains much of Connary's writing dating from the early 1880s to 1897, and much of this records the
experience of reading and enhancing the volume itself. Indeed, as we noted in
the previous chapter, this book memorializes specific moments and a setting
and allows us to understand something about the concrete experience of reading it in certain kinds of domestic spaces. It is very possible that Connary felt
a particular affinity with the medieval visionary and anchoress because the
spirituality of both centers, to varying extents, on the possibility of withdrawal
and private reading. For Connary this takes place in his study, "the room in
which I am busy much of my time," where, surrounded by books and images
of holy people, he routinely retires from the duties of managing a large household. A note dated February 9, 1890, inserted between pages 20 and 21,
indicates that Connary indeed regards some measure of confinement (to the

extent that this was compatible with domestic obligation) as a calling and a prerequisite for prayer and reflection: "Now all who know me well must know the reason that I have not ever spent much of my time away from my own house—I cannot, my mind is in my business—that business of everlasting life, which never can be done too well. . . . Nothing earthly can ever pay me for that time which I have to spend with our Divine Creator." For Julian, withdrawal meant total dedication to the life of prayer, contemplation, and communion with God in the anchorhold, that enclosed yet liminal space attached to a church and with a window to the world through which she could offer counsel and guidance to those in need. For both, it was retirement and enclosure that offered precious moments for reading, introspection, and religious reflection.

What little we know of Julian's life can be briefly stated. Born probably in 1342, she fell severely ill in May 1373: "And when I was thirtie yeares old and a halfe, God sent me a bodilie sickness, in which I lay three daies and three nights, and on the fourth night I tooke all my Rights of Holie Church, and went [thought] not to have liven till daie."[18] What ensued on the following day was a series of sixteen revelations (or "shewings") that lasted until Julian suddenly recovered from her illness by a seeming miracle: "I marvailed of this sodaine change: for me thought that it was a privie working of God and not of kind [human nature]."[19] Her own short account of her revelations appears to have been written before 1388, while she produced her so-called Long Text possibly as late as the early fifteenth century, after having reflected on the meaning of her visions for decades.[20] We know Julian was still alive in 1416, by which time she would have been enclosed in her anchorhold for more than twenty years.

If one activity unites Julian of Norwich and Thomas Connary, it is that of glossing, understood in its widest sense. Julian, who is both a visionary and an exegete, provides a prolonged gloss on her own spiritual experiences in her Long Text. She probes and questions her visions, which always have Christ's Passion as the focal point. Through this gloss, she augments and complicates the "shewings," transforming them into vibrant, at times audacious, theological reflections on Christian community, salvation, and the nature of evil. Thomas Connary, similarly and in his very distinct way, provides a gloss on his own fervent spiritual experiences. But first and foremost, of course, he provides his comprehensive gloss of prayer and religious proclamation written in the margins and interleaved into his many books. In the cases of both Julian and Connary, we see a remarkably self-documenting book-centered spirituality. "Laboring in my Books"—writing books and writing inside them—is a labor of love, a devout, prayerful exercise, and a route to theological comprehension.

Of no other individual does Connary talk with such overwhelming sympathy as Julian of Norwich: she is praised for being "whole in every Heavenly pure gift, and persecuted persistently for choosing to obey our Divine Creator incessantly in harmony with His Eternal endless designed full purpose," and he notes that "she suffered much and was not scholarly in English words." We may query his assessment, as we have no evidence that Julian was ever persecuted for her belief or doctrine, although she evidently struggled productively to reconcile her theology with the official orthodox line and to some degree liberated herself from it, notably on the subject of salvation. Moreover, the characterization of Julian as "not scholarly" and as a "simple creature unlettered" ignores the vibrant and sophisticated intellectualism that pervades her writing, and which has led one recent commentator to describe her language as "a vernacular version of a scholastic discourse, a reasoning inquiry with carefully articulated questions and answers deploying pointedly abstract terms."[21] The appeal to Julian's and indeed to Connary's own lack of conventional schooling is, of course, a *topos*: it is a version of the humility gesture so common in medieval visionary writing, where authority is derived from being (as Connary says of Julian) "fully schooled by God." It is a *topos* particularly useful to him for asserting proximity with this female recipient of God's grace and revelation.

But to cast doubt on Connary's understanding of Julian as persecuted and unlearned somehow misses the point. It deflects attention from the extraordinary sympathy and indeed reverence that Connary had for the life and writing of this holy woman who "never really died anywhere." "I understand her well without her glossary" and "I understand the full force of the Divine blessed holy Heavenly words without explanation thank God": Connary reiterates this point throughout his annotation of the *Revelations*, as if comprehension was brought about by an act of divine mediation. A note dated November 21, 1884, is written in his characteristic idiosyncratic prose with its convoluted syntax and provides us with further insight into his particular esteem for Julian as an epitome both of holiness and of the obedience to God's will that is always a positive moral choice:

> She never was schooled much in human literature anywhere, through her very painful duties of her secluded blessed and holy vocation, through her very firm endless Faithful willingness to live perpetually with our Divine Creator fully in the most pure unending thankful obedience to

Him everywhere, nothing has ever disappointed or really injured her anywhere—nothing can ever disappoint or really injure her anywhere—so exactly with every personal one member of the whole human family thankfully willing to choose our Divine Creator in the most pure faithful endless obedience to Himself everywhere—nothing of mystery in this but the one Great Heavenly pure mystery of Godliness.

Connary thus sees in Julian the special virtue of obedience that is not merely a single transitory act, but a conscious choice of according one's will with God's: a choice, ultimately, of salvation. That he finds in her example considerable inspiration for his own work becomes evident when he continues in what reads like a signed declaration: "I have faithfully and long worked in humble obedience to our Divine Creator for real human improvement in every respect everywhere, my confidence in him is unlimited—no power can ever disappoint Him be sure. Thomas Connary." Below I will comment on some of the differences and similarities in the theological positions of Julian and Connary. For now we may note the special value that the material book of Julian's *Revelations* holds for Connary and that leads him to interact with it and to augment its material complexity in myriad creative ways. Julian's book, which is now considered one of the highlights of medieval English spiritual literature and generates a vast amount of scholarly interest, was not widely known even among Catholic readers in the nineteenth century. But Connary seems to have treasured the work as an instance of past spiritual authority as relevant in his own time as it ever was, and he enters into his own eccentric form of dialogue with it.

In Dialogue with Julian

We must confront two caveats as we compare the theological positions of Julian of Norwich and Thomas Connary and consider the possible ways in which Connary was influenced by the contents of the book into which he so emphatically inserts himself. Firstly, relating his handwritten annotations to the books in which they appear can be challenging because they show a tendency to become texts unto themselves, often glossing other annotations and responding only indirectly, if at all, to the print. Secondly, we see two rather different processes, as Julian's labors merge experience and its interpretation to produce a comprehensive theological experiment of progressive, deepening understanding. Connary's rhetoric at all stages is that of the confident and didactic assertion. Although the experiential dimension is important to his religious identity, it is not the essence of it, and his recorded narratives are never glossed at any length, except indirectly and through a concatenation of moral and theological declarations.

Furthermore, Connary remains largely unaffected by the predominant feature of Julian's theology, namely her unrelenting focus on Christ and his Passion. Her visions commence after she has been shown a crucifix, and we remain essentially within the parameters of what Berndt Hamm has termed a "normative centring" of late medieval theology and piety, that is to say, a theology in which the omnipresent image of the Christ of the Passion, in which is also presented the exemplary compassion of Mary, serves as the locus of devotion and as the most characteristic representation of God's mercy and grace.[22] Julian remains throughout her text, in her own words, "fulfilled of feeling, and mind of Christ's passion, and his dying."[23] Though she can be said to move toward deeper contemplation of the divinity, Christ never leaves her field of vision, and most often her reflections alternate between the received Christ-centered visions and thoughts about the transcendent Godhead. It is as if, for her, the full reality of the divinity and the Trinity is contained in the complex "shewings" of the tortured humanity of Christ, susceptible to suffering and pain: "He lighteth our heart, and giveth us in party knowing, and loving in his blessed-ful God-head, with gracious mind in his sweet Manhood, and his blessed passion."[24] When we turn to Connary's annotations in the *Revelations*, we find Julian's searching Christocentrism replaced with an insistent theocentrism—a focus on God, the "Heavenly High Priest," the "Best and Purest School Teacher," "our own National Sovereign."

Where Connary and Julian seem to converge, however, is in formulating a highly optimistic perspective on the subject of human salvation. Connary is brought to a general understanding and assurance regarding human salvation, which is similar in many respects to the "sovereign comfort" and "sickerness [certainty, assurance] in hope of bliss of heaven" that Julian derives from her visions of Christ. The following statement offers striking articulation of Connary's optimism in his vision of the elect. As he himself indicates, it is inserted meaningfully at the very end of the *Revelations* as his own personal declaration and ultimate endorsement of Julian's words:

> I now say very truly that thoughts constantly coming continually for the entire human family of immortal heavenly creatures everywhere, from the only True Living God, in His entire unlimited unfathomable creations, every one of them all, and all of them collectively together, are

perpetually Living with Him, and His entire heavenly family of immortal creatures everlastingly, in His heavenly kingdom: this one of my papers in Book, "Revelations of the unschooled Mother Juliana," in 214 printed pages, published in Boston, Massachusetts, By the protestant publishers Ticknor And Fields, in the year 1864, with a Glossary, proves mathematically everywhere in Creation thank God.[25]

Such an assertion resonates strongly with Julian's text. In her elaborate "reading" and gloss of Christ's body revealed to her, she too finds "sicker [certain] trust" in God's promise and grace. Julian's extensive commentary on her fourteenth revelation, for instance, states that even in mankind's "frailty and fallings," God "keepeth us in this time as tenderly, and as sweetly to his worship, and as surely to our salvation, as he doth when we be in most solace and comfort."[26] This is given further substance by her when she characterizes the soul's union with God, in the words of Joan Nuth, as "not only a static ontological reality, but also a relational one; it means being united to God in Love."[27] Julian writes, "Our soul is oned to him, unchangeable goodness: and between God and our soul is neither wrath nor forgiveness in his sight; for our soul is so fulsomely oned to God of his own goodness, that between God and our soul may be right naught."[28] In Julian's optimistic and inclusive salvation theology, "we be all bound to God for kind, and we be bound to God for grace." As she emphasizes in numerous places, she is brought to an understanding of this reality as a principle of generality for all mankind: "But no man, ne woman take this singularity [Julian's Middle English has "syngulary"] to himself; for it is not so, it is general."[29]

Finding Comfort in Julian: Reflections on Incorporation and Salvation

When we take into account Julian's optimistic view on salvation as a possibility for all, we can understand why Connary would declare that "Mother Juliana never will fail as encouragement."[30] Julian's meditations about salvation center on the permanent and unchanging union of herself and her "even Christians" with God, and it is in her book that Connary formulates his most positive views on the graces accorded by God to all. These views continue to revolve around the exercise of free will ("human creatures may sinfully refuse to believe our Divine Creator in this world") and the possibility of eternal torment.[31] But the degree of comfort and assurance conveyed in his notes in the *Revelations* is unmatched in any other of his annotated books. Central to his thoughts, as it is to Julian's, is the idea of incorporation into "the entire human family of immortal heavenly creatures everywhere" made possible by divine grace. God is "peaceful" and he "lives purely everywhere," Connary writes. "God alone in His merciful endless goodness, has done all during the entire eternity of His Noble Life Time to help and really befriend all."

Connary's understanding is thoroughly social when he affirms that, for those who choose to work for God, "no controversy is required or expected—all perfectly reasonable—perfectly peaceful." These words concern not just his closest family, but all of humanity, "every one of them all, and all of them collectively together." This theme of incorporation and generality is similarly addressed in a note from 1884 found in *The Spirit of St. Francis de Sales*. It requires a sentence without punctuation or division to convey the idea of an integrated company of righteous souls: "As I know I am one member of the whole human family I know I am related to every one member of the whole human family from first to last and from last to first unchangeably everywhere under that one unchangeably perfect Eternal Government Law of our Divine Creator's Life Time." As already observed, Connary derives assurance about his own salvation from his vision of the Lady and company, which led him to understand "that God and His whole heavenly creatures were fully with me for endless Eternity." But his annotations in the *Revelations* concentrate on the corporate, inclusive nature of such affirmation. We may reasonably speculate that one of the things that Julian has taught Connary is how a comprehensive vision of incorporation and the availability of salvation may profitably be understood, in her terms, not as "singulary" but as "general." Connary, in other words, appears to have read and absorbed Julian's message that "if I look singularly to myself, I am right nought; but in general I am, I hope [believe], in one-head of charity with all my even Christian; for in this one-head standeth the life of all mankind that shall be saved."[32]

As these readings indicate, it is obvious how Connary could derive comfort from Julian, this medieval visionary who recounts the uplifting words spoken to her by Christ, "Sin is behovely [necessary, beneficial], but all shall be well, and all shall be well, and all manner of thing shall be well."[33] A statement rich in soteriological implication, it is hardly surprising that several modern commentators on Julian have seen in her thinking an impetus toward universal salvation.[34] We might do well to exercise caution in this respect, for Julian nowhere claims with confidence and explicitness that all humans will ultimately be saved.[35] But it seems to be the case, nonetheless, that, on the basis of her conscientious inner negotiation, she arrives at an understanding of the corporeal body of Christ as an image of a shared, transhistorical community of compassionate "even Christians," in which the term "even Christians" becomes the marker for a boldly speculative and, in some respects, radically inclusive vision of a salvation potentially available to all.

The simple point I want to make here is that Julian's thoughts on salvation resonate very strongly with Connary's religious annotations, particularly and understandably with those inserted into his copy of the *Revelations*. Ultimately, Connary can consent to Julian's optimistic views as "all purely devotional and strictly pure in thought design and creation." Both voices, it seems, become aligned with the idea of an inclusive Christian community united eternally to God.

For Connary, such a notion of inclusion involves agreement on essential doctrine across the Protestant-Catholic divide and their respective printed Bibles. He insists that contradiction is full in "painful living death for human immortal creatures, as the entire Book of Creation with Roman Catholic Bible and protestant Bible fully prove." And in a rhetorical address also inserted in the *Revelations* he emphasizes a similar universal appeal: "in Roman Catholic Bible and in protestant Bible please read every word of Chapter vi, in Saint John's Gospel: I say to all never forget the encouraging words of the Chapter anywhere."[36] Developing this idea of an inclusive Christian community further, Connary never tires of noting that the publishers of the *Revelations* are Protestants. To him, this fact appears to be particularly reassuring and loaded with meaning. Thus he writes, for instance, "[this book is] published by Ticknor and Fields, in Boston, in the year 1864, they are protestant publishers, and have done justice to the whole human family in publishing this Book," and later he notes, "The Book of Revelations as will be seen, was published by protestant publishers and was plainly credited by them as purely remarkable."[37] Such Protestant approval of pre-Reformation English spirituality is particularly meaningful to Connary, to whom common ground for religious belief clearly matters more than controversy and doctrinal disagreement.

These observations about a shared religious interest and belief can usefully be seen against a backdrop of widespread struggle between Protestants and Catholics in many places in New England, rural as well as urban, beginning in the 1830s and '40s, during the first significant wave of immigration from Ireland. Religion could, and often did, exercise great divisive potential in a place and time that witnessed the development of dual institutional systems, primarily in industrial towns and cities, and not infrequent acts of aggressive self-assertion on the parts of both Catholics and Protestants.[38]

But Connary, in a remarkably sympathetic, if rather bizarre, statement, extends his rhetoric of tolerance and communality to apply across gender and race:

> I speak again of the small Indians as men, and as women—they are now in Lilliput here, as Dean Swift had them years ago, as about four feet in bodily form—the common Indians are good, and peaceful naturally. I am well acquainted with them—so with the black men and women. All of our best people are most sound and most happy with God, and they choose to be so for endless time—so they Live for endless heavenly felicity. No thing can be any better than endless Heavenly felicity I am sure with God and His pure heavenly Hosts of Immortal Creatures.[39]

This statement is inserted into a book in which the author struggles to reconcile her conviction that "all shall be well" with the teaching of the Church that some people will be damned, specifically "tho that be heathen: and also many that hath received Christendome, and liveth unchristen life, and so dyeth out of charity."[40] In reflecting on this, Julian arrives at an impasse: she understands that what is impossible to her is not impossible to God. She can do nothing but reassert her faith in the orthodox exposition, "and sadly [firmly] believe, that all manner thing shall be well, as our Lord shewed in the same time."[41]

Such comfort and optimism is paralleled in Connary's annotations that enter into some productive exchange with the theology of Julian. Her reflections on salvation, which lean toward belief in the possibility of salvation even for those not pledging allegiance to the Christian creed, acquire new resonance in the specific time and locale that is late nineteenth-century New England. They prove particularly enabling to Connary's desirous anticipation of an inclusive Christian community sustained by divine grace and homeliness.

"The Social Joys of Heaven" and the Problem of Contention

Two concepts stand out in Connary's commentary on St. Francis of Sales and Julian of Norwich, namely, "cordiality" and "contention." Both terms are given theological substance by him and are understood to function crucially in the scheme of salvation. Through the virtue of "cordiality," man can enter into a true reciprocal relationship with his neighbor and with God; through it, he can be disposed toward salvation and toward incorporation into "the social joys of heaven where God is King and Judge of all."[42] "Contention," on the other hand, is a concept that Connary returns to time and again, especially in his writing in Julian's *Revelations*, and it signifies to him the willful choosing of wrong and voluntary rejection of God's gifts. A cluster of notes dated January 29, 1889, and inserted after page 214 of the *Revelations* revolves around the concept of "contention" understood as contradiction of God's moral law. Connary notes that "the whole of contradiction is full to overflowing in contentious everlasting unfaithful evil sinful infernal tormenting painful living death for human immortal creatures." Like so many of his annotations, this one leads almost inevitably toward observations about paratext and ownership, before returning briefly to the subject at hand:

> This one of my papers in Book "Revelations of the unschooled Mother Juliana" in 214 printed pages, published in Boston, Massachusetts, by the protestant publishers Ticknor And Fields in the year 1864 with a glossary, proves mathematically everywhere in creation thank God. I think the Book has been mine continually since 1864: I understand every word of it as Theologically Truthful everywhere. No glossary required for me in this Book. Now and continually during unending eternity human family members may be guarded against contention. Thomas Connary.

It seems safe to say that both Julian and Connary identify man primarily with the will to do good and with an innate inclination to follow God's moral law. As Connary states, man "will choose to be Ruled and Governed by God and His pure family of Immortal Creatures forever Eternally, never to be sinfully wrong anywhere." Julian similarly thinks of her "even Christians" predominantly in terms of that "high substance" in which is found the "godly will that never assented to sin, ne never shall. Which will is so good that it may never will evil."[43] In the writings of both, however, the image of sin occupies a central place as the contradiction or blindness that makes man lose his vision of God.[44]

Julian conceives of sin as an abstraction and as a privation of the good. This person, who lived in the time of the Black Death and the Peasants' Revolt of 1381—cataclysmic events widely understood and rationalized as divine punishment for human sinfulness—never associates sin with any specific event or deed in her own time. For Connary, on the other hand, human contention finds a strikingly concrete manifestation in one harrowing historical event, the American Civil War (1861–65), whose duration and magnitude took most if not all Americans by surprise and led to the deaths of more than half a million soldiers, mostly nonprofessionals who fought in mass citizens' armies.[45] Like so many in postwar America, Connary felt compelled to seek meaning in war's unfathomable destruction, and in his annotations he frequently glosses the event as a conscious, chosen act of rebellion against God and as the epitome of human sinfulness.[46] "We are sure that God forbids fighting and unnecessary controversy, as all sinfully and painfully wrong," notes Connary in his book *Memoirs of a Guardian Angel,* and the Civil War—sometimes referred to by him as the "uncivil war"—returns as a leitmotif throughout his annotations. In Julian's *Revelations* we find the clearest indication that the war brought about a profound crisis in his life and led him to formulate with such insistence the rigor and severity of his moral demands: "Then during the war of the Rebellion, I was fully confirmed in the belief that the whole fight was against God, and all parties who were instrumental in causing that sinful work must live in painful sin during endless Eternity—I have seen more in this direction, than words can ever represent thank God."[47]

"A figure and a likeness of our foul, black deed" is how Julian describes the image of the face of Christ discolored and disfigured in his Passion, and it sums up what the Civil War represents for Connary: it is the willfully determined act of injustice that most hauntingly manifests man's alienation from God. In her book *This Republic of Suffering,* Drew Faust offers an illuminating discussion of the ways in which Americans on the eve of the Civil War "found their traditional systems of belief both powerfully challenged and fervently reaffirmed." She comments, "The Civil War carnage transformed the mid-nineteenth century's growing sense of religious doubt into a crisis of belief that propelled many Americans to redefine or even reject their faith in a benevolent and responsive deity."[48] The next chapter will make further observations about Connary's crisis—religious and psychological—brought about by the experience of the war, but what specifically characterizes the notes in Julian's *Revelations* (produced two to three decades after the event) is a focus on the moral and transcendent purpose of profound upheaval. In the end, Connary clearly affirms divine rule and the punishment of sinful human agency, recognizing a moral triumph in an event that challenged notions of unity and integrity.

With his leanings toward figurative and quasi-mystical discourse, Connary proceeds to dramatize the nature of "the uncivil war" through the use of personification and his oft-employed visionary *topos* of "seeing plainly." The war is an event to be interpreted and narrated in literary terms:

> At the time of the great Rebellion here in the year 1860 . . . when this our government was in danger of being dismembered, I plainly saw the

sinful unpeaceful King of endless warfare standing near me as a man
very large in body: I saw him as nothing but painful evil when I saw no
thing good in him. He then had no power to stand on his feet, my own
Divine heavenly Commander was personally present with me unlimited
in heavenly power, but not as large as a young man as I have often seen
in body: my evidences are numberless and perpetual I cannot be mis-
taken. Thomas Connary.[49]

The same apparition of a personified "King of endless warfare" is recounted
in a note dated April 8, 1893, in James Balmes's *Fundamental Philosophy*:
"When I was in the divine presence of God, at the time this, our government
was in danger of being dismembered rebelliously, our heavenly King conde-
scended to show me the very large King of endless warfare, and he then had
no power to remain on his feet when I saw nothing good in him—he is now
sinfully infernal and must be so with his entire full family of Immortal creatures for endless Eternity." A sense of spiritual and civil crisis, however, gives
way to manifest optimism in a note which takes comfort in the idea of a rees-
tablished American polity and in a sense of divine restoration and Christian
eschatology: "In 1860 we were very busy here with our wartroubles. Now
thank God, our Government business is right, in the coming future our real
business must be heavenly in a peaceful way, for all endless eternity."[50]

Simply and uncompromisingly, human contention is perceived as antithet-
ical to the sovereign goodness and peacefulness of God. It has been observed
by many commentators that Julian can attribute no wrath to God, as this
would mar her image of God as "unchaungeable goodnesse." I suggest here
that Connary follows Julian in understanding wrath as predominantly a
human phenomenon and a symptom of man's "contrariness" against God.
Even in the epiphanic account of his nocturnal excursion to Lancaster (discussed in the interlude following chapter 3), during which he is granted a
vision of "a bottle of wrath" that must come as punishment for sin, wrath can
be understood as internal to man. Nowhere does Connary state that this can
be a relational reality between man and God. In fact, this specific apparition
of the bottle of wrath recalls some of the striking visionary images that we find
in the *Revelations*: it recalls especially Julian's brief abstract vision of the entirety
of creation lovingly sustained by God, presented before her as "a litle thing,
the quantitie of a hasel-nutt, lying in the palme of my hand" (presented in
chapters 5 and 10 of the *Revelations*). For both Connary and Julian, the short
and pregnant vision provides lasting insight into the nature of cordiality, contention, and the reality of human salvation.

The following narrative by Connary brings together many of these themes in a remarkable record of a corporeal spiritual vision. It is inserted into the front of St. Francis of Sales's *Spiritual Conferences*—like Julian's *Revelations*, a book through which man may be "schooled by God Himself for endless Eternity."

EPIPHANY

"No Priest or Bishop in this Church but Himself Alone"

I plainly saw Him as a very firmly built strong man, but perhaps less than five feet eight inches in height apparently, purely noble in every respect, hair and beard long and white, fully dressed in every respect as infinitely perfect heavenly high priest last night, walking in a firmly built plainly finished Roman Catholic church in Ireland—I found myself without any expense in money in time—in labor—in preparation with Him and with His own not very large congregation of young and old persons including many children, all over the commonage of infancy as He measures human life in this world everywhere—no priest or bishop in this church but Himself alone—appearances indicated a beginning of Divine Service—with my hat in one of my hands, and my soul full to overflowing with pure heavenly love for Him and for His whole congregation of blessed and holy worshippers flowing freely incessantly from Himself alone in my favor in justice, mercy and charity to the whole family of immortal creatures endlessly—I humbly fell on my knees instantly for His Blessing which I thankfully received in common communion with his whole congregation—my Happiness Heavenly pure never will end thanks unspeakable incessantly to Him from me—I never will forget to remember the full force of His English words pronounced sweetly with very plain Old Irish accent, He slowly walked and talked as Teacher to all of the people, giving them full time to understand, that though He, in appearance was then leaving them slowly as a human pastor must move when required to move, He Himself will never leave them—I plainly saw Him blessing the people immediately before He disappeared from human sight—all of the people sung that endless Eternal Heavenly song of Divine worship which He alone can ever teach— no day light in the church during the time referred to—common material light—nothing more handsomely connected with very plain surrounding church furniture, all disappeared instantly from my view with His last words of blessing the people.

"For our Lord himself is sovereign homely-head [intimacy, familiarity], and so homely as he is, as courteous he is; for he is very courteous": Julian's words aptly sum up Connary's epiphanic narrative.[1] This account of God's blessing of the congregation in an Irish Roman Catholic church is found on a note dated "eleven O'clock in the forenoon Wednesday January 31, 1883" and inserted at the front of the *Spiritual Conferences* by St. Francis of Sales. No other narrative captures more fully the imaginative and experiential dimension of Connary's piety. We note again the strikingly literal and corporeal nature of "plain" seeing and hearing (what Julian refers to as a "seeing with bodily sight"), together with the theocentrism and topographical familiarity that determine and enrich his experience. Although no specific church is referred to, annotations by Connary in several of his books mention the Ballyouskill Catholic church, founded in 1822, that he helped build in his childhood days near his home in Ireland. As he remarks in a note in Chardon's *Memoirs of a Guardian Angel*, "since I left that place, I have been there in my mind power very much more than here." He would be able to visualize very concretely the space in which the above narrative is set. And what expression of belonging and Irish identity could be more manifest than that of the divinity appearing in the local Irish Catholic church, addressing the congregation "sweetly with very plain Old Irish accent"!

We saw in the previous epiphany that, for Connary, the road to Lancaster becomes a theological *via positiva*, providing positive affirmation of God's guidance and of the suffering that must follow disobedience. But even more so here; more than mere affirmation, we see the extraordinary domestication of a God who is "condescending" (one of Connary's favorite terms), appearing in plain sight in a familiar locale, his height, hair, and accent manifest and describable. Throughout his writings, Connary labors to give creative linguistic expression to a deity graspable and familiar yet transcendent. Among his many epithets are "Bountiful Creator," "Divine Landlord," "Heavenly High Priest," "Unlimited Powerful Worker without wages," "Holy Father," "Best and Purest School Teacher," "the Best Business Schoolmaster," "Director and Schoolmaster," "Schoolmaster First," "Treasure and Treasurer," "Commander," "Keeper of the Vineyard," "our own National Sovereign," and "Divine Book unbound as a Book."

Consolation is derived from invoking God in terms of familiar reference. This recalls one of the central themes in Julian's *Revelations*, namely that of the "homeliness" and "courtesie" of God and the comfort and reassurance he offers to man. Beginning with her reflections on her first showing, it is clear that she glosses her experience of the divine as an instance of supreme familiarity and courtesy: "It is the most joy that may be as to my sight, that he that is highest and mightest, nobliest and worthiest, is lowest and meekest, homliest and courtesiest . . . for the most fulhed of joy that we shall have is this marvellous courtesie and homeliness of our Father."[2] For Connary, and truly in the spirit of Julian, such an unmediated experience of divine "homeliness" is intricately associated with a sense of communion and incorporation with God's congregation—what he elsewhere refers to as "the social joys of heaven." In this account of divine blessing and communal rejoicing, Connary's love is inherently social and relational, directed both toward God and "his whole congregation of blessed and holy worshippers," while he remains safe in the knowledge that "all shall be well."

5

BOOK KEEPING, LONGING, AND BESETMENT

> For nineteen (19) days I was silent so.
>
> **—Thomas Connary, undated note between pages
> 70 and 71 in Philippe, *The Six Hundred Thousand
> Combatants***

In a Room of His Own: Book Enhancement and Besetment

Thomas Connary was insane. His recorded condition was not stated with
further diagnostic precision, but it was official. The United States census
records of 1870 and 1880, in the section that registers "whether deaf and dumb,
blind, insane, idiotic, pauper, or convict," note "insane" next to Connary's
name. When these two census records were compiled, Connary was in his late
fifties and late sixties, respectively. The seventh and eighth United States census records, compiled in 1850 and 1860, were the first to separately enumerate
what in the psychiatric parlance of the day was termed "insane" and "idiotic,"
and they note nothing unusual or abnormal about him or any of his family.
Similarly, nothing is noted in the census of 1890.

Connary partook in what was a veritable explosion of diagnosed cases of
insanity in the United States from the middle to the end of the nineteenth
century. The years 1850 to 1880 saw a doubling of the population of the United
States (from twenty-three million to fifty million) but a sextupling of the
number of "insane, idiots, blind, and deaf-mutes." In that period, the number
of those categorized specifically as insane went from 15,000 to 92,000, nearly
half of whom were committed in asylums for the insane.[1]

The preceding chapters have examined Connary's strong set of convictions
regarding salvation and incorporation into the "social joys" of an eternal
Christian community. We now have to acknowledge a very different sort of
social incorporation for him, namely, into that approximately one percent of
the American population which in 1880 was categorized as "the defective
classes." This was a category within which the "insane" and "idiotic" out-
numbered any other grouping, including the blind, homeless, prisoners, and

paupers in almshouses.[2] In his *Report on the Defective, Dependent, and Delinquent Classes*, completed for the Department of the Interior in connection with the 1880 census, Frederick H. Wines regrets the terms "defectives" and the "defective classes" as titles offensive to many and largely nondescriptive: "I should have preferred some other term, had I been able to think of a better, but no one has suggested a better." Some justification for the term, notes Wines, is that it conveys to administrators the precise numbers of those whose "claim to the protecting care of the government is based upon a physical or mental defect." The "defective classes" are those that sustain "a peculiar relation with the public": "the governments of the several states and territories are invoked to make provision for their maintenance, tuition, or medical treatment in institutions created by law and supported at the expense of the public treasury."[3]

The system that Connary came into contact with was one increasingly prone to incarceration, and we know that Connary had a history of repeated institutionalization, for he states so himself. His striking account (inserted in *The Sinner's Guide*) of his walk to Lancaster in the middle of the night at God's bidding is prefaced by the following remark: "Immediately before I was taken the third time from this, my own home, to the Asylum for the Insane in Concord, New Hampshire, I had full power to know positively continually what our Divine Creator really required me to do—I had no power to disobey Him— no inclination to disobey Him." His purported experiencing of apparitions and divine instructions very possibly played a role in his hospitalization, as he was brought to the only state asylum in New Hampshire, the New Hampshire Asylum for the Insane, founded in Concord in 1842 (fig. 29). I have been unable to ascertain when precisely Connary was hospitalized for insanity, and whether he underwent brief or prolonged periods of confinement. Probably he had several shorter stays (at least three, as we know) during the 1860s and 1870s and possibly later.

Many in the nineteenth century took great pride in the high degree of organization and development of public institutions as well as in the vast network of asylums for the treatment of the insane, which, the census report for 1860 concludes, presented one of the preeminent "evidences of progressive science and enlightened philanthropy."[4] As the report proclaims further, a new stage of advancement had been entered, in which treatment through "liberal employment of blisters, purgatives, cupping, and blood-letting" had given way to the administering of "stimulants and tonics."[5] The fact is, however, that this predated any modern psycho-pharmacological revolution, and there were no very effective treatment modalities available to doctors or staff. Care of the "men-

N. H. Insane Hospital, Concord, N. H.

FIG. 29   Postcard of the New Hampshire Asylum for the Insane, Concord, ca. 1910

tally alienated" was in large measure restricted to the custodial and disciplinary rather than the curative. The experience for Connary must have been degrading: in the Concord hospital, he would have been subjected to some form of incarceration or seclusion, which, as Wines notes, toward the end of the 1880s functioned as "a form of restraint. . . . [consisting] in shutting up a lunatic, by night only, or both by day and night, in a room by himself, in order to prevent him from wandering, or from injuring himself or others, or from irritating others to injure him."[6] He would also, in all probability, have been subjected to an occupational or "moral" treatment, involving the exercise of "mild but firm directive and disciplinary power over the actions of the patient," and this probably meant some labor in the asylum grounds, where a 120-acre farm colony re-created the conditions of a typical New England farm (fig. 30).[7] In all likelihood, the asylum was a religion-free zone, a place to calm the passions and the protean mind, where the reading of spiritual literature was not permitted.

It was largely at the judgment and discretion of the local census enumerator to assess whether a report of a person's insanity was worthy of confidence.[8] In a way that suggests the secrecy and social stigma that often surrounded an afflicted member of a household, the enumerator was instructed to make inquiries about "defective" individuals—not just of their closest family, who

Concord, N.H., Scene in State Hospital Grounds.

FIG. 30   Postcard of a scene in the New Hampshire Asylum grounds, Concord, ca. 1910

might not always, it was suspected, give reliable witness, but also of neighbors and others in the local community—in an effort to establish as accurate an assessment as possible.[9] Importantly, as we learn from Wines's *Report* for the 1880 census, the enumerators' compilations were supplemented by "correspondence with physicians, in all parts of the United States, to the number of nearly 100,000, all of whom were furnished with blank forms of return, and were invited and urged to report to the Census Office all idiots and lunatics within the sphere of their personal knowledge."[10]

The report by Wines provides some valuable insight into how the label "insane" was understood within the context of the U.S. census enumeration. The term was to prove long-lived in the psychiatric profession, while the word "idiotic" was replaced in the 1890 census with "feeble-minded." Where "idiots" "lack the full development of their mental powers," the insane "have lost, to a greater or less extent, the faculty of reason or the balance between the intellectual powers of which, before becoming insane, they were possessed, and which the most of them still partially retain."[11] In remarks replete with confidence in the reliability of modern psychiatric diagnostics, Wines invokes the New England Psychological Association and other "expert alienists" for the official nomenclature of mental disorders grouped together as "insanity."

This comprises mania ("which manifests itself in a state of nervous, intellectual, and emotional exaltation and excitement"), melancholia ("a state of depression"), monomania ("fixed delusions on particular subjects"), paresis ("general paralysis of the insane"), dementia ("the condition of imbecility into which mania and melancholia ultimately degenerate"), dipsomania ("alcoholic insanity"), and epilepsy.[12] Mania, dementia, and melancholia appear in that order as the three major categories of insanity, and Wines can conclude that "the tendency to nervous excitement among the insane is about twice as great as that to depression."[13]

When Connary was recorded as "insane" in the U.S. census of 1870, he was one of the 37,432 to which the diagnosis was attached, of which just over 11,000 were foreign born, indicating a disproportionately high rate of the diagnosed condition among immigrants.[14] In 1870, Connary was one of the 18 men and 33 women born in Ireland who were diagnosed as insane in the state of New Hampshire.[15]

The observations above present us, naturally, with a very different perspective on the enhanced books in which the owner claims narrative power, speaking passionately and autobiographically. The challenge, for this study, is to acknowledge the diagnosis—to acknowledge some degree of psychological instability and the concomitant suffering of an individual and a family—while avoiding the approach to Connary's writings through the label of "insanity." An approach to his writing through the dimension of deviance and social exclusion would risk reducing it to a curiosity or (at best) to a study of language and madness. The precise diagnosis should not preoccupy us much here. What is important is the fact that Connary had the label attached to him that was, in the words of Allan Ingram, "the ultimate in alienation, the most damaging of social stigmas, the most personally invasive of definitions, potentially the most remote and inaccessible of narrative positions."[16]

Connary himself is not overly concerned with diagnosis either. He often mentions *en passant* a mental crisis in the past without any indication of shame, and he offers nothing in the sense of vindication, such as insisting on his sanity or complaining of mistreatment or of being misunderstood. He often returns to one specific instance of paralysis, referring to it as "my nineteen (19) days of unconsciousness, beginning Monday, June 10, 1889, ending Friday June 28, same year."[17] As we learn from a close study of his notes, Connary wrote copiously in his diary on June 8 and 9 of that year: "my words were purely Truthful, when I wrote them, they are so now, and will be so for everlasting Eternity thank God." Following this bout of productivity, perhaps weary from his daily combats with malice, he is visited by a paroxysm "when for nineteen days of time, I had no power to speak one word to anyone of you." This state of paralysis is later associated with a near-revelatory insight into God's moral law and the urgent need to communicate this: "For nineteen (19) days I was silent so, I see all thank God. Controversy, fighting, and wilfully deceiving, determined human rascality, however long continued into everlasting Infinitude in Rebelliously opposing the one only true Living God, never can be right anywhere—remember."[18]

One way of approaching this account of rapid decline and subsequent recovery is to see it as aligned with numerous mystical accounts, such as that of Julian of Norwich, in which sickness and a temporary insensibility to the world around are associated with revelation and an experience of the divinity. It points to another side to the imitative dimension of Connary's writing, where he models himself on inspirational mystical accounts by invoking mental and physical crisis as part of the process of spiritual growth. But the account is also, undoubtedly, the record of a real lapse into melancholy and a state of immobility—a numbing of the senses, being thrust into the depths of darkness and silence. The period, as Connary recounts it, is surrounded by periods of impassioned articulation. He appears to emerge from it with redoubled vigor and scrupulosity, even more confirmed in his opinions.

We have, of course, already noted a particularly eccentric, even obsessive, mental constitution. The extravagance and inordinate repetition of his sentences, and the insisting, meandering form of his admonition; all point to an obsession with moral rigor and exactitude. If the following writing by Connary does not directly constitute proof positive of madness, it labors hard to mask his sanity:

> I prove in this very small paper, that in living with God for endless Eternity, our real home is heavenly. We are very sure that what is purely right is so everywhere into heaven. We are very sure that what is impurely wrong everywhere, is so into heavenly felicity with God. We will now see very plainly, the tormenting sinful refractory infernal gods, who have sinfully continued warfare in this world everywhere against the only True Living God, who commands us to love our enemies, to be merciful to those who hate us, and to pray for those who persecute and calumniate us. We are sure that we never can be more obedient to God than He requires us to be. Human power we have from God as our Gift: this Gift is everlasting, every moment of it is the Book of everlasting heavenly pure lifetime for every one of us all, and I am now much more than very

happy to know well, that our Divine Creator and His heavenly family of Immortal creatures, never can be injured anywhere.[19]

"Language is the first and last structure of madness, its constituent form: on language are based all the cycles in which madness articulates its nature," observes Michel Foucault in *Madness and Civilization*.[20] The elaborate, even baroque, architecture of Connary's overloaded sentences shows him caught in an endlessly self-referring affirmation and linguistic self-assertion, and in this he clings to words and syllables, slightly rephrasing his assertions in each repetition. This is a person who takes language extremely seriously, establishing a humor- and irony-free zone and forging a reliability and security of language to accommodate his complex of convictions. His distinct linguistic style is meandering but precise, made up of ordered classifications and rigorous assertions: it remains entirely single-minded, displaying a remarkable firmness of moral perspective and linguistic choice, conveyed in the idiosyncratic, saturated prose in which strings of descriptive adjectives accrue.

We see a Connary who gets carried away when he relates the spiritual epiphany that produces special insight into the realm of metaphysics. This is when he is "much more than very happy" and stretches the resources of language to convey emotional intensity. In the following statement, where theological assertion and the account of a vision form a coherent whole, everything is conveyed in a single enveloping sentence whose structure can hardly sustain any more weight:

Saturday, October 4, 1884, Stratford, Coös County, New Hampshire, cloudy and rainy in the morning calm and beautiful—I think rain continued most of last night here, and with its purely refreshing Heavenly sweet Balm, two beautiful Angels dressed and blessed in robes of celestial bright sunlight assured me positively, that the whole infernal sinful thick heavy cloud of painful tormenting evil darkness in this world is now fully and entirely sundered, as a very slow passing vapour, never again to extend far below or above the range of that centre point in space permanently fitted as the endless Eternal grave of living death, for every personal one member of the whole contradictory refractory unpeaceful unhappy immortal infernal tormenting evil power, including in that range as many members of the whole human family evil, as will never choose to be just or faithful any where—fully infernal in every respect they must centre together in that one only infernal place in space—no infernal property for any one of them all in Heaven remember.

The passage, preserved in Connary's book *The Sinner's Guide*, would not look out of place in a publication such as Allan Ingram's *Voices of Madness*, an anthology of writings by people regarded as mad. In one eighteenth-century voice, Ingram identifies an "obsession with packing all relevant information into a single sentence," a tendency "indicative of a powerful desire to leave nothing to chance. Every scrap of information has to become evidence and be marshalled into some kind of order, whether the syntactic patterns of English writing lend themselves to it or not."[21] With Connary, the formulations display extreme simplicity of moral content: faith is not treated as an internal process involving temptation or a waxing and waning of fervor, but rather in terms of iron-clad certainties judged as fixed stars in the firmament of revelation. Many striking Connarisms are minimalist verbal strategies and convey the essence of his moral demands: "Heaven has no contention," "there is no right way to be wrong," "good Books cannot be bad," "we cannot go both ways to be right," "God is justice and justice is heavenly."

Much in Connary points to the physical and mental state of melancholia, where the mind may undergo periods of melancholic immobility and is attached to a fixed idea, "imposing unreasonable proportions upon it."[22] Above all, his copious book annotations reveal the indeterminacy of the border between reason and unreason, and they suggest what we might refer to as a mental and linguistic "besetment," with Connary being conditioned, even haunted, by a few specific thoughts and motifs.

In his 1896 presidential address delivered at the annual meeting of the Medico-Psychological Association in London, W. Julius Mickle talked on the subject of "Mental Besetments."[23] The person suffering from mental besetment is plagued by the insistency of imperative thoughts and conceptions, and is, in Mickle's words, "engrossed by the vivid reality and validity of the feeling or thought, so that by it the life is essentially altered, and the acts are largely dominated—in which, therefore, a truly delusive impress characterises the mind."[24] This is a state of incessant labor of thought in which a ruling idea, question, or metaphysical problem can tend to fixation and take possession of the mind. As Mickle notes, this unceasing train of thought appears irrepressible to the sufferer. It is associated with limited powers of self-control and can potentially lead to isolation or alienation from the community. I use Mickle's concept of mental besetment only very loosely here (the concept did not become standard in psychology, "obsession" and "obsessive disorder" becoming the preferred terms). And I use "besetment" primarily in a linguistic sense, a sense that Mickle also intends, when he notes that often in the articulations of the beset "we find, for example, the formation of new words; the veneration for and the formal worship of words; a belief in the discovery of truth, or in the penetration of mysteries, by pronouncing words; the attribution of enormous importance to mere words, or of extraordinary potencies to them."[25] So far we have examined the material traces of a mental and linguistic besetment with both creative and corrosive powers, as these have been preserved in numerous books enhanced by Connary in his private room. But his declarations were also public, disseminated utterances that insisted on public attention outside the family sphere.

"We Must Never Be Too Full of Words": Preaching in Stratford

Thomas Connary's protean mental constitution was widely recognized in the Stratford community and even receives mention in Thompson's *History of the Town of Stratford*. In it we find the following observations, which recognize aspects of the aging Connary's melancholia and mental besetment: "Owing to the severe strain upon his sympathetic nature, he suffered a nervous breakdown which left his mind somewhat clouded. Those who were living in Stratford during those later years of his life will remember the kind old gentleman, with his high ideals, his intense love of learning, living among his townspeople, and striving to impress upon them his own high principles of thought and action."[26]

One part of the story of Thomas Connary in the last decades of his life (but only one part) is that of an individual performing his labor of love inside books in a room of his own, absorbed by the vivacity of religious ideas, and with minimal resonance with what is consensually defined as reality or normative behavior. There can be little doubt that he came to be regarded in his community increasingly as a proselytizer and a religious fanatic. To "prove," "tell," "instruct," and "teach" are some of the terms he uses when summoning family and acquaintances to acts of the greatest probity, to lives of the utmost virtue and scruple.

Being enveloped in a world of judgment and moral requirement entails the urgent call for reform, and books are the vehicles for disseminating his message: of the several visitors to the Connary farm, we often read in the diary-like records that they return from Stratford Hollow to their homes, whether by foot, horse, or by railroad ("the cars"), with an enhanced book in their bags. But it is through letter writing that we see the more public side to the urge to instruct and proclaim that cannot be subdued. The Stratford post office, as the institution that serves as platform for the dissemination of a message, acquires an importance equal to that of the church. Connary receives the bulk of his books at the post office and conducts his correspondence with publishers such as Patrick Donahoe in Boston and D. & J. Sadlier in New York. It is here, also, that he commits to the care of the U.S. postal service innumerable letters of religious exhortations, many of which he transcribes in notes inserted into his books. Several letters are addressed to postmasters in Coös County—for instance to Joseph H. Danforth (postmaster at North Stratford, 1861–85):

Stratford, Coös County, New Hampshire, June 25, 1881.

Postmaster for Coös, North Stratford, Coös County, New Hampshire.

Justly respected dear Sir:—You know me now exactly as well as you can now or ever know yourself—when I was last in your office I left a Book in it for you—I now most respectfully call your attention in this way to that Book and to the words which I marked in it as true in every respect, in justice to the whole family of human creatures from the first to the last and from the last to the first unchangeably everywhere . . . God knows I am positively certain that human creatures to be ever really safe anywhere must continue to be purely peaceful just and faithful everywhere for endless Eternity.[27]

Among those addressed in these letters (excluding family) are several individuals in Stratford, Lancaster, and Island Pond in Vermont, the town clerks of Stratford, various book publishers, and the president of the United States. Like the postmaster, the priest, and the town clerk, Connary sees himself as employed in the service of the town of Stratford, performing a function like that of a pastor who toils for the spiritual health of souls: "I will this day, say to all my neighbours in this way everywhere, in doing all of the good you can ever do, be purely faithful everywhere to all, and you live with God."[28] In this endeavor, the book enhancements and letter writing are part of the same ambition to promulgate and edify, and they involve considerable labor and expense: "Now think of this very slow work which I have most faithfully done during my whole life. Letters written and postages paid on them by myself saying nothing of my very long journeys in mailing them: my helpers and directors God and His heavenly pure family of Immortal creatures."[29] The North Stratford post office thus played an important part in the logistic operation of Connary's "Book keeping" and didactic communication. And Connary obviously felt compelled to pontificate on the unrelenting rigor of his ethical and dogmatic demands. "Now thank God, I have lived here in the United States of America so long, that my neighbours are well acquainted with me, and with my words and works," he remarks in one of the final years of his life in a note that he inserts into his copy of *The Six Hundred Thousand Combatants.*

It seems unavoidable that such indomitable, magniloquent proclamation would have caused some resentment in the local community, particularly when we factor in the enduring religious tension in the New England region between Catholics and Protestants, beginning in the 1840s when the first big wave of Irish Catholic immigrants arrived in the United States. Several questions present themselves. Did Connary address his fellow townspeople with the peremptory proclamations that he used in his annotations, and did his attempt to "impress" on them the firmness of his moral habits spark indignant responses? Did his neighbors report him as a case of insanity to the census enumerator? Was the diagnosis as "insane" in part a reaction to a violation of social norms? Was it a reaction to what was perceived to be a behavioral problem by a society unable or unwilling to accommodate his utterings? His rather public attempts to correct behavior that appeared to be under the immediate inspiration of the fiend may have been viewed as the devout antics of a "kind old gentleman" whose mind was "somewhat clouded" (to repeat the characterization in Thompson's *History of Stratford*). But they were also part of an ostentatious religious self-assertion by the first Catholic resident in the town and the person who established the local parish church on Main Street in North Stratford (where there were also Baptist and Methodist churches).

As regards those labeled (without exact semantic distinction) "mad," "insane," "beset," "melancholic," "alienated," "defective," "unreasonable," it matters, of course, who determined the diagnosis. In his article "Irish Immigrants, Pauperism, and Insanity in 1854 Massachusetts," John W. Fox refers to an important early study by the psychologist Edward Jarvis on cases of insanity among Irish immigrants. Jarvis's study, notes Fox, indicates the impact of social bias and intolerance, which could influence and even determine diagnosis: "The prejudice of physicians and others against foreign-born immigrants may have 'increased' their rates of insanity, especially for poor Irish Catholic famine immigrants. For example, a Boston physician reported to Jarvis: 'Very many of the foreign Irish population, say one in ten, imported into this city for the last six years, are idiots or at least no better. Three fourths of the remaining Irish importations, are monomaniacs, being the dupes of Catholic Priests. One half of the whole receive aid from charitable institutions, the City or State.'"[30]

The statement by the Boston physician shows prejudice, indeed, but also an abject racism that vilifies a community on an ethnic and cultural basis and associates it indiscriminately with psychic dysfunction. The clear majority of "Irish importations" are seen as suffering from monomania, defined as "fixed delusions on particular subjects" in the taxonomic scheme of the day, and a close cousin, of course, to Mickle's concept of mental besetment. Had the physician—who connects insanity with the influence of a Catholic upbringing and Catholic priests—known of Thomas Connary, he would undoubtedly claim affirmation of his stereotype of the mercurial Irish passions. Yet the statement, from the place and time when religious tension rode highest in New England, shows the degree to which social and sectarian bias could influence the diagnostic process and likely lead to increased findings of insanity among foreign-born immigrants, the Irish in particular.

Connary is a person extravagant in his eccentricity, one who calls attention to himself as someone who speaks publicly and claims to have "understood on a large scale." But the truth is, of course, that he finds a rural setting where his Catholic values and preachiness are accommodated or tolerated and not too much at odds with American secular values. It would undoubtedly have been difficult for him to function in the city. As he was sufficiently preoccupied with chastising the waywardness that he observed in Stratford, the city would have proved too much for Connary—and no doubt any firsthand experience of anti-Catholic riots, such as the so-called Bible Riots in Philadelphia in 1844, could bring about a deeper mental collapse. Connary shows some interest in these sectarian tensions when he pastes into *The Sinner's Guide* a printed article about the burning of the Ursuline Convent in Charlestown, Massachusetts, by a rioting mob in the summer of 1834, the year after his arrival in the United States.

Although the first resident Catholic in Stratford, Thomas Connary was able to achieve a measure of assimilation, cultivate his conservative Irish Catholicism, and rise to respectability in the local community. The Connary that we read about in printed sources is an individual with a continuum of activities in work and in public life who found ways of rendering himself useful to the town. According to the *New Hampshire Annual Register*, he served as county officer during the Civil War in the years 1861–63. Also in the 1860s, according to Thompson's *History*, he served as town treasurer and selectman (one of a board of three elected town officials).[31] Connary's library, with its numerous titles relating to history, politics, and administration, demonstrates that he took a particularly active interest in governance at national and local levels.

The records of Connary's involvement in town administration end with the early 1870s, at the time when his project of "Book keeping" begins to acquire momentum. But this by no means implies withdrawal from social participation in the community. He remained on cordial terms with many, and until a year or so before his death he interacted with a wide range of individuals, often recording in his books how he traveled by horse-drawn carriage or sleigh to see friends in the area, most often bringing with him enhanced books as gift objects. Such social activity, it seems, was punctuated by periodic visits to the asylum in Concord, where he would have been subject to treatment and regulation in attempts to assuage the religious passion and besetment that consumed his life.

"Madness finds its first possibility in the phenomenon of passion," it has been noted.[32] For Connary, passion meant the irresistible urge to disseminate his creed prodigiously, whether vocally, or through writing and book enhancements, or even, as we have seen, through the medium of a one-page print paratext. In the declining years of his life, when his mind retreated into a rather solipsistic mode of spiritual affirmation, he actively and publicly sought recognition for himself and his religious convictions.

Madness in the Books

The nature of the material considered here has not allowed a detailed time line of Connary's mental decline, but it is evident that in old age he hovered increasingly on the border between sanity and insanity. Such a decline is manifested not in a withdrawal from language, but instead in its opposite—an increasing reliance on language and written testimony. With time (and we have enough material to see change over time), we see Connary's tendency to reinforce the power of words and their regular arrangement. The syntax becomes increasingly complex and reiterative, packing as many descriptive adjectives and superlatives as possible into a sentence. Moreover, as Connary becomes increasingly absorbed in the discipline of empowering, redemptive reading, we see no attempt on his part to dispense with the materiality of the printed book. In fact, as he progresses with his project of book enhancement, and as his pious annotation becomes more fervent and sustained (also more dogmatic and conceited), he highlights even more the status of his books as material objects and works harder to enhance their material complexity. Accompanying an increasing longing for salvation is an increasing attention on the enhancements themselves—on the visible, tactile instantiation of the enhanced book and on comprehensive self-articulation.

Undoubtedly, being enshrined in a bookish universe, dedicated to the enhancement of books, is what soothes Connary's declining years. This work serves as his main source of consolation (especially when no spirit of levity nor a healthy dose of irony is present to alleviate his distress), and we see Connary at his most engaged and resourceful, finding in books a world of familiar certainty—a place to affirm, narrate, and rejoice, and not least, a place to long for and to belong. If a recurring experience is that of a disturbance of the self and the world, the pursuit of "Book keeping" where a library is personalized as a testimony to faith could provide some palliation through an experience of control and empowerment. Here could be found a protocol for literate discipline and high moral seriousness, with each signed page scrupulously avoiding the printed area, precisely filling the writing space. Also, laboring in books would keep Connary's mind occupied with creative composition, being a process of interleaving much of himself and of proclaiming a sense of belonging. This diegetic dimension of Connary's book enhancements is marked by the use of literary and rhetorical features, often with bombastic rhetorical flourishes. Even the account of his nineteen days of unconsciousness becomes a leitmotif in his inserted book writings, being communicated in different ways clearly calculated for rhetorical effect and occurring in various contexts of religious assertion.[33] We might thus perceive a link between book enhancement and self-recovery. Indeed, for Connary, it is in his "Book keeping" that he experiences some retrieval of character and what he understands to be an infusion of textual grace. From this discipline he derives a sense of rootedness, both in the sacred and in a long textual tradition of Catholic Christianity.

Allowing for remarkable eccentricity on Connary's part, it is also possible to see him as in large measure shaped by what he reads and certainly validated by the Catholic books issuing forth in great numbers from Irish American presses. The writings of Julian of Norwich, St. Francis of Sales, and various other saints present Connary with a past contemplative tradition of disciplined and concentrated spiritual meditation. This is a literature of the highest spiritual ambition that captures moments of intense experience and divine intervention, sometimes in the form of individual mystical visionary activity, as in the case of Julian of Norwich. A broader devotional appeal is found in a range of popular pious literature designed to stir the passions and produce affectionate ardor. Texts such as *The Dove of the Tabernacle*, Kempis's *Imitation of Christ*, Faber's *All for Jesus*, Chardon's *Memoirs of a Guardian Angel*, and St. Bernard of Clairvaux's *Glories of the Virgin Mother and Channel of Divine Grace* all encourage an affective mode of piety that would guide Catholic devotional practices (e.g., the Angelus and the Benediction of the Holy Sacrament) and the many popular devotions that Connary pursues (to the sacrament of the

Eucharist, guardian angels, Christ's Passion, the name of Jesus, Our Lady, the Sacred Heart, the five wounds, and so on).

A body of writing including *The Sinner's Guide* and Rodriguez's *Practice of Christian Perfection*, as well as Aesop's *Fables* and Martin's *Secrets of the Great City*, offers an explicit didacticism, insisting on the urgency of moral and spiritual reform. These titles clearly spur Connary's motivation to exhort and edify—and a range of rhetoric and elocution manuals offer practical advice on articulation and the power of the spoken word to move an audience.

In the closely studied authorities of Baine (*An Essay on the Harmonious Relations between Divine Faith and Natural Reason*), Leatherman (*Elements of Moral Science*), and Balmes (*Fundamental Philosophy*), Connary becomes acquainted with probing philosophical exercises marked by stringency of thought and rigor of articulation. Especially in the systematic commonsense philosophy of Balmes is found a model of exactitude in the determination of, and adherence to, a very simple core of general ideas. Reasoning of a different sort is found in the body of religious apologetics and controversy read by Connary. If anything, such controversial material leads Connary to formulate with particular urgency his conviction about the universality of God's love and the necessity for toleration.

One final category of formative literature consists of works of eschatology, offering reassurance regarding Connary's convictions about the requirements for salvation and the certainty of his own. Examples of this literature are Philippe's *Six Hundred Thousand Combatants* and Gaudentius Rossi's *Christian Trumpet*, with the informative subtitle *Previsions and Predictions about Impending General Calamities, the Universal Triumph of the Church, the Coming of Antichrist, the Last Judgment, and the End of the World*.

Thus, despite the original and single-minded stamp to Connary's religious opinion and practice, we need to recognize in them a normative dimension. He absorbs what he reads, and he embodies and mobilizes the didacticism inherent in the books that a culture puts at his disposal. Borrowing words from the Italian historian Carlo Ginzburg, we may say that Connary's interaction with books "permits us to define the latent possibilities of something (popular culture) otherwise known to us only through fragmentary and distorted documents, almost all of which originate in the 'archives of the repression.'"[34] Ginzburg's remarks are made in connection with his fascinating investigation of the bookish, intellectual world of a sixteenth-century miller by the name of Menocchio from the Pordenone province of northeast Italy. It is possible to draw a number of interesting parallels between Ginzburg's now-classic case study and the study of our New England farmer. Separated by geography and three centuries, both Connary and Menocchio lived in periods that saw notable printing initiatives and an increase in the accessibility of books. Menocchio, like Connary, was an avid reader of a wide range of books, including the Bible and possibly the Koran, Voragine's *Golden Legend, Travels of Sir John Mandeville,* and Boccaccio's *Decameron.* He read with considerable license and constructed from his books (in lively exchange with popular oral traditions of his day) a radical cosmology, much of it genuinely bizarre and irreconcilable with Christian dogma. As Ginzburg notes, "a century or so later Menocchio probably would have been committed to an insane asylum, as someone affected by 'religious delirium.'"[35] However, Menocchio, whose opinions were baffling and radical to an extent that Connary's are not, lived at a time when the standard response to nonconformism was prosecution as an heretic. He came up against the apparatus of the Inquisition, which condemned him to death in 1599.[36]

With Connary and Menocchio we have two comparatively rare instances where we are able to study individual personalities from non-elite culture and their formation through texts. Both are creative and receptive minds, reading selectively and in a rather one-sided way. The remark made by Ginzburg about his sixteenth-century miller is equally true of Connary: he reads as if "searching for confirmation of ideas and convictions that were already firmly entrenched."[37] With these representatives of peasant culture (what Connary refers to as "the commonage"), reading is never just passive consumption, and books ferment in the minds of their readers, compelling them to respond and propagate in their own highly idiosyncratic ways. But, as we see, an inclination to proselytize can mobilize languages of exclusion—whether judicial, in the form of early modern inquisitorial concepts, or psychiatric, in the form of a nineteenth-century nomenclature of mental alienation. Ultimately, the realities of struggle, institutionalization, and exclusion can function, with certain individuals, as the tests that enable a clearer, more persistent, articulation of opinion and exhortation.

Not much can prepare us for what may happen when books meet with the passion and conviction that can engross a whole mind. Readers can find in books validation for their opinions, sometimes with astonishing determination and creativity—often in such single-minded ways that the authors of these books would be mystified. And books can converge and be instrumental in shaping subjectivity and devotional identity, sometimes in remarkably direct ways. The discussion here has listed a range of literature that we may see as influencing Connary's understanding of himself, his religion, and his mission. But so far, we have failed to engage the most significant body of literature

and enhancement that enables Connary to experience a sense of belonging—
namely, works pertaining to Irish identity and culture. As we shall now explore,
a sense of rootedness in the parental homeland can make itself most strongly
felt through the medium of books.

Vessels of Nostalgia

Thomas Connary's account of seeing God and his congregation is a vision not
of fantasy or longing, but of fulfillment, and it speaks volumes about his emo-
tive and imaginative rootedness: "I plainly saw Him . . . in a firmly built
plainly finished Roman Catholic church in Ireland." In this manifestation of
the supreme condescension and homeliness of God, the sacred is never of a
wholly different order, but appears in visual and audible ways that are reassur-
ingly familiar: "I never will forget to remember the full force of His English
words pronounced sweetly with very plain Old Irish accent." The Irish commonage is addressed directly by God in the accent and rhythm of speech
which Connary himself must have spoken. This is a God assimilated to the
experience, nostalgia, and embellishing imagination of an Irish immigrant. In
the narrative, the familiar place—half-real, half-imaginary—takes on the significance of the sacred, as a unique, prelapsarian setting. Connary records this
as a powerfully emotional experience of the sacred, of what is perceived as
all-important and ultimate, but equally, we might regard it, to quote Vincent
Gillespie about the mystical experience, as "a highly enculturated outcome of
a fertile and visually hyperstimulated subconsciousness."[38]

Ireland and Irish descent signify powerfully to Connary, who departed his
paternal homeland at the age of nineteen. In many of the book enhancements
that pertain to Irish memories, "Old Ireland" becomes associated with adoration and celebration. The narrative referred to above is perhaps the most sustained and striking example. In these many records we find expressions of what
Rev. John O'Hanlon, in his *Irish Emigrant's Guide*, refers to as the "deep feeling," so strong "in the sons of the Green Isle," which "brings to recollection and
heart the memories, hopes, and interests of the land of our birth."[39] From
Ireland are derived strong religious impulses, and in retrospect, the Irish experience is invoked as being of a spiritual and sacred nature. A note pasted opposite page 1 of *The Lives of the Fathers of the Desert*, dated May 5, 1893, reflects
on the discipline of "Book keeping" and associates Ireland with the rich spiritual life: "I have said often to the members of my family, that I would in this
way, and in every such way, live with our Divine bountiful Creator, and with

His heavenly family of Immortal creatures, as I had power to live so, in my native home Old Ireland before I left for this country. My words in this, and in me, are my thoughts. Thomas Connary."

It was in Ireland in the halcyon days that Connary was struck by an intense religious conviction and found the impetus for his book enhancement labors. A note dated May 16, 1894, traces the foundational spiritual impulse back to Ireland: "The Law as God's Law cannot change as I saw in my native home Old Ireland. We cannot improve endlessly in being right today, and wrong periodically." A note in *The Council of the Vatican* indicates that it was in Ireland that he commenced his moral and religious declaration (and maybe his book enhancement work): "Now think of this very slow work which I have most faithfully done during my whole life, beginning in Old Ireland, and continued to this passing moment."

These are the statements by an immigrant in old age asserting his pious formation and the continuity of labor dedicated to God. But they are also invocations of Irish descent as the important imaginative resource, the place of the most deep-seated emotions and religious impulses, what O'Hanlon names the "deep feeling." In this sense, Ireland has the status of what Vincent Buckley, a third-generation Irish Australian writer, has termed a "source-country": Ireland "contains a knowledge which goes very deep into the psyche, and it has an almost superstitious integrity. The country is a source in the sense that the psyche grows from and in it, and remains profoundly attuned to it."[40] Buckley further observes, "Religion, like poetry, takes its flavour, its dimensions, its very shape and guiding concepts, from place, from the complex imaginative eco-system, involving human, animal, and earth."[41] Connary's remark "since I left that place, I have been there in my mind power very much more than here" is surely the crucial acknowledgment of one's "source-country."

Echoing Buckley, I suggest that "Old Ireland," for Connary, comes to harbor individual religious consciousness (with its quasi-mystical flavoring) and a sense of rootedness in a deeper psychic, almost archetypal way. Childhood and adolescent memories and moods become an imaginative repository that is enhanced by a fertile mind, and then preserved in the books that are understood to remain in his family for posterity. The many records of genealogy, place, and past recollection work to secure a consciousness of Irish roots and may reflect some anxiety that an experience of a "source-country" is a tenuous one, not easily sustained in a family without firsthand experience of the country of origin. A wealth of place names and proper names from a primal landscape occur in the annotations, signifying the "home" of Connary's memory and imagination. They trace the relationship of a family to locale as much as they trace the foundation of a deep conviction: "When I lived in my Native home Old Ireland, I was fully schooled in my youthful days in a very old Roman and Catholic Church, it was very near my home then—the cemetery, Rosconnell, very old also, and very near—a few years before I lift [*sic*] that home, we built in the Locality, very near a good firm Roman Catholic Church, well covered with slate, there we have Landford cemetery. Then I felt bound to be right. Thomas Connary."[42]

Thinking of Ireland means endlessly romantic ruminations about people, sacred places, and benign landscapes left behind. The focus is almost exclusively on the parochial scene—on the reiterated rhythms of religious affirmation and church activity. This is a nostalgic immersion almost void of political engagement or consciousness. Although Connary keeps well informed about political and social events in Ireland through the multitude of books and periodicals accessed, he comments only very rarely on such issues. A corpus of literature on the history, topography, and religion of Ireland shows his desire to surround himself with treasured books pertaining to his native country and to cultivate a mythology of Ireland. This literature includes *The Lives of the Irish Martyrs and Confessors* by Brennan and O'Reilly, James Miller's *Reference Book of Ireland*, Thomas Mooney's *History of Ireland*, and two unidentified books referred to by Connary as his "Life of Saint Patrick" and an "Illustrated History of Ireland in green cover."[43]

In his many enhanced books we find an entire anthology of Irish poetry in the form of magazine cut-outs, most of which date from the last two decades of Connary's life, clearly a fertile period for nostalgic meditation. Examples of this poetry include "Songs of Our Land" by Frances Browne, "the Blind Poetess of Donegal," inserted in John Newman's *Discourses*, and "Song" by a "T. D. S." found in the *Spiritual Conferences* of St. Francis of Sales, with the lines "But, oh! For fond affection, / Howe'er your fate befall / There is no land like Ireland / Anywhere at all!" These are representative of a corpus of mostly forgotten voices steeped in sentimentalism and patriotism of the deepest dye.

Being prone to nostalgia was in fact for nearly two centuries primarily considered a medical and mental condition, a form of melancholy. Coined in the latter part of the seventeenth century, and originally relating to persons in the military stationed abroad, nostalgia (from the Greek *nostos*, homecoming, and *algia*, pain, ache) was approached as a category of disease, a home-sickness, in which a painful yearning to return home was understood to degenerate often into a melancholic depression.[44] The decades when Connary was devoted to enhancing books saw a transition in the understanding of nostalgia, which

came less to be seen as a medical condition and more as the mode of sentimental longing that we associate with the term today. I suggest that when Connary
goes back "in my mind's power" to piquant memories and sensations this is
not expressive of a homesickness, a melancholic suffering, or even a mournful
longing for a better age that is no longer. If anything, it works for him rather
like an "anti-depressant." It becomes a way of enriching the present moment,
and perhaps a reaction to disruptive experience and some emotional anguish.[45]
An exercise of summoning memories or imagining events of the past may
elicit pleasurable emotions, feelings of warmth, comfort, and belonging: being
of a different nature than recollection or reminiscence, it can involve an imaginative adoration of the past and a paternal homeland. In nostalgia, as Fred
Davis reminds us, "more than 'mere past' is involved. It is a past imbued with
special qualities."[46] For Connary, we may conclude, the past is all the more
potent for being to a certain extent imaginary.

Of course Connary, like so many early Irish immigrants, never returned to
his "Old Ireland." He remained in his Stratford homestead, dedicated to his
family and the farm and to the discipline of "conforming all of my power fully
strictly entirely to my paper surface room." On page 214 of *The Council of the
Vatican* is inserted an advertisement for tickets to "The Old Country" by
White Star Line steamer (later of *Titanic* fame) for sale through the agency of
Patrick Donahoe in Boston (fig. 31). Connary remains silent about much, and
we cannot know for certain if he contemplated actually revisiting places and
family in Old Ireland. Most likely is that he thrives on the longing itself,
which works as a source of comfort and proves highly enabling within the
discipline of book enhancement. In itself, the creative act of pasting the advertisement for tickets into a treasured book can provide a rich imaginative link
to the homeland. Besides, we may speculate that it will be anything but
unproblematic to return in senior age to a place that has acquired the status of
a "source-country," the home and the privileged space of the imagination.
Nostalgia seems to have been a stable component of Connary's life in the
United States, and it is associated with the impulse to preserve and reaffirm.
Books, as we see, can serve as potent stimuli for nostalgia, but they can also
become the carriers of nostalgic inscription, providing opportunity and space
for the imaginative exploration of a native country.

It is insufficient, however, to regard Ireland as the sole locus of Connary's
affective belonging, because the United States signifies deeply and emotively
as well. As Vincent Buckley remarks, this country has perhaps more than any
other successfully established itself as a "source-country" in the minds of many,
in part by "driving a sense of allegiance deep into people by making America

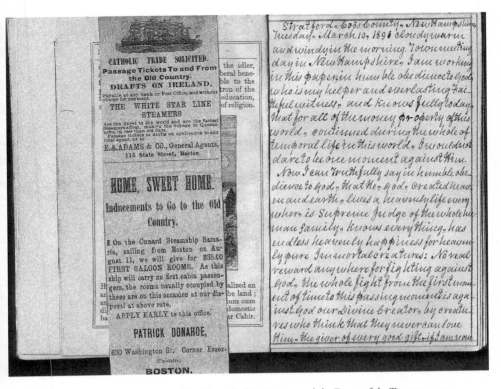

FIG. 31   Thomas Canon Pope, *The Council of the Vatican and the Events of the Time*, page 214

itself the myth" and by placing "an emphasis on primal innocence . . . and on the goodness of nature."[47] Where we can identify a range of books in Connary's library on the themes of Irish history, geography, and religion, we can, of course, find similar books relating to the United States—and more of them. We should understand Connary not simply as having a consuming nostalgic yearning in the direction of his native Ireland, but as being powerfully tied to Ireland *and* to the United States. Like so many of his books, Connary is a unique Irish American product, and it would be difficult, if not impossible, to imagine the archive of enhanced books without the productive and creative dynamic between two nations: one the country of birth and the site of imaginative, nostalgic projection, and the other the adopted country (in which he ended up by pure chance, as he often points out). Both are places of strong, though not equal, resonance for Connary, who displays both adoration of his Irish past *and* profound praise of the non-native land. Ireland provides a language, an accent, a genealogy, memories of people, places, and schooling, and the foundation of belief.[48] In America, Connary established a family and a home "more valuable than property and money power": here are found a measure of economic security, participation in public life, and the foundation of a church, a congregation, and a private library. Moreover, in America Connary found confirmation of his divine mission and participation in the American myth.

"We are blessed here in the United States of America," he asserts in his reference book *New Hampshire as It Is*, and what is seen as the divine foundation of the United States, together with the sacrosanct nature of its government and institutions, receives frequent affirmation. In an appeal to his children in *Memoirs of a Guardian Angel*, Connary stresses the link between a sacred nation and the joys of heaven when he asserts the power of "the Divine Creator to help every one of you constantly into His own Eternal Heavenly Kingdom from this, our very beautiful New England home Republic, created and continued by Himself alone fully, in every respect." It took time for the American experience to root itself deeply in Connary's mind, and, of course, for him to turn his focus from agricultural labor to his "theological work" in the "millions of acres in Book room." Only after having spent more than two decades in Stratford was he ready to embark on his project of pious book enhancement.

Judging from the many writings of an autobiographical nature inserted into his books, Connary experienced two traumas in his adult life in America, traumas that shook his world to its foundation and help account for the etiology of his mental disorder. The first of these was the death of his daughter Anne in 1880 at the age of twenty-one. The bond between the two must have been surpassing strong, for he often remembers her with the tenderest affection in his writing and offers prayers on her behalf. Another profound trauma of a very different order was the Civil War, this moment in American history when the nation became bound up with violence and sacrifice on an unprecedented scale. As we saw in chapter 4, Connary's late annotations show that he understood the Civil War, with the clarity of an epiphany, as a rebellion by sinful man and the devil personified against a divinely instituted government. Whereas Connary's nostalgic writing about Ireland remains largely detached from contemporary social and political issues (no mention is made, for instance, of the Great Famine and only very little of the issue of Irish self-government), the one cataclysmic historical event that he returns to time and again with brooding reflection was that attempted overthrow of divine rule in the United States. The war is an umbrage that overshadows Connary's later years. With the event being richly documented in the news media of the time through the new medium of photography, it is likely that he was haunted in old age by graphic depictions of war's destruction and death. To a person who thinks of family unity and filial bonds as sacred and inviolable, images of dead soldiers away from home, nearly half of whom were buried unidentified while their families were left in harrowing suspense, must have been distressing at the deepest level.[49]

Perhaps as a way of transcending war's affliction and mitigating a personal crisis, he deals with the disaster only at the abstract level of metaphysical assertion: we find no mention, for example, of battlefield deaths or of a confrontation of North and South, Union and Confederacy. The war comes to cement a set of moral convictions—it makes him "understand on a large scale," signifying a moment of searing moral clarity about the triumph of God's eternal law over the subversive forces of human contention. In fact, Connary makes it clear that one of his early spiritual visions, when God pictured to him "a large bottle of wrath which must come everywhere in this world as punishment for incessant disobedience," was granted him during the time of the war: "When we had our last Rebellion here, I am sure that the sinful power had no chance to induce me to be sinfully wrong—then I found that God himself required me to Leave my bed and follow Him I did so, and my conversation with Him was long and heavenly." For Connary, epiphany and moral conviction become associated with a belief in America and the American polity as divinely authorized. With the end of the war came the restoration of God's design and inspired nationhood.

When Connary turns to his book enhancement project in the final decades of his life, an understanding of an American mythology has had time to blend productively with a deep-seated Irish nostalgia and patriotism, in which a few remaining recollections had imprinted themselves with a certain gravity and density. The result is a double tie that proves imaginatively and spiritually enabling, being preserved in the Irish American printings that were understood to have a lifetime far beyond that of their original owner.

Peace and Communality

Thomas Connary may serve as an example of the ideal of "peaceful assimilation" into American society that O'Hanlon advocates in his *Irish Emigrant's Guide* from 1851. Central to the life of the immigrant should be the "punctilious discharge of private, social, and moral obligations," with social duties ranging "from the most contracted, but endearing sphere of family engagements, which must be regulated by religious observances and precepts, to more extended circles."[50] Moreover, the head of a family should endeavor to participate in the institutions of the adopted country and actively "require a general stock of knowledge to be communicated to those around him," all the while ensuring that "the religious character [is] preserved inviolable."[51] With the adoption of a new citizenship comes also a new opportunity for moral assertion, for a reinvention of the self as a morally responsible individual. In O'Hanlon's words, the integration in a new society should entail "the assimilation of our character to a more perfect, but not ideal standard." The situation of the Irish immigrant, he insists, requires an aspiration to renewed "piety, integrity, sincerity, temperance, regularity of conduct, an obliging disposition, self-respect and respectful consideration for the feelings of others, punctuality, generosity, industry, firmness, and fortitude."[52] Nothing more, nothing less.

Connary spent five decades in Stratford, a period during which he made lasting contributions to the community, especially with regard to the Catholic mission, but also a period in which pious and moral assertion became a besetment that dominated his thought and linguistic expression. This besetment brought with it some marginalization in the community and a diagnosis of insanity, yet it also exercised a sustaining and harmonizing power on him. Through the repeated rehearsal of a few incandescent ideas such as free will, common profit, and eschatological glory, Connary is able to be at his most articulate and fixed. But ultimately it is the two central concepts of peace and communality that provide the foundation for his thinking about the spiritual community. These are constantly brought to the fore in his writings, and they are as central to his moral drive as they are to an eschatological vision of an ideal American society governed by an unchangeable God, fundamentally benevolent and peaceful.

Connary holds a firm conviction about the urgent need for universal and all-encompassing peace. Lapidary exhortations, found in all the enhanced books, voice his categorical pacifist imperative to avoid harmful enmity at all times: "warfare is abominable contention hateful to God"; "to return injury for injury is sinfully and hatefully wrong"; "controversy and contention is unsafe for all"; "never cherish any feelings of hostility against any human creature." These are the succinct and demanding maxims that constitute the cornerstone of Connary's ethical identity. Preserved among the pages of the enhanced books are the traces of this most demanding moral-theological discipline never to entertain feelings of hostility towards anyone.

As we have already seen, when Samuel Croxall calumniates Catholics in his preface to *Fables of Aesop and Others* we find Connary initially condemning

Croxall's position, but then responding that "I am thankful for his Book and have nothing in my mind for him but purely just faithful charitable feelings of affection." The library of enhanced volumes becomes the training ground for applying such stringent ethical precepts. This is where he labors to assert cordiality as a stable feature of the moral life and an essential part of having one's attention directed toward God and the social joys of heaven. Even when it comes to the one area where we might anticipate Connary's indignation or bitterness—namely, the British administration in Ireland—he remains unagitated and optimistic, voicing a hope for a peaceful and mutually beneficial coexistence. While he mostly manages to transcend many of the corroding controversies of his time, Connary provides a rare commentary on the political situation in Ireland in the second volume of Balmes's *Fundamental Philosophy* (fig. 32). Here, a short composition by a W. O. Farmer, entitled "The Spirit

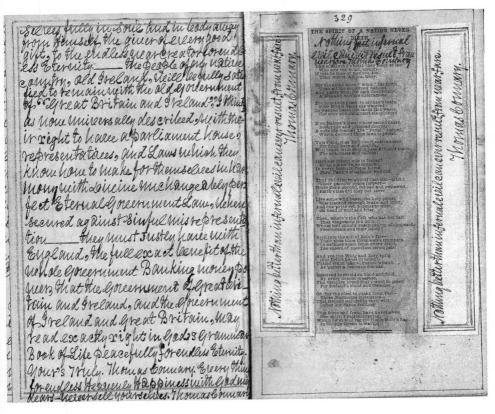

FIG. 32   James Balmes, *Fundamental Philosophy*, volume 2, pages 328–29

of a Nation Never Dieth," has been affixed to a blank page, and the final two stanzas suffice to convey its spirit:

Oh! For the steel to make them feel–
Those Northcote Legislators–
That Ireland still defies their will,
Defies her Saxon traitors!

That force and fraud have never awed
Her spirit's patriot craving,
Which ne'er will lag till Home Rule's flag
In College Green is waving.[53]

Though steeped in Irish nationalism, such a verse is irreconcilable with Connary's impulse of large benignity. Surrounding the composition are three identical assertions, all signed: "Nothing better than infernal evil can ever result from warfare. Thomas Connary." Connary, who characterizes war as "hell upon earth" and whose opposition to dissension is pertinacious, would have entertained no sympathy at all for any militant campaign seeking to sever the union. As suggested by another note opposite Farmer's verse, dated June 29, 1881, Connary avoids agitation about the Irish political scene, seeing instead an opportunity for the reconciliation of Ireland with the British state and a beneficial monetary cooperation (but still with the protection of Irish domestic affairs). The handwritten note is highly topical and offers an eccentric perspective on a contemporary movement. (Less than a year after Connary wrote the note, Charles Stewart Parnell had formed the Irish Parliamentary Party, more commonly known as the Home Rule Party, which pressed for land reforms and legislative independence on the path towards Irish self-government.)

The people of my native country, Old Ireland, will be fully satisfied to remain with the old Government of "Great Britain and Ireland," I think as now universally described, with their right to have a parliament house, representatives, and Laws which they know how to make for themselves in harmony with Divine unchangeably perfect Eternal Government Law. . . . They must Justly have with England, the full exact benefit of the whole Government Banking money power that the Government of Great Britain and Ireland, and the Government of Ireland and Great Britain, may read exactly right in God's Grammar Book of Life peacefully for endless Eternity.

Here Connary's familiar ideas of incorporation and common profit become operant inside the book and dominate over the theme of Irish independence. The principles of cordiality in relationship and the harmony between the divine law and human institutional governance (principles articulated so richly in the enhanced books of Julian of Norwich and St. Francis of Sales) receive strikingly concrete application, just as they do in the many notes concerning the American Civil War. Given his firm opposition to any kind of contention and bellicosity, we can speculate that Connary may have been profoundly troubled in his later years by his own participation (in his capacity as one of Stratford's selectmen) in the recruitment process for the Civil War. The involvement in recruiting never receives mention by Connary, for whom the war seems to have become increasingly an allegory of the conflict between divine government and man's "unpeaceful contradiction."[54]

If we can talk about a social vision in Connary's writings, and even a teleology, then inseparable from the values of peace and cordiality are those of communality and toleration. As we saw in the previous chapter, Connary follows Julian of Norwich in formulating a particularly optimistic view on the subjects of salvation and the incorporation of righteous souls in an inclusive Christian community. There is, in his writings, not much talk of heaven, hell, or purgatory, but instead of a social union of the righteous and what he refers to as "the social joys of Heaven" (a formulation undoubtedly borrowed from the Jesuit Florentin Boudreaux's *Happiness of Heaven*, which has a chapter by that title: this could be echoing the hymn "Jerusalem the Golden," J. M. Neale's translation of Bernard of Cluny's *Urbs Sion aurea*). In addition, peculiar Connarisms such as "neighborship," "eternal family," and "God's Goodship" denote such lasting inclusion. Offered in his writings is a hopeful eschatological vision of restoration and eternal life, and a multifaceted concept of government plays the key part: this comprises God's eternal government or "National Guardianship," the political "general government" of America, and, crucially, the moral governance of the individual, at the heart of which is the voluntary human act of choosing God's law.

Connary's association of future eschatological glory and the concepts of inclusion and (religious) toleration is reflected in several of the titles in his library. We find, for example, a copy of George Lynn-Lachlan Davis, *The Day-Star of American Freedom, or, The Birth and Early Growth of Toleration, in the Province of Maryland*, a book that advocates toleration and presents the history of the state of Maryland as a model of American religious liberty. Connary's broad interest in religions and in the various Christian denominations is indicated, too, by his copy of John Hayward's *Religious Creeds and Statistics of*

Every Christian Denomination in the United States and British Provinces: with some Account of the Religious Sentiments of the Jews, American Indians, Deists, Mahometans, &c. The respectful recognition of other Christian denominations is urged by the verse composition "One Faith in Many Forms," which Connary transcribes in 1881 on a page in Balmes's *Fundamental Philosophy* (fig. 33) and opposite the title page of Boudreaux's *Happiness of Heaven*, a book with copious musings on the "perfect social pleasures of Heaven." The composition, attributed to M. A. Jevons and transcribed "from the Spectator," notes the many ways of Christian worship, all of which are comprehended by God, "as some great cathedral includes each separate shrine." Connary responds to it in the following manner: "M. A. Jevons has done very well in his wording—all who choose God in spirit and in Truth really in this world know Him fully in this world—love Him purely in this world exactly through His own Loving Divine Spirit of Purity, and really live with Him infinitely more in Heaven

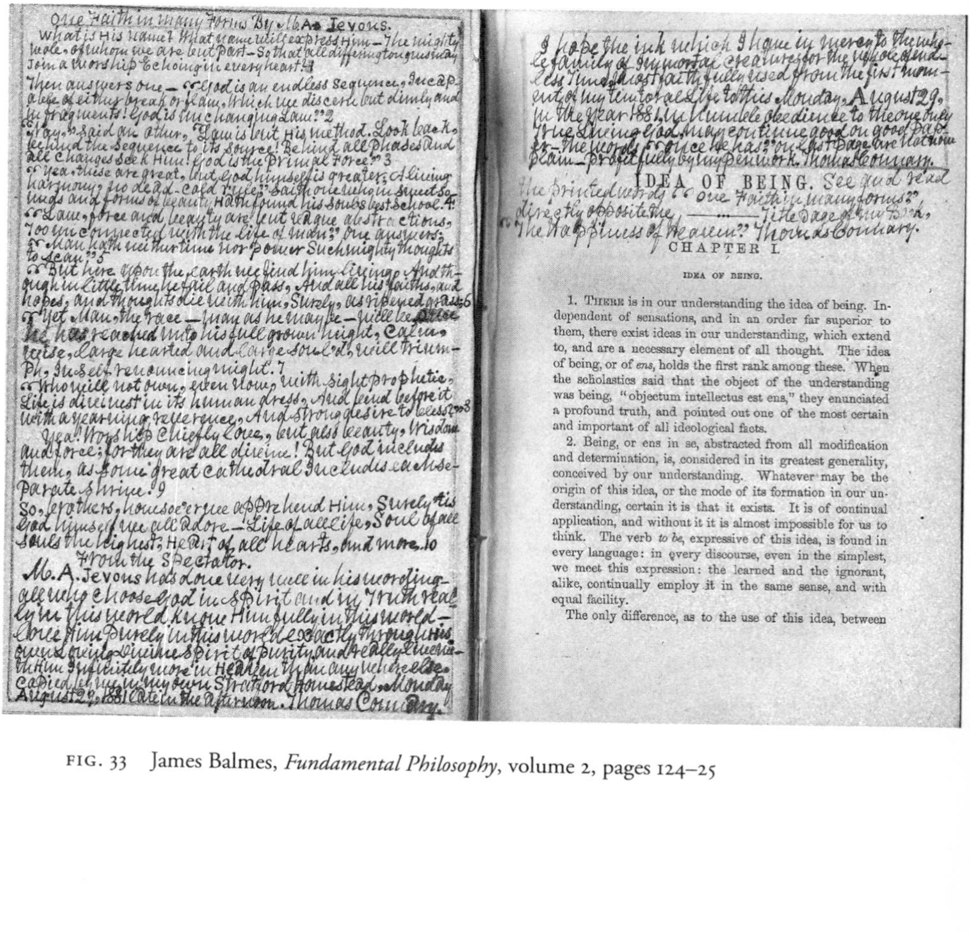

One Faith in Many Forms By M. A. Jevons.
What is His name? What name will express Him—The mighty whole, of whom we are but part—So that all differing tongues may Join a worship echoing in every heart? 1
Then answers one—"God is an endless sequence, Incapable of either break or flaw, Which we discern but dimly and in fragments! God is unchanging Law." 2
"Nay," said another, "Law is but His method. Look back, behind the sequence to its source! Behind all phases and all changes seek Him! God is the Primal Force." 3
"Yea, these are great, but God himself is greater; A living harmony, no dead-cold rule;" saith one who in sweet songs and forms of beauty Hath found his soul's best school. 4
"Law, force and beauty are but vague abstractions, Too unconnected with the life of man;" One answers; "Man hath neither time nor power Such mighty thoughts to scan." 5
"But here upon the earth we find him living, And though in little time he fail and pass, And all his faiths, and hopes, and thoughts die with him, Surely, as ripened grass: 6
"Yet Man, the race—man as he may be—will be, once he has reached unto his full grown height, Calm, wise, large hearted and large soul'd, will triumph, In self renouncing might. 7
"Who will not own, even now, with sight prophetic, Life is divinest in its human dress, And bend before it with a yearning reverence, And strong desire to bless?" 8
Yea! Worship chiefly Love, but also beauty, Wisdom and force; for they are all divine! But God includes them, as some great cathedral Includes each separate shrine. 9
So, brothers, howsoe'er we apprehend Him, Surely 'tis God himself we all adore—Life of all life, Soul of all souls the highest, Heart of all hearts, and more. 10
From the Spectator.
M. A. Jevons has done very well in his wording—all who choose God in Spirit and in Truth really in this world know Him fully in this world—love Him purely in this world exactly through His own Loving Divine Spirit of Purity and really live with Him infinitely more in Heaven than anywhere else. Copied by me in my own Stratford Homestead, Monday August 29, 1881 late in the afternoon. Thomas Connary.

I hope the ink which I have in mercy to the whole family of immortal creatures for the whole endless Time almost faithfully used from the first moment of my temporal Life to this Monday, August 29, in the year 1881, in humble obedience to the one only True Living God, may continue good on good paper—the words "once he has" on last page are not now plain—perfectly by my penwork. Thomas Connary.

IDEA OF BEING. See and read the printed words "One Faith in Many Forms" directly opposite the ——— Title Page of my Book, "The Happiness of Heaven." Thomas Connary.

CHAPTER I.

IDEA OF BEING.

1. There is in our understanding the idea of being. Independent of sensations, and in an order far superior to them, there exist ideas in our understanding, which extend to, and are a necessary element of all thought. The idea of being, or of *ens*, holds the first rank among these. When the scholastics said that the object of the understanding was being, "objectum intellectus est ens," they enunciated a profound truth, and pointed out one of the most certain and important of all ideological facts.

2. Being, or ens in se, abstracted from all modification and determination, is, considered in its greatest generality, conceived by our understanding. Whatever may be the origin of this idea, or the mode of its formation in our understanding, certain it is that it exists. It is of continual application, and without it it is almost impossible for us to think. The verb *to be*, expressive of this idea, is found in every language: in every discourse, even in the simplest, we meet this expression: the learned and the ignorant, alike, continually employ it in the same sense, and with equal facility.

The only difference, as to the use of this idea, between

FIG. 33 James Balmes, *Fundamental Philosophy*, volume 2, pages 124–25 than anywhere else. Copied by me in my own Stratford Homestead, Monday August 29, 1881 late in the afternoon. Thomas Connary."

Connary does not restrict any understanding of the elect to a white Christian community, and he praises the native Indians as "good and peaceful naturally," "most sound and most happy with God." Whenever the "black men or women" receive mention, they are people of dignity, purpose, and personality.[55] Eschatological glory remains firmly bound up with the ideas of incorporation and common profit: "He, Himself, and His whole family of human creatures everywhere in space, cheerfully feel firmly bound together individually personally and collectively, unlimited in power as one Happy Immortal family of peacemakers for endless Eternity."[56] These ideas about morality and soteriology are all refracted through the activity of "Book keeping." Connary's enhanced "Book" becomes the conveyor of a happy message about a community of the righteous bound together.

For our farmer-bibliophile, the very culmination of the spiritual life is found in the freedom, originality, and passion with which the discipline of "laboring in my Books" is pursued. Through this discipline he enters into dialogue with his religious works and occupies part of the same experiential space as the visionaries and saints whose books he reads attentively. It is a discipline, also, in which the brief declarative statement "I am here" becomes a nostalgic "being there," a being in Ireland, a place more psychic than physical. First and foremost, however, laboring in books means augmenting the books with what is referred to as "my theological work," that is, the elaborate creed that proclaims his perspective on redemption, moral improvement, and the nature of evil. As we have seen, Connary's writing is not one that looks much to the Bible or to the virtuous life of Christ for moral guidance, but it constantly refers to self-examination and correction of the individual conscience in order to ascertain conformity with God's unchangeable moral law.

In proclaiming his high-minded moral admonitions, Connary believes that he acts on an impulse from on high. For the common profit of himself, his family, and his friends, he tirelessly extends the didactic repertoire of the books he acquires through the insertion of what he refers to as "my pen and ink work small and crowded for paper surface room." It is as if he willfully sets out to subvert any habitual assumption that the text itself is essential, while the material properties of the book (e.g., the paper, margins, flyleaves, layout, and annotation) are secondary and contingent. Connary literally emblazons his presence and conscience on the books themselves in an unerring deposition of his faith, making the books bear historical witness, imbuing them with iconic power as the material objects that can embody belief and sacrality.

With some of Connary's book enhancement strategies we see the poaching reader who takes liberties with texts and conducts acts of selective appropriation. But more pertinently, I believe, we see the pilgrim of the book who labors across the topography of the page and records on it a variety of spiritual encounters. The idea that Connary carries out his very own pilgrimage inside the material book is a suggestive one. There is no indication that Connary ever went on a pilgrimage himself: it appears that he undertook only one major voyage in his life. But the idea of the pilgrimage exercised a particularly powerful hold on his mind. Abounding in his enhanced books are articles and poems about holy places such as St. Peter's Basilica, the Sanctuary at Loretto, the Church of the Holy Sepulchre, and the monasteries of Mount Athos. The inserted short composition "The Message Judea, A.D." found in O'Leary's *History of the Bible* addresses the "pilgrim, worn and gray" and provides consolation for the person devout and advanced in years with tidings of the birth of Christ and the joys of eternal life.

Part of Connary's language and experience becomes the symbolic representation of pilgrimage. The peregrine Connary arrives from abroad and longs for his native and spiritual homeland. He is a traveler in the books that provide him with a perspective on the world and which he understands as the shrines enriched by divine blessing. As the pilgrim's diary, his writings are record of both comfort and discomfort, and they are never far removed from social and political complexities. Yet finally they are oriented to the mystical dimension of the Christian life. The many signed and dated notes deployed throughout his library record the itinerary of his wanderings in books, and they show how each book visited becomes a site of religious reflection and assertion: they make of each book and each instance of laboring in it an event in which is found great moral and spiritual significance. The complex ways in which he foregrounds the material instantiation of his books provide some suggestive parallel to the attraction that tangible and measurable religious relics hold for the pilgrim. Like the pilgrimage, the entire discipline of "Book keeping" possesses an eschatological dimension, signifying not just an existential spiritual affirmation of the divine but the devoted labor toward a state of beatitude.

Furthermore, like the pilgrim venturing forth, Connary's bookish peregrinations are oriented toward both the exterior and the interior. To labor in books means to be on an individual spiritual path and to pursue a discipline in a manner enclosed and withdrawn. But at the same time the activity is motivated by a sense of communality and by the impulse to proclaim and participate socially. As he provides elaborate records of daily regularities, prayer, friendship and kinship, churchgoing, and participation in the sacraments, Connary understands his religious identity in terms of incorporation and shared meaning. His desire is for the social joys of heaven, a participation in the collective of the righteous.

The Sinner's Guide, Louis of Granada's sixteenth-century exhortation to virtue, was one of Connary's most cherished books, amply enhanced with extra-illustration and numerous appeals to his family. As a conclusion to this enhanced "Book," as a form of extension of the printed text, Connary has pasted Oscar Wilde's pilgrim poem "Rome Unvisited" (fig. 34).[1] The poem, Wilde's first publication in America, was published in the *Month and Catholic Review* in 1876 (as "Graffiti d'Italia"), and it appeared the same year in the *Pilot*. Of all of Wilde's poetry, this work expresses best his profound attraction to the Catholic Church—to its ritual, liturgy, and aesthetics—and it was written in response to travels in Italy in 1875, when Wilde ran out of funds and had to abandon a planned visit to Rome.[2] The poem proved prophetic, as Wilde traveled to Rome in 1877 (during which he had an audience with Pope Pius IX) and again in 1900, the year of his deathbed conversion to Catholicism. The tone is replete with longing and a desire for conversion.

> And here I set my face toward home,
> For all my pilgrimage is done,
> Although, methinks, yon blood-red sun
> Marshals the way to Holy Rome.

The poem culminates with the poet's response to the Pope's elevation of the consecrated host, that most exalted of mysteries that is the revelation of God under the appearance of bread and wine.

> A pilgrim from the northern seas—
> What joy for me to seek alone
> The wondrous Temple, and the throne
> Of Him who holds the awful keys!
>
> When, bright with purple and with gold,
> Come priest and holy Cardinal,
> And borne above the heads of all
> The gentle Shepherd of the Fold.
>
> O joy to see before I die
> The only God-anointed King,
> And hear the silver trumpets ring
> A triumph as he passes by!
>
> Or at the altar of the shrine
> Holds high the mystic sacrifice,
> And shows a God to human eyes
> Beneath the veil of bread and wine.

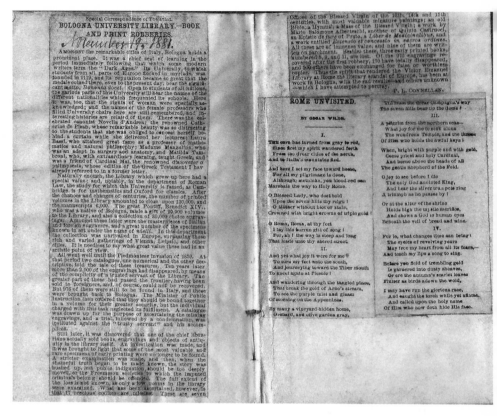

FIG. 34   F. Lewis [Louis of Granada], *The Sinner's Guide*, end pastedown

This sense of religious desire and longing finds its culminating expression in an imagined participation in the sacrament of the Eucharist. Wilde's poem provides an interesting echo of Connary's vision of God revealing himself to administer Holy Communion in an Irish church—a genuine sacramental and spiritual meeting, in which Connary is the recipient of God's blessing, together with the congregation of the commonage. However, metaphysical mystery lies at the heart of Wilde's desire for God ("Him who now doth hide His face"). Less so with Connary: for him there is little sense of an emanation of an unreachable, unknowable Godhead, but rather the "plain sight" of a manifest deity, the very embodiment of homeliness and cordiality.

Connary preserves Wilde's eloquent statement about the pilgrim's longing on the final pastedown of *The Sinner's Guide* together with an article about the extensive robberies of manuscripts and early prints from the library of Bologna

University in the nineteenth century. This article essentially confirms the priceless nature of books. Here is another juxtaposition which is anything but arbitrary, pointing to a perceived relation between books and the sacred. Wandering through books, and preserving one's marks in a discipline of prayerful "Book keeping," is to celebrate and make a connection. It means to experience through enhanced books a vibrant world of blessing, common profit, and the longing of the pilgrim.

No catalogue exists of the full contents of Thomas Connary's library. To reconstruct the collection requires the painstaking detective work of piecing together references to individual titles that are found on literally hundreds of Connary's handwritten pages inserted into those of his books I have been able to examine. The task of providing an overview of the library is further complicated by the fact that individual titles are often referred to in abbreviated form, with no author (e.g., "Farmer's Treasure"), or with reference to their material properties, such as bindings and page numbers (e.g., "my little Illustrated Catechism of 183 pages").

However, it is possible to reconstruct a library from myriad sporadic references with what I believe to be a tolerable degree of accuracy. The following represents my best attempt to catalogue the books in Connary's possession. Approximately 110 titles have been tentatively identified (omitting periodicals and newspapers): to say that this constitutes an incomplete list is undoubtedly an understatement at best. The main shortcoming of this overview is that it has been compiled only from the twenty-nine titles (in thirty-one volumes) that I have been able to examine. When more of Connary's books are found and examined, they will no doubt mention of additional book titles. The list, however, provides a clear sense of the titles available to this Irish Catholic farmer-bibliophile in nineteenth-century New Hampshire—and indicates the dedication and expenditure with which he built his library.

It has been necessary to divide the list into five sections. The first lists the volumes that I have examined and on which my research is based. With no exception, these titles are in my possession, having been purchased through an antiquarian book dealer.

The second category shows those titles of whose existence I am aware and that are known to have survived. I have been unable to access the specific volumes that belonged to Connary, and I know them by titles only. For that reason, publisher and date of publication are uncertain. In providing full bibliographic details, I use "e.g." when a book has been subsequently reprinted, possibly with a different publisher. I try to list early (or the earliest) editions of the title by an American publisher, but it is of course highly likely that Connary would have acquired a later edition (and, in some cases—probably very few—not necessarily from an American publisher).

The third category lists Connary's handwritten references to various titles in his library. I have not been able to locate and examine any of these titles, and their survival is uncertain. With no exception, these references are found on notes inserted into those of his books that I have examined, where they are part of Connary's own carefully recorded lists of books and plans for his reading program. I first list Connary's own reference as it appears in his records and below it the full bibliographic details as I have been able to ascertain them. Many of these references are from his book *The Sinner's Guide*, in which long lists of books are provided in a manner such as this: "my six books, "God Our Father," "Duties of Young Men," "The Family," "Memoirs of a Guardian Angel," "The Child," "Youth's Director." Given the ambiguities of such references, the activity of compiling this list is partly interpretive. As in the second category, I use "e.g." with publisher and year of publication when multiple versions are known, and I strive to list early American editions—often the editions that Connary would have been likely to procure. In a few instances I list two (nearly) identical titles when it is uncertain to which of these Connary refers. We should acknowledge the possibility that some of the titles referred to could have been borrowed rather than purchased and thus did not form part of Connary's collection. However, in most cases, a reference to a title is prefaced with "my Book," or Connary refers to "my work" (i.e., his annotations and inserted pages) in these titles. Space constraints prevent these notes from being reproduced here.

The fourth category lists Connary's references to book titles in his possession, which, because of his habit of providing only abbreviated titles (intended, it seems, as references to himself), I have been unable to identify. I include here references to Connary's Bibles: though he quotes frequently from the Douai-Rheims version, the printing is unknown. The final section provides a list of the newspapers, periodicals, notebooks, and miscellaneous papers used by Connary and mentioned in his notes.

Extant and Examined Titles

[Aesop et al.] *Fables of Aesop and Others.* Translated by Samuel Croxall. New York: Derby & Jackson, 1859.

Anon. *Historical Selections from The London Rambler and Other Periodicals.* St. Louis: Duggan, 1860.

Anon. *In Heaven We Know Our Own: or, Solace for the Suffering.* Translated by Father Blot. New York: The Catholic Publication Society, 1865.

Anon. *The Lives of Eminent Saints.* Boston: Patrick Donahoe, 1853.

Anon. *The Lives of the Fathers of the Desert, and of Many Holy Men and Women who Dwelt in Solitude.* Baltimore: Fielding Lucas, Jr., n.d.

Baine, A. C. *An Essay on the Harmonious Relations between Divine Faith and Natural Reason. To which are Added Two Chapters on the Divine Office of the Church.* Baltimore: John Murphy, 1861.

Balmes, James. *Fundamental Philosophy.* Translated by Henry F. Brownson. 2 vols. New York: D. & J. Sadlier, 1858.

Balmes, James. *Protestantism and Catholicity Compared in Their Effects on the Civilization of Europe.* Baltimore: John Murphy, 1851.

Bodenham, Elizabeth de. *Mrs. Herbert and the Villagers: or, Familiar Conversations on the Principal Duties of Christianity.* 2 vols. (vol. 2 only). Baltimore: Fielding Lucas, Jr., 1853.

Breckenridge, John, and John Hughes. *Controversy between Rev. Messrs. Hughes and Breckenridge, on the Subject "Is the Protestant Religion the Religion of Christ?"* Philadelphia: Eugene Cummiskey, 1864.

Camus, Jean-Pierre. *The Spirit of St. Francis de Sales.* New York: P. O'Shea, 1867.

Chardon, M. A. G. *Memoirs of a Guardian Angel.* Baltimore: John Murphy, 1873.

Charlton, Edwin A. *New Hampshire as It Is*. Claremont, N.H.: Tracy and Co., 1856.

Cowper, William. *Poems*. 3 vols. (vol. 3 only). Boston: Water Street Bookstore, 1833.

Faber, Frederick W. *All for Jesus: or, The Easy Ways of Divine Love*. Baltimore: John Murphy, 1857.

Francis of Sales. *The True Spiritual Conferences of St. Francis of Sales*. London: Thomas Richardson and Son, 1862.

Fredet, Peter. *Modern History: From the Coming of Christ and the Change of the Roman Republic into an Empire, to the Year of Our Lord 1850*. 4th ed., "enlarged and improbed [*sic*]." Baltimore: John Murphy, 1850.

Haskins, George Foxcroft. *Travels in England, France, Italy, and Ireland*. Boston: Patrick Donahoe, 1856.

Julian of Norwich. *Sixteen Revelations of Divine Love*. Boston: Ticknor and Fields, 1864.

Kinane, T. H. *The Dove of the Tabernacle*. New York: P. M. Haverty, 1876.

Leatherman, P. R. *Elements of Moral Science*. Philadelphia: James Challen & Son, 1860.

Lewis, F. [Louis of Granada.] *The Sinner's Guide*. Philadelphia: Henry M'Grath, 1845.

Livingston, Vanbrugh. *An Inquiry into the Merits of the Reformed Doctrine of "Imputation," as Contrasted with Those of "Catholic Imputation"; or, The Cardinal Point of Controversy between the Church of Rome and the Protestant High Church*. New York: Casserly & Sons, 1843.

Newman, John Henry. *Discourses Addressed to Mixed Congregations*. Boston: Patrick Donahoe, 1853.

O'Leary, J. *A History of the Bible, Its Origin, Object, and Structure*. New York: D. & J. Sadlier, 1873.

Philippe. *The Six Hundred Thousand Combatants; or, The Children of the Patriarchs Conquering the Promised Land*. Translated by Christine Farville. New York: P. O'Shea, 1864.

Pope, Thomas Canon. *The Council of the Vatican and the Events of the Time*. Boston: Patrick Donahoe, 1872.

Rodriguez, Alphonso. *The Practice of Christian and Religious Perfection*. 3 vols. (vols. 1 and 3 only). New York: Edward Dunigan and Brother, 1853.

Spalding, Martin J. *The History of the Protestant Reformation, in Germany and Switzerland, and in England, Ireland, Scotland, and the Netherlands, France, and Northern Europe*. Louisville: Webb & Levering, 1860.

Extant but Unexamined Titles

The publisher and date of publication for titles in this category are uncertain.

Davenport, Richard A. *The Universal Biographical Dictionary, Embracing the Most Eminent Characters of Every Age, Nation, and Profession*. E.g., Boston: Otis, Broaders, 1847.

Gibbon, Lardner. *Exploration of the Valley of the Amazon, Made under the Direction of the Navy Department*. E.g., Washington: R. Armstrong, 1853.

Martin, Edward Winslow. *The Secrets of the Great City: A Work Descriptive of the Virtues and the Vices, the Mysteries, Miseries and Crimes of New York City.* Philadelphia: Jones Brothers, 1868.

Mooney, Thomas. *A History of Ireland, from Its First Settlement to the Present Time; Including a Particular Account of Its Literature, Music, Architecture, and Natural Resources.* E.g., Boston: Patrick Donahoe, 1845.

Wiseman, Nicholas P. S. *Recollections of the Last Four Popes and of Rome in Their Times.* E.g., Boston: Patrick Donahoe, 1858.

Connary's References to Books in His Possession

The publisher and date of publication for titles in this category are uncertain.

"Catholic Pulpit"
Anon. *The Catholic Pulpit: Containing a Sermon for Every Sunday and Holiday in the Year, and for Good Friday.* E.g., Baltimore: John Murphy, 1851, and Pittsburgh: George Quigley, 1856.

"Youth's Director"
Anon. *The Youth's Director: or, Familiar Instructions for Young People; which Will Be Found Useful also to Persons of Every Sex, Age and Condition in Life; with a Number of Historical Traits and Edifying Examples.* New York: P. J. Kennedy, Excelsior Catholic Publishing House, 1878.

"History of the United States Secret Service by General L. C. Baker in 704 pages"
Baker, La Fayette C. *History of the United States Secret Service.* Philadelphia: L. C. Baker, 1867. (704 pages)

"The Glories of the Virgin Mother, And Channel of Divine Grace"
St. Bernard of Clairvaux. *The Glories of the Virgin Mother and Channel of Divine Grace.* Boston: Patrick Donahoe, 1867.

"Juvenile Companion, small, pages 300"
Blake, John L. *The Juvenile Companion: Being an Introduction to the Historical Reader.* E.g., Boston: Bowles and Dearborn, 1827. (300 pages)

"Parables and Stories of Saint Bonaventura"
[Bonaventure.] *The Parables and Stories of Père Bonaventure.* New York: P. O'Shea, 1867.

"God Our Father"
Boudreaux, Florentin J. *God Our Father.* Baltimore: John Murphy, 1873.

"Happiness of Heaven"
Boudreaux, Florentin J. *The Happiness of Heaven.* E.g., Baltimore: John Murphy, 1871, and New York: Catholic Publication Society, 1871.

"Bourdaloui's Sermons"
Bourdaloue, Louis. *Sermons and Moral Discourses in the Important Duties of Christianity.* E.g., Dublin: James Duffy, 1843.

"History of the Lives of Irish Martyrs published 1878"
Brennan, Richard, and Myles O'Reilly. *Lives of the Irish Martyrs and Confessors.* New York: James Sheehy, 1878.

"Christ in His Church"
Businger, Lucas C. *Christ in His Church: A Catholic Church History.* New York: Benziger Brothers, 1881.

"Butler's Feasts and Fasts"
Butler, Alban. *The Moveable Feasts, Fasts, and Other Annual Observances of the Catholic Church.* E.g., New York: E. Dunigan and Brother, 1854.

"my Catechism of the Council of Trent"
The Catechism of the Council of Trent. E.g., Baltimore: Fielding Lucas, Jr., 1829, and New York: Catholic Publication Society, 1829.

"A Mad World"
Chambers, Julius. *A Mad World and Its Inhabitants.* New York: D. Appleton, 1877.

"Touchstone of Character"
Chassay, Frédéric-Edouard. *The Touchstone of Character.* E.g., New York: M. T. Cozans, 1853.

"Palestine or the Holy Land by Le Chateaubriand"
Chateaubriand, François-René de. *Palestine, or, The Holy Land.* Baltimore: Fielding Lucas, Jr., 1835.

"Lacon by G. G. Colton in 507 pages"
Colton, Charles C. *Lacon: or, Many Things in Few Words; Addressed to Those Who Think.* E.g., New York: E. Bliss and E. White, 1822, and Philadelphia: Porter and Coates, 1871. (507 pages)

"The Life and Revelations of Saint Gertrude"
Cusack, Mary Francis. *The Life and Revelations of Saint Gertrude, Virgin and Abbess of the Order of St. Benedict.* E.g., Boston: Patrick Donahoe, 1871, and New York: Benziger, 1871.

"the Life of Father Mathew"
Cusack, Mary Francis. *The Life of Father Mathew, the People's Soggarth Aroon.* New York: D. & J. Sadlier, 1872.

"Day Star of American Freedom"
Davis, George Lynn-Lachlan. *The Day-Star of American Freedom, or, The Birth and Early Growth of Toleration, in the Province of Maryland.* New York: C. Scribner, 1855, and Baltimore: John Murphy, 1855.

"Signers of the Declaration of Independence"
Several titles have been identified that appear to have been often reprinted.
Dwight, Nathaniel. *The Lives of the Signers of the Declaration of Independence;*
Goodrich, Charles A. *Lives of the Signers to the Declaration of Independence;*

Judson, Levi Carroll. *A Biography of the Signers of the Declaration of Independence, and of Washington and Patrick Henry*;

Lincoln, Robert W. *Lives of the Presidents of the United States, with Biographical Notices of the Signers of the Declaration of Independence*;

Lossing, John Bensing. *Biographical Sketches of the Signers of the Declaration of American Independence*; or

Sanderson, John. *Sanderson's Biography of the Signers to the Declaration of Independence.*

"a New English General Dictionary, printed in London, England, in the year 1744"

Dyche, Thomas, and William Pardon. *A New General English Dictionary: Particularly Calculated for the Use and Improvement of Such as Are Unacquainted with the Learned Languages.* London: Richard Ware, 1744.

"Farmer's Treasure"

Falkner, Frederic. *The Farmer's Treasure: A Practical Treatise on the Nature and Value of Manures, Founded from Experiments on Various Crops.* New York: D. Appleton, 1844.

"Complete Farmer"

Fessenden, Thomas G. *The Complete Farmer and Rural Economist.* E.g., Boston: Lilly, Wait, and Company, 1834.

"my little Book, Devout Life By Saint Francis of Sales in 339 pages"

Francis de Sales. *Introduction to the Devout Life, to which Is Prefixed an Abstract of His Life.* E.g., Baltimore: Fielding Lucas, Jr., 1833. (339 pages)

"read my work now in the Book Love of God, next to page 356, number of pages in that Book 591"

Francis de Sales. *Treatise on the Love of God.* New York: P. O'Shea, 1867. (591 pages)

"Devout Instructions by Goffine, the book has 901 numbered pages"

Goffine, Leonard. *Devout Instructions on the Epistles and Gospels for the Sundays and Holydays.* New York: P. J. Kennedy, 1859. (901 pages)

"Gordon's America"

Gordon, Thomas Francis. *The History of America, Containing the History of the Spanish Discoveries prior to 1520.* E.g., Philadelphia: Carey & Lea, 1831.

"My three large Books of A New and Complete Dictionary of the Arts and Sciences by G. Gregory published in 1822"

Gregory, G. *A New and Complete Dictionary of Arts and Sciences.* New York: William J. Robinson, 1822. (3 vols.)

"Religious Creeds and Statistics By John Hayward"

Hayward, John. *The Religious Creeds and Statistics of Every Christian Denomination in the United States and British Provinces: with some Account of the Religious Sentiments of the Jews, American Indians, Deists, Mahometans, &c.* Boston: J. Hayward, 1836.

"'History of the Great Rebellion,' By J. T. Headley"
Headley, Joel Tyler. *The Great Rebellion: A History of the Civil War in the United States.*
E.g., Baltimore: Jones Brothers, 1864, and Hartford: Hurlbut, Scranton, 1864.

"The Lives of the early Martyrs, by Mrs. Hope in 388 small pages"
Hope, Anne. *The Lives of the Early Martyrs.* New York: D. & J. Sadlier, 1856. (388 pages)

"Charity in Conversation"
Huguet, P. *On Charity in Conversation.* London: Catholic Publishing and Bookselling Co., 1860.

"Half Hours with the Saints pictorial"
Kenny, Charles. *Half-hours with the Saints and Servants of God.* E.g., New York: Benziger Brothers, 1882; or
Lecanu, Auguste François. *Pictorial Half Hours with the Saints.* Dublin and London: James Duffy, 1865.

"Farmer's Own Book"
Koogle, J. D. *The Farmer's Own Book: A Treatise on the Numerous Diseases of the Horse.* E.g., Baltimore: McCoull & Slater, 1857.

"Blanche Leslie; or the Living Rosary, printed in the year 1865"
Leslie, Blanche. *Blanche Leslie, or The Living Rosary.* New York: P. J. Kennedy, 1865.

"Preparation for Death"
Liguori, Alphonso M. de. *Preparation for Death; or, Considerations on the Eternal Maxims.* E.g., Boston: Thomas Sweeney, 1854.

"the debates of Lincoln and Douglas"
[Lincoln, Abraham, and Stephen A. Douglas.] *Political Debates between Hon. Abraham Lincoln and Hon. Stephen A. Douglas, in the Celebrated Campaign of 1858, in Illinois.* Columbus: Follett, Foster and Co., 1860.

"The American Reader by Asa Lyman A. M. published in the year 1811"
Lyman, Asa. *The American Reader: Containing Elegant Selections in Prose and Poetry: Designed for the Improvement of Youth in the Art of Reading and Speaking with Propriety and Beauty, and for the Cultivation of a Correct Moral Taste.* Portland: A. Lyman, 1811.

"Homilies on the Book of Tobias, old book"
Martyn, Francis. *Homilies on the Book of Tobias: or, A Familiar Explication of the Practical Duties of Domestic Life.* Baltimore: Fielding Lucas, Jr., 1831.

"History of the Irish Settlers in North America, By Thomas D. Arcy Mcgee"
McGee, Thomas D'Arcy. *A History of the Irish Settlers in North America: From the Earliest Period to the Census of 1850.* E.g., Boston: Patrick Donahoe, 1851.

"Intelligent Reader"
Merriam, George. *The Intelligent Reader, Designed as a Sequel to The Child's Guide.* Springfield: G. and C. Merriam, 1834.

"Reference Book of Ireland"
> Miller, James. *Reference Book of Ireland: Contains a Complete List of Provinces, Counties, Baronies, Cities, Parishes, and Villages, with their Location, Population etc.* New York: Cooke and Cobb, 1877.

"Milner's end of Controversy as published in the year 1843, in 352 pages"
> Milner, John. *The End of Religious Controversy, in a Friendly Correspondence between a Religious Society of Protestants and a Roman Catholic Divine.* New York: D. & J. Sadlier, 1843. (352 pages)

"History of the Catholic Church by Noethen"
> Noethen, Theodore. *A History of the Catholic Church, from the Commencement of the Christian Era to the Ecumenical Council of the Vatican.* Baltimore: John Murphy, 1871.

"Nouet's Meditations for every day in the year"
> Nouet, Jacques. *Meditations for Every Day in the Year.* E.g., New York: Catholic Publication Society, 1855.

"O'Hanlon's 'Guide'"
> O'Hanlon, John. *The Irish Emigrant's Guide for the United States.* Boston: Patrick Donahoe, 1851.

"Duties of Young Men"
> Pellico, Silvio. *On the Duties of Young Men.* New York: D. & J. Sadlier, 1872.

"Geographical View of the World"
> Phillips, Richard. *A Geographical View of the World, Embracing the Manners, Customs, and Pursuits of Every Nation.* E.g., New York: E. Hopkins and W. Reed, 1826.

"Rhetorical Reader, old book"
> Porter, Ebenezer. *The Rhetorical Reader: Consisting of Instructions for Regulating the Voice with a Rhetorical Notation Illustrating Inflection, Emphasis, and Modulation, and a Course of Rhetorical Exercises.* E.g., Andover, Mass.: Flagg, Gould, & Newman, 1831.

"the Family by Auguste Riche"
> Riche, Auguste. *The Family.* Translated by Mary Anne Sadlier. New York: D. & J. Sadlier, 1875.

"Traveller's Guide Through Ireland"
> Robertson, Joseph. *The Traveller's Guide through Ireland: or, A Topographical Description of that Kingdom.* Edinburgh: Denham and Dick, 1806; or
> Anon. *The Traveller's New Guide through Ireland: Containing, a New and Accurate Description of the Roads, with Particulars of all the Different Towns . . .* E.g., Dublin: John Cumming, 1815;

"Domestic Life in Palestine"
> Rogers, Mary Eliza. *Domestic Life in Palestine.* E.g., Cincinnati: Poe & Hitchcock, 1865.

"Christian Trumpet"

Rossi, Gaudentius. *The Christian Trumpet: or, Previsions and Predictions about Impending General Calamities, the Universal Triumph of the Church, the Coming of Antichrist, the Last Judgment, and the End of the World.* E.g., Boston: Patrick Donahoe, 1873.

"Scudder's History of the United States"

Scudder, Horace E. *A History of the United States of America, Preceded by a Narrative of the Discovery and Settlement of North America.* Philadelphia: J. H. Butler, 1884.

"my little Book Spiritual Combat"

Scupoli, Lorenzo. *The Spiritual Combat: to which Is Added The Peace of the Soul and the Happiness of the Heart which Dies to Itself in Order to Live to God.* E.g., Baltimore: Metropolitan Press, 1843. (book size 32mo)

"Governmental Instructor"

Shurtleff, J. B. *The Governmental Instructor, or, A Brief and Comprehensive View of the Government of the United States and of the State Governments, in Lessons Designed for the Use of Schools and Families.* E.g., New York: Collin, Brother, & Co., 1845.

"Miscellanea By M. J. Spalding"

Spalding, Martin J. *Miscellanea: Comprising Reviews, Lectures, and Essays, on Historical, Theological, and Miscellaneous Subjects.* E.g., Louisville, Ky.: Webb, Gill & Levering, 1855, and Baltimore: J. Murphy, 1866.

"Statesman's Manual"

The Statesman's Manual: The Addresses and Messages of the Presidents of the United States, Inaugural, Annual, and Special, from 1789 to 1858. E.g., New York: E. Walker, 1858.

"Judge Story's two books"

Story, Joseph. *Commentaries on the Constitution of the United States.* E.g., Boston: C. C. Little and J. Brown, 1851. (2 vols.)

"Following of Christ"

Thomas à Kempis. *The Following of Christ.* E.g., Baltimore: Fielding Lucas, Jr., 1821; New York: D. & J. Sadlier, 1862; Boston: Patrick Donahoe, 1863; and Philadelphia: Eugene Cummiskey, 1865.

"Garden of Roses"

Thomas à Kempis. *The Little Garden of Roses and Valley of Lilies.* Baltimore: John Murphy, 1851; or

Egan, Maurice F. *A Garden of Roses: Stories and Sketches.* E.g., Boston: T. B. Noonan, 1887.

"Catholic Offering Pictorial"

Walsh, William. *The Catholic Offering: A Gift Book for all Seasons.* E.g., New York: E. Dunigan and Brother, 1852. (illustrated)

"My Primary School Dictionary By W. G. Webster"
>Webster, Noah, William G. Webster, and William A. Wheeler. *A Primary School Dictionary of the English Language*. E.g., New York: Ivison, Blakeman, Taylor, 1874.

"Wells Everyman his own Lawyer"
>Wells, John G. *Every Man His Own Lawyer, and United States Form Book; Being a Complete Guide in All Matters of Law, and Business Negotiations, for Every State in the Union*. E.g., New York: J. G. Wells, 1856.

"Willard's United States History"
>Willard, Emma. *History of the United States, or Republic of America*. E.g., New York: White, Gallaher & White, 1828.

Connary's References to Books in His Possession— Unidentified Titles and Bible Editions

"The American Farmer"
"The Ballads of Ireland, a large Book, by Thomas Moore"
"Catholic Dictionary"
"The Child"
"Gregory's Dictionary"
"'Illustrated History of Ireland,' green cover"
"Life of Saint Patrick"
"my Blessed and Holy Bibles large"
"my Book Holy Week"
"my large red cover family Bible"
"my little gilt edged Book"
"my little Illustrated Catechism of 183 pages"
"My New American Cyclopedia in 16 volumes"
"my very beautiful clasped Family Bible"
"2 more Books of Fables, one in 344 pages. The other in 224 pages" (these are not the *Fables of Aesop and Others* translated by Samuel Croxall above)
"the Works of Rt. Rev. John Hughes as I have them fully"

Connary's References to Newspapers, Periodicals, Notebooks, and Miscellaneous Papers

"The Boston Weekly Globe"
"Christian parlor Magazine"
"Coös County Democrat"
"The Coös Republican"
"Department of Agriculture Report. 1879"
"Department of Agriculture Special Report—No. 22. Contagious Diseases for Domestic Animals for 1880"
"Harper's Magazine"

"Illustrated Catholic Family Annual for 1885 and 1888"
"The Lamp for 1860"
"The Lancaster Gazette"
"Massachusetts Plowman, Boston, for October 28, 1876"
"my Book 'Metropolitan Magazine,' marked VOL. IV on back"
"my Diary for 1866"
"my journal of 400 pages"
"my little Book of 100 pages very closely written by myself red and white paper"
"New England Homestead"
"No. 1, of volume 2, Monthly American Spectator, from the publishers in Boston"
"People and New Hampshire Patriot"
"pictorial Catholic Home Almanac"
"The Pilot"

NOTES

Preface

1. Quoted from Robert K. Merton and Elinor Barber's remarkable book about serendipity, *The Travels and Adventures of Serendipity: A Study in Sociological Semantics and the Sociology of Science* (Princeton: Princeton University Press, 2004), 2.

2. See also the classification of various forms of serendipity in Pek van Andel, "Anatomy of the Unsought Finding: Serendipity; Origin, History, Domains, Traditions, Appearances, Patterns, and Programmability," *British Journal for the Philosophy of Science* 45 (1994): 631–48.

3. Ibid., 644.

4. *The Book of Margery Kempe*, ed. Barry Windeatt (Cambridge: D. S. Brewer, 2004).

Introduction

1. The details of this particular reading experience are recorded on a page inserted by Connary between the front flyleaf and the title page of Julian of Norwich, *Sixteen Revelations of Divine Love* (Boston: Ticknor and Fields, 1864).

2. Note inserted between pages 208 and 209 of Thomas Canon Pope, *The Council of the Vatican and the Events of the Time* (Boston: Patrick Donahoe, 1872).

3. The key work for the history of Stratford is Jeannette R. Thompson, *History of the Town of Stratford, New Hampshire, 1773–1925* (Concord, N.H.: The Rumford Press, 1925). In addition to this, useful material can be found in Georgia D. Merrill, *A History of Coös County, New Hampshire* (Syracuse: W. A. Fergusson, 1888), 744–82, and *A Pictorial History of the Town of Stratford, New Hampshire, on the Occasion of Her 200th Birthday: 1773–1973* (Stratford, N.H.: Bicentennial Committee, 1973).

4. Thompson, *History of the Town of Stratford*, 350. This book contains a short genealogy of the Connary family (350–52).

5. Ibid., 185–86. Thompson incorporates statements from Mr. Prescott and Father Routhier, resident priest of Sacred Heart Church in Stratford from 1916. Before Thomas Connary settled in Stratford in 1846, he lived in Lancaster, New Hampshire, where his brother Patrick also resided. Somers's *History of Lancaster* notes the following about the small Catholic community in this town: "The great tide of Irish immigration that set in this direction about 1830, reached Lancaster in 1833. That year the Connary family settled in Lancaster, where ever since they have been prominent Catholics, and highly respected citizens. The first mass celebrated in Lancaster was at the dwelling-house of Patrick Connary, May 4, 1850. . . . There were present at that service, Patrick Connary and wife, John Connary and wife, Thomas Connary and wife, Patrick Clarey and wife, then all the Catholics in Lancaster, or near it." Amos N. Somers, *The History of Lancaster, New Hampshire* (Concord, N.H.: The Rumford Press, 1899), 449.

6. For this information I am indebted to Mr. Edward Harlan Connary, great-great-grandson of Thomas Connary and still resident in Stratford. Private correspondence, January 30, 2010.

7. Thompson, *History of the Town of Stratford*, 261–62.

8. Jefferson to John Adams, June 10, 1815, in *The Adams-Jefferson Letters*, ed. Lester J. Cappon (Chapel Hill: University of North Carolina Press, 1987), 443. The Borges quotation is doubtful; it is probably a free adaptation of the lines "I that used to figure Paradise / In such a library's

guise," in Jorge Luis Borges, "Poem About Gifts," in *Dreamtigers*, trans. Mildred Boyer and Harold Morland (Austin: University of Texas Press, 2006), 55.

9. Note in Julian of Norwich, *Revelations*, inserted between 40–41.

10. On Harvey, see, for example, Anthony Grafton and Lisa Jardine, "'Studied for Action': How Gabriel Harvey Read His Livy," *Past and Present* 129 (1990): 30–78. On Coleridge, see Heather J. Jackson, *Marginalia: Readers Writing in Books* (New Haven: Yale University Press, 2001), 150–65. For an edition of Coleridge's annotations, see Coleridge, *Marginalia*, ed. George Whalley and Heather J. Jackson, vol. 12 of *The Collected Works of Samuel Taylor Coleridge*, 6 pts. (Princeton: Princeton University Press, 1980–2001). Søren Kierkegaard's marginal annotations in his copy of the New Testament are discussed in Bradley Rau Dewey, "Kierkegaard and the Blue Testament," *Harvard Theological Review* 60 (1967): 391–409.

11. I note my indebtedness to several studies within the field of book-historical studies and studies of the history and sociology of reading. The following titles in particular have influenced my thinking: Mark Amsler, "Affective Literacy: Gestures of Reading in the Later Middle Ages," *Essays in Medieval Studies* 18 (2001): 83–109; Stephen Barney, ed., *Annotation and Its Texts* (Oxford: Oxford University Press, 1991); Matthew P. Brown, *The Pilgrim and the Bee: Reading Rituals and Book Culture in Early New England* (Philadelphia: University of Pennsylvania Press, 2007); Michel de Certeau, *The Practice of Everyday Life*, trans. Steven Rendall (Berkeley: University of California Press, 1988); Roger Chartier, *The Order of Books: Readers, Authors, and Libraries in Europe Between the Fourteenth and Eighteenth Centuries*, trans. Lydia C. Cochrane (Stanford: Stanford University Press, 1994); Bradin Cormack and Carla Mazzio, *Book Use, Book Theory: 1500–1700* (Chicago: University of Chicago Library, 2005); Stephen Colclough, *Consuming Texts: Readers and Reading Communities, 1695–1870* (Basingstoke: Palgrave Macmillan, 2007).

12. Jackson, *Marginalia*. See also her *Romantic Readers: The Evidence of Marginalia* (New Haven: Yale University Press, 2005), where she usefully narrows the temporal scope of the investigation of readers' marginalia. See also William H. Sherman, *Used Books: Marking Readers in Renaissance England* (Philadelphia: University of Pennsylvania Press, 2008), and Roger Stoddard's pioneering exhibition catalogue *Marks in Books, Illustrated and Explained* (Cambridge, Mass.: Houghton Library, 1985). Two studies of printed marginalia in Renaissance books provide a useful taxonomy of annotating purposes and examine the strategies of authors, editors, and translators to control the reading experience in the face of readers' diverse approaches to texts: Evelyn B. Tribble, *Margins and Marginality: The Printed Page in Early Modern England* (Charlottesville: University Press of Virginia, 1993), and William W. E. Slights, *Managing Readers: Printed Marginalia in English Renaissance Books* (Ann Arbor: University of Michigan Press, 2001).

13. See especially Jackson, "History," chap. 2 in *Marginalia*, 44–80. See also the valuable review of *Marginalia* by David C. Greetham, who calls attention to the rich pre-1700 tradition of marginal annotation largely excluded in Jackson's study; the review appears in *Papers of the Bibliographical Society of Canada* 40, no. 1 (2002): 61–73.

14. Jackson, *Marginalia*, 149–78.

15. Sherman, *Used Books*, 3. For another theoretically adept study which similarly prefers the term "use" to "reading," see Cormack and Mazzio, *Book Use, Book Theory*.

16. Sherman, *Used Books*, 126.

17. Jackson, *Marginalia*, 81.

18. Sherman provides a particularly interesting analysis of a manuscript Book of Common Prayer of ca. 1560, in which illustrated initials excised from a medieval manuscript prayer book have been pasted in to create a strikingly original hybrid of printed text features, manuscript, and pictorial embellishment. Such creative *mise-en-page* and retrofitting of images find a parallel in the devout book labors of Thomas Connary. See "An Uncommon Book of Common Prayer," chap. 5 in *Used Books*, 87–112.

19. Anthony Grafton, "Is the History of Reading a Marginal Enterprise? Guillaume Budé and His Books," *Papers of the Bibliographical Society of America* 91 (1997): 141; Jackson, *Marginalia*, 178.

20. Brown, *The Pilgrim and the Bee*, 14, 137.

21. See especially the carefully argued and polemical "Introduction: Toward a Reader-Based Literary History," in ibid., 1–20.

22. From a slightly different angle, Jardine and Grafton's study of Gabriel Harvey's reading of Livy's *History of Rome* also examines a reiterated reading over three decades and shows the unfolding of a single reader's response as the purposes and circumstances of reading change; see "'Studied for Action.'"

23. Leah Price provides a very useful overview of scholarship on the history of reading, and how it has "extensively discussed and intensively criticized" historical contrasting models such as those of intensive and extensive reading, vocalized and silent reading. Price, "Reading: The State of the Discipline," *Book History* 7 (2004): 303–20.

24. Useful discussion and bibliography can be found in Andrew Elfenbein, "Cognitive Science and the History of Reading," *PMLA* 121, no. 2 (2006): 484–502.

25. Gérard Genette, *Paratexts: Thresholds of Interpretation*, trans. Jane E. Lewin (Cambridge: Cambridge University Press, 1997); Genette, "Introduction to the Paratext," *New Literary History* 22 (1991): 261–72.

26. Genette, *Paratexts*, 1.

27. Ibid., 344. Genette states that "in principle, every context serves as a paratext," and in this he includes historical periods, but he also clarifies the textual focus of his investigation: "almost all the paratexts I consider will themselves be of a *textual*, or at least verbal, kind: titles, prefaces, interviews, all of them utterances that, varying greatly in scope, nonetheless share the linguistic status of the text" (ibid., 7, 8).

28. Genette determines paratext as "authorial or more or less legitimated by the author": "By definition, something is not a paratext unless the author or one of his associates accepts responsibility for it, although the degree of responsibility may vary" (ibid., 2, 9). He understands paratext as functioning always in service of the text whose meaning it clarifies or moderates; "subordinate" and "auxiliary" are words used to describe its status (ibid., 2, 12).

29. For an excellent collection of studies of English Renaissance books that extend and challenge Genette's work on the paratext, see Helen Smith and Louise Wilson, eds., *Renaissance Paratexts* (Cambridge: Cambridge University Press, 2011).

30. Stallybrass, "Afterword," in ibid., 219. In the essay "Unannotating Spenser" in the same volume, Jason Scott-Warren extends Genette's taxonomy by considering handwritten annotations as paratexts (153–64).

31. In the conclusion of *Paratexts*, Genette acknowledges "the immense continent" of illustration as an important paratextual form, but sees it as outside the scope of his investigation (406). For a recent study that shows the value of reading illustrations as a form of paratext, see Hester Lees-Jeffries, "Pictures, Places, and Spaces: Sydney, Wroth, Wilton House, and the *Songe de Poliphile*," in Smith and Wilson, *Renaissance Paratexts*, 185–203.

32. Scott-Warren, "Unannotating Spenser," 163–64.

33. Employing the language of speech act theory, Genette makes a brief observation about the illocutionary and even performative force of the paratext; see *Paratexts*, 10–12.

34. Adrian Johns, *The Nature of the Book: Print and Knowledge in the Making* (Chicago: University of Chicago Press, 1998), 29.

35. The value of the unusual and idiosyncratic in our study of reading cultures has been asserted by several, including Stephen Colclough, "Readers: Books and Biography," in *A Companion to the History of the Book*, ed. Simon Eliot and Jonathan Rose (Oxford: Blackwell, 2007), 50–62, and Colclough, "Introduction," in *Consuming Texts*, 1–27. See also H. J. Jackson,

"'Marginal Frivolities': Readers' Notes as Evidence for the History of Reading," in *Owners, Annotators, and the Signs of Reading*, ed. Robin Myers, Michael Harris, and Giles Mandelbrote (London: British Library, 2005), 137–52.

36. Jackson, *Marginalia*, 203, 182.

37. Ibid., 203.

38. Ibid., 182–85.

39. Hans Ulrich Gumbrecht's personalized polemic *The Production of Presence: What Meaning Cannot Convey* (Stanford: Stanford University Press, 2004) offers an assessment of the preference within the humanities for theory and the interpretation of the meaning of cultural artifacts. The consequence of this preference, he argues, is that our study of cultural productions has become disconnected from the experiential dimension of affect and aesthetics. In his challenge to this status quo, Gumbrecht argues for increased attention to the "dimension of presence," where cultural phenomena impact our senses and bodies and provide nonconceptual moments of sensuous, aesthetic intensity. In a way that resonates with my argument here, Gumbrecht makes a case for three central forms of "presence phenomena" that he refers to as epiphany, presentification, and deixis. "Epiphany/Presentification/Deixis: Futures for the Humanities and Arts," chap. 4 in ibid., 91–132.

Chapter 1

1. For an excellent study of this early development of mass communication in America, see David Paul Nord, *Faith in Reading: Religious Publishing and the Birth of Mass Media in America* (Oxford: Oxford University Press, 2004).

2. Charles Fanning, *The Irish Voice in America: 250 Years of Irish-American Fiction*, 2nd ed. (Lexington: University Press of Kentucky, 2000), 6–71.

3. Fanning provides a very useful survey of the fictional literature of the nineteenth-century Famine generation in "The Famine Generation: Practical Fiction for Immigrants," chap. 3 in ibid., 72–113.

4. J. B. O'Connor, "Ven. Louis of Granada," in *The Catholic Encyclopedia*, vol. 9 (New York: Robert Appleton, 1913), http://www.newadvent.org/cathen/09385b.htm.

5. *The Sinner's Guide* was printed frequently in Dublin in the nineteenth century, including by P. Wogan in 1790, Richard Coyne in 1825, Richard Grace in 1837, and Warren in 1848. It was printed in Philadelphia in 1833 by Eugene Cummiskey, in 1845 by Henry M'Grath, and in Boston in 1886 by T. B. Noonan and Co.

6. Anon., review in *The Irish Monthly* 1, no. 1 (1873): 56.

7. Thomas H. Kinane, *The Dove of the Tabernacle* (New York: P. M. Haverty, 1876), 559–60.

8. Fanning, *Irish Voice*, 114–15.

9. See Alban Butler, *The Lives of the Fathers, Martyrs, and Other Principal Saints*, 3 vols. (New York: D. & J. Sadlier, 1846); *The Holy Bible Translated from the Latin Vulgate* (New York: D. & J. Sadlier, 1845); and *Die Heilige Schrift des neuen Testamentes* (New York: D. & J. Sadlier, 1850). Sadlier also published a Catholic treatise on the controversy of Bible translation: Thomas Ward, John Lingard, and John Milner, *Errata of the Protestant Bible, Or, the Truth of the English Translations Examined: In a Treatise, Showing some of the Errors that Are to Be Found in the English Translations of the Sacred Scriptures, Used by Protestants, against such Points of Religious Doctrine as Are the Subject of Controversy between Them and the Members of the Catholic Church* (New York: D. & J. Sadlier, 1844). For discussion of the writings of Mary Anne Sadlier, see Liz Szabo, "'My Heart Bleeds to Tell It': Women, Domesticity, and the American Ideal in Mary Anne Sadlier's 'Romance of Irish Immigration,'" http://xroads.virginia.edu/~hyper/SADLIER/Intro.htm; Michele Lacombe, "Frying Pans and Deadlier Weapons: The Immigrant Novels of Mary Anne Sadlier," *Essays on*

Canadian Writing 29 (1984): 96–116; Fanning, "Mrs. Sadlier and Father Quigley," chap. 4 in *Irish Voice*, 114–52.

10. The anecdote about Balmes's reading is plausible but unverified: it is recorded in a brief printed biography cut from a newspaper and inserted by Connary on page iv of vol. 1 of the *Philosophy*. The source is uncertain. A useful introduction to Balmes's system is Kelly James Clark, "Spanish Common Sense Philosophy: Jaime Balmes' Critique of Cartesian Foundationalism," *History of Philosophy Quarterly* 7, no. 2 (1990): 207–26.

11. Balmes's *Protestantism and Catholicity* was published in London in a translation from the French by C. J. Hanford and R. Kershaw (London: James Burns, 1849). The same text appeared in America from John Murphy in Baltimore in 1850; this is the version owned by Connary. Murphy published a sixth edition in 1858.

12. Balmes, *Fundamental Philosophy*, 2:488.

13. From the first page of the publisher's advertisements at the rear of George Foxcroft Haskins, *Travels in England, France, Italy, and Ireland* (Boston: Patrick Donahoe, 1856).

14. See Nord, *Faith in Reading*, esp. chap. 4, "The New Mass Media: National Institutions," 61–88.

15. From the advertisements at the back of Haskins's *Travels*.

16. This is the only edition published of Haskins's *Travels*. He also wrote *Six Weeks Abroad in Ireland, England, and Belgium* (Boston: Patrick Donahoe, 1872). On the history of the House of the Angel Guardian, of which Haskins was the rector, see Peter C. Holloran, *Boston's Wayward Children: Social Services for Homeless Children, 1830–1930* (Rutherford: Fairleigh Dickinson University Press, 1989), esp. chap. 2, "Boston Catholic Charity for Children," 63–105.

17. Holloran, *Boston's Wayward Children*, 83.

18. Holloran notes that Haskins toured European reform schools, many housing juvenile delinquents, in 1843, 1851, and 1870 (ibid., 86).

19. Haskins, *Travels*, 5.

20. Ibid., 152–53.

21. Ibid., 278.

22. Ibid., 291, 292.

23. Ibid., 285.

24. See also Francis R. Walsh, "Who Spoke for Boston's Irish? The Boston *Pilot* in the Nineteenth Century," *Journal of Ethnic Studies* 10, no. 3 (1982): 21–36. *The United States Catholic Miscellany* dates back further than the *Pilot*. It was published from 1822 to 1861 as the official newspaper of the Roman Catholic Diocese of Charleston.

25. On a note inserted between pages 6–7 in Julian of Norwich, *Revelations*, Connary records the following payments: "My receipts at post office, signed by Postmaster Kenny date January 15, 1890, to go by mail, Wednesday 16, prove that I send in sealed letter $1.00, to publisher Colby of Lancaster, N.H. $1.25, to publishers of People and New Hampshire Patriot to Concord, N.H., and $2.75 to Pilot Publishing Company, no. 597, Washington Street Boston, Mass."

26. This is found on pages inserted between the Preface ("To the Reader") and the first page of Julian of Norwich, *Revelations*. *The New England Homestead* was published in Springfield, Massachusetts, weekly from 1842 to 1969.

27. John O'Hanlon, *The Irish Emigrant's Guide for the United States* (Boston: Patrick Donahoe, 1851), 177. In the advertisements appended to Haskins's *Travels*, Donahoe offers this title for sale in a cloth-bound volume for 25 cents. On a note inserted in *The Sinner's Guide*, Connary refers to "O'Hanlon's 'Guide'" as being in his possession, and I assume it to be this book.

28. Connary refers to these titles as being part of his library on a note inserted in *The Sinner's Guide* between pages 182 and 83. In all probability they refer to *The Youth's Director, or, Familiar Instructions for Young People: which Will Be Found Useful also to Persons of Every Sex, Age and*

Condition in Life: with a Number of Historical Traits and Edifying Examples (New York: P. J. Kennedy, Excelsior Catholic Publishing House, 1878), and Silvio Pellico, *On the Duties of Young Men*, trans. R. A. Vain (New York: D. & J. Sadlier, 1872).

29. Frederic Falkner, *The Farmer's Treasure: A Practical Treatise on the Nature and Value of Manures, Founded from Experiments on Various Crops* (New York: D. Appleton, 1844). Connary mentions the other two works in a note in *The Sinner's Guide* and is probably referring to J. D. Koogle, *The Farmer's Own Book: A Treatise on the Numerous Diseases of the Horse* (Baltimore: McCoull & Slater, 1857), and Thomas G. Fessenden, *The Complete Farmer and Rural Economist* (Boston: Lilly, Wait, and Company, and G. C. Barrett, 1834). This last title was reprinted many times; the copy printed with A. O. Moore, Agricultural Book Publisher, New York, in 1858 states that it is the 10th edition.

30. Edwin A. Charlton, *New Hampshire as It Is* (Claremont, N.H.: Tracy and Sanford, 1856).

31. O'Hanlon, *Irish Emigrant's Guide*, 165–67.

32. Ibid., 164–65.

33. This is probably *The Catechism of the Council of Trent*, trans. J. Donovan, published by Fielding Lucas Jr. in Baltimore in 1829 (and since reprinted several times). This volume comprises 413 pages and is thus not identical with Connary's "little illustrated catechism."

34. *The Catholic Spectator*, 3rd ser., vol. 1 (1824). The magazine was published in London by Keating and Brown, and the praise of *Mrs. Herbert and the Villagers* is found on the their advertisement page at the back of the volume (the book is priced at 4s, 6p). The title was also printed in Dublin several times from the 1820s on. Connary's copy was published in 1853 by Fielding Lucas Jr. in Baltimore.

35. Louis Gaston de Ségur, *Plain Talk about the Protestantism of To-Day* (Boston: Patrick Donahoe, 1868), 7.

36. Connary's edition was published by Eugene Cummiskey in 1864. The title appeared first in 1833 from the three publishers Joseph Whetham, Eugene Cummiskey, and Isaac Bird, all in Philadelphia.

37. *Controversy between Rev. Messrs. Hughes and Breckenridge, on the Subject "Is the Protestant Religion the Religion of Christ?"* (Philadelphia: Eugene Cummiskey, 1864), xii.

38. Two additional titles of Catholic apologetics and polemic include Balmes, *Protestantism and Catholicity*, and the work by Vanbrugh Livingston with the informative title page *An Inquiry into the Merits of the Reformed Doctrine of "Imputation," as Contrasted with Those of "Catholic Imputation;" or, The Cardinal Point of Controversy between the Church of Rome and the Protestant High Church* (New York: Casserly & Sons, 1843).

39. Fanning, *Irish Voice*, 120.

40. See the survey of Sadlier's fiction in ibid., 114–40.

41. O'Hanlon, *Irish Emigrant's Guide*, 167.

Epiphany: "Seeing Very Plainly"

1. These classifications are discussed in greater detail in Lucien Roure, "Visions and Apparitions," in *The Catholic Encyclopedia*, vol. 15 (New York: Robert Appleton, 1912), http://www.newadvent.org/cathen/15477a.htm.

Chapter 2

1. Jackson, *Marginalia*, 179–81.

2. Ibid., 179.

3. Extra-illustration is defined as "illustrations added to the book after publication, normally done by the owner of the book, not the book's publisher." See Independent Online Booksellers Association, "book terminology," http://www.ioba.org/terms.html.

4. Jackson, *Marginalia*, 186–91. Jackson corrects the common understanding that Granger himself published his works with blank spaces for portraits—a misconception that appears to have "arisen from later practice and from the fact that some of the few extant copies of the first edition [of Granger's *Biographical History*] were printed on only one side of the leaf" (187).

5. Ellen Gruber Garvey, *Writing with Scissors: American Scrapbooks from the Civil War to the Harlem Renaissance* (Oxford: Oxford University Press, 2012).

6. On this depiction and devotion to the Holy Name, see Frederick Holweck, "Holy Name of Jesus," in *The Catholic Encyclopedia*, vol. 7 (New York: Robert Appleton, 1910), http://www.newadvent.org/cathen/07421a.htm.

7. We find many detailed instructions by Connary to himself that point to such purposeful insertion of material between specific pages. A two-page rumination found between pages 66 and 67 of *The True Spiritual Conferences of St. Francis of Sales* (London: Richardson and Son, 1862) concerns itself with the necessity of obedience as a positive moral choice, and then notes the following: "We are now speaking in this paper for pages 66 and 67 for my Book Spiritual Conferences of Saint Francis of Sales in 330 pages. Read all that I have written in this Book. That especially which I have written in it next to page of title and picture. This one Book is worth much more than money is worth thank God. Thomas Connary."

8. From a note inserted between pages 16 and 17 of *Lives of the Fathers of the Desert*.

9. Stallybrass, "Afterword," in Smith and Wilson, *Renaissance Paratexts*, 219.

10. Croxall, *Fables of Aesop and Others*, note between pages 24 and 25.

11. Ibid., xvii.

12. Ibid., 58.

13. Ibid., 253.

14. On a note inserted opposite the title page of *The Spirit of St. Francis de Sales*, dated August 28, 1892.

15. Leatherman, *Elements of Moral Science*, 17.

16. Unusually, this note is undated by Connary. It is inserted between pages lii and 1 of the *Spiritual Conferences*.

17. See also the essay by Simon Eliot, "The Reading Experience Database; or, What Are We to Do About the History of Reading?," http://www.open.ac.uk/Arts/RED/redback.htm. Here I am adding to Eliot, who lists two caveats and important reminders in the discipline of the history of reading: first, that "to own, buy, borrow or steal a book is no proof of wishing to read it, let alone proof of having read it," and, second, that "quoting, or misquoting, a text is no proof of having read it."

18. Michel de Certeau, "Reading as Poaching," in *The Practice of Everyday Life*, 165–76. Useful discussion is found in Jeremy Ahearne, *De Certeau: Interpretation and Its Other* (Cambridge: Polity Press, 1995), 164–76.

19. Ibid., 169.

20. Brown, *The Pilgrim and the Bee*, 138.

21. Ryan Perry, " 'Some Sprytuall Matter of Gostly Edyfycacion': Readers and Readings of Nicholas Love's *Mirror of the Blessed Life of Jesus Christ*," in *The Pseudo-Bonaventuran Lives of Christ: Exploring the Middle English Tradition*, ed. Ian Johnson and Allan Westphall (Turnhout: Brepols, 2013), 79–126.

22. Note in Pope, *The Council of the Vatican*, dated August 5, 1888, and inserted between pages xviii and 1.

23. Jacques Derrida, "This Is Not an Oral Footnote," in Barney, *Annotation and Its Texts*, 194.

24. David Paul Nord, "How Readers Should Read," chap. 6 in *Faith in Reading*, 113–30. See also chap. 7, "How Readers Did Read," 131–50, which assesses the evidence for actual readers' encounters with books.

Epiphany: The Lamp

1. Richard Rolle, *The Fire of Love*, quoted from *The Law of Love: English Spirituality in the Age of Wyclif*, ed. and trans. David Lyle Jeffrey (Grand Rapids, Mich.: W. B. Eerdmans, 1988), 183. Rolle's Middle English has the following: "I felt first my herte wax warme and—truly, not ymagyngly, bot als it were with sensibill fier—byrned! I was forsoth mervaylde as the byrnynge in my saule byrst up, and of an unwonte solas. For uncuthnes of slike helefull habundance oftymes have I gropyd my breste, sekandly whedyr this byrnynge were of any bodily cause utwardly. But when I knewe that onely it was kyndylte of gostely caus inwardlye—and that this brynnynge was nought of fleschly lufe ne concupiscens—in this I consayvyd it was the gyfte of my makar: glad therefore I am moltyn into the desire of grettyr luf." Quoted from *English Mystics of the Middle Ages*, ed. Barry Windeatt (Cambridge: Cambridge University Press, 1994), 15.

Chapter 3

1. William H. Sherman, "'The Book thus Put in Every Vulgar Hand': Marking the Bible," chap. 4 in *Used Books*, 71–86; Jackson, *Marginalia*, 182–84; Peter Stallybrass, "Books and Scrolls: Navigating the Bible," in *Books and Readers in Early Modern England: Material Studies*, ed. Jennifer Andersen and Elizabeth Sauer (Philadelphia: University of Pennsylvania Press, 2002), 42–79.
2. Brown, *The Pilgrim and the Bee*, 20, 139.
3. Connary makes several references to his own binding of books, and he probably sought to ensure the durability of some of books that might have been purchased unbound or in temporary paper bindings. One reference is to "my Book, Life of Saint Joseph, Life of Maria of Jesus of Agreda, and Saint Patrick, bound firmly by me as one Book": on a note between pages 526 and 527 in the second volume of Balmes's *Fundamental Philosophy*.
4. Genette, *Paratexts*, 7. The significance to the reading experience of space and the spatial positioning of the reading body has not been subject to much analysis. Some aspects are considered in Stephen Colclough, "Representing Reading Spaces," in *The History of Reading*, vol. 3, *Methods, Strategies, Tactics*, ed. Rosalind Crone and Shafquat Towheed (Basingstoke: Macmillan, 2011), 99–114; see also Andrew Taylor, "Into His Secret Chamber: Reading and Privacy in Late Medieval England," in *The Practice and Representation of Reading in England*, ed. James Raven, Helen Small, and Naomi Tadmor (Cambridge: Cambridge University Press, 2006), 41–61.
5. Lees-Jeffries, "Pictures, Places, and Spaces," 203.
6. For an argument along similar tracks, see Walter Benjamin's famous essay "The Work of Art in the Age of Mechanical Reproduction." Benjamin explores what he refers to as the "aura" of the material artifact, associating this with the experience of presence, singularity, and authenticity that are part of cult and ritual. Benjamin understands the "aura" of an artifact to wither with the facile technological reproduction of a commodity. "The Work of Art in the Age of Mechanical Reproduction," trans. J. A. Underwood, in Benjamin, *The Work of Art in the Age of Mechanical Reproduction*, Great Ideas 56 (London: Penguin, 2008), 1–50.
7. Collins's poem can be found online at http://www.poemhunter.com/poem/marginalia/.
8. Balmes, *Fundamental Philosophy*, 1:336.
9. Note dated April 1, 1891, in *The Council of the Vatican*, between pages 218 and 219.
10. Genette considers oral confidences and personal letters to recipients of volumes as examples of the private epitext; see *Paratexts*, 371–404.

11. The same Theresa McGoldrick was the recipient of at least one more book from Thomas Connary, as is recorded on a note dated Monday, January 30, 1893, and inserted in the second volume of Balmes's *Fundamental Philosophy*: "Miss Theresa A. McGoldrick here Saturday night last, Sunday last she was with us all day, so Sunday night last, this morning early she goes from our Diamond Crossing in the Cars to Lancaster, New Hampshire: she has from me as her own Book, a very good History of the Roman Catholic Church, it has in its proper place, one paper of my work as finished early today, and I am very sure, that the words now in that paper, as my own thoughtful words, never can be sinful, and for the good reason, that all of my thoughts are centred in heaven."

12. Charles Lock, "Book History and the Metonymies of the Text," in *Movable Type, Mobile Nations: Interactions in Transnational Book History*, ed. Simon Frost and Robert W. Rix, Angles on the English-Speaking World 10 (Copenhagen: Museum Tusculanum Press, 2010), 149.

13. Ibid., 149.

14. Amsler, "Affective Literacy," 83–84. For an illuminating discussion of the relation between private reading and vocalized performance, see also Peter Kivy, "The Experience of Reading," in *A Companion to the Philosophy of Literature*, ed. Garry L. Hagberg and Walter Jost, Blackwell Companions to Philosophy 44 (Chichester: Wiley-Blackwell, 2010), 106–19.

15. Note inserted after the final contents page of *The Council of the Vatican* and dated August 5, 1888.

16. Note dated February 24, 1891, inserted between pages 68 and 69 in the *Spiritual Conferences* of St. Francis of Sales. The literature on the medieval book metaphor is considerable: foundational is Ernst Robert Curtius, "The Book as Symbol," in *European Literature and the Latin Middle Ages* (Princeton: Princeton University Press, 1953), 302–47. Vincent Gillespie gives examples of this rich tradition from medieval English literature in "Lukynge in Haly Bukes: *Lectio* in Some Late Medieval Spiritual Miscellanies," in *Spätmittelalterliche Geistliche Literatur in der Nationalsprache*, ed. James Hogg, Analecta Cartusiana 106 (Salzburg: Institut für Anglistik und Amerikanistik, Universität Salzburg, 1984), 10–13.

17. This in *The Council of the Vatican* between pages vi and vii of the contents pages and dated September 18, 1889.

18. This in a note inserted between pages 236 and 237 in *The Six Hundred Thousand Combatants* and dated October 29, 1893.

19. On a note dated June 29, 1881, inserted between pages 328 and 329 of volume 2 of Balmes's *Fundamental Philosophy*.

20. In *Mrs. Herbert and the Villagers*, between pages viii and ix.

21. On notes from 1884 and 1891 found in *The Spirit of St. Francis de Sales, Mrs. Herbert and the Villagers*, and *An Inquiry into the Merits of the Reformed Doctrine of "Imputation."*

22. At times Connary appears daunted or exhausted with the magnitude of the work that he feels called to carry out: "I am doing my best most peacefully, in all of my papers to prove that God never can be wrong anywhere"; "Now I will try to help all as much as possible, I cannot do any better than I can do anywhere, but I try to do so. I never can do better than I can do." Notes in the second volume of *Fundamental Philosophy* by Balmes and in Fredet's *Modern History*, from 1893 and 1898, respectively.

23. This poem is the same as that printed under the authorship of Ellis Gray in *The Cambridge Book of Poetry and Song: Selected from English and American Authors*, ed. Charlotte Fiske Bates (New York: Thomas Y. Crowell, 1832), 823. Connary's source for the poem is uncertain, and I have found no reference in his notes to *The Cambridge Book of Poetry and Song*. Connary has also transcribed it on an end flyleaf in the second volume of *Mrs. Herbert and the Villagers*, and here it is followed by three biblical quotations on the subject of salvation that give some indication of Connary's deep familiarity with the Bible: " 'Then shall the just shine as the sun, in the Kingdom of their Father. He that hath ears to hear let him hear.' Saint Matthew Chapter XIII. 43

verse. For lo, the Kingdom of God is within you. Saint Luke XVII. 21. Fear not, little flock, for it hath pleased your Father to give you a Kingdom. Saint Luke XII. 32. No power has ever reasoned Divine Justice away anywhere thank God."

24. *Hours with the Muses* (Manchester: J. B. Rogerson, 1841). The poem also found its way into Isaac Pitman's *A Manual of Phonography*, first printed in London in 1842, where it forms one of the exercises in Pitman's system of stenographic shorthand (in improved form the most widely used system of phonetic shorthand to this day). See *A Manual of Phonography, or, Writing by Sound* (London: S. Bagster and Sons, 1842). Pitman's work was available in the United States from 1844, printed by J. Donlevy in New York, but there is no indication that Connary owned a copy.

25. Wendy Scase, "Reginald Pecock, John Carpenter, and John Colop's 'Common-Profit' Books: Aspects of Book Ownership and Circulation in Fifteenth-Century London," *Medium Aevum* 61, no. 2 (1992): 261–74. Margaret Connolly examines the contents and relationships of six 'common-profit' compilations in "Books for the 'helpe of euery persoone that thenkith to be sau ed': Six Devotional Miscellanies from Fifteenth-Century London," *Yearbook of English Studies* 33 (2003): 170–81.

26. The Middle English is quoted from Scase, "Reginald Pecock," 261. The quotation is from a fifteenth-century manuscript of English religious writings, now Cambridge University Library, MS Ff.vi.31.

Chapter 4

1. I have been unable to examine the two last titles by St. Francis of Sales, and it is uncertain if they have survived.

2. Several of the books owned by Connary and printed on Irish American presses were available in England in earlier editions printed by Thomas Richardson and Son—e.g., Frederick Faber's *All for Jesus* and John Milner's *End of Religious Controversy*.

3. From St. Francis of Sales's preface to *Introduction to the Devout Life*, Christian Classics Ethereal Library, www.ccel.org/ccel/desales/devwww.ccel.org/ccel/desales/devout_life.i.i.htmlout _life.i.i.html.

4. Michael Winship, *American Literary Publishing in the Mid-Nineteenth Century: The Business of Ticknor and Fields* (Cambridge: Cambridge University Press, 1995). See esp. chap. 3, "The Publications of Ticknor and Fields," 39–93.

5. Ibid., 54–56.

6. Ibid., 189.

7. Ibid., 104.

8. Julian of Norwich, *Sixteen Revelations of Divine Love: shewed to a devout servant of our Lord called Mother Juliana, an anchorete of Norwich, who lived in the dayes of King Edward the Third*, ed. Serenus Cressy (n.p.: "published by R. F. S. Cressy," 1670). For a brief biography of Cressy, see George Hind, "Hugh Paulinus Serenus Cressy," in *The Catholic Encyclopedia*, vol. 4 (New York: Robert Appleton, 1908), http://www.newadvent.org/cathen/04486b.htm. An edition of Julian of Norwich, *Revelations*, edited by G. H. Parker, was published in London in 1843 (no publisher stated), which prints verbatim from Cressy's edition of 1670.

9. Some useful discussion of the recusant interest in Middle English devotional and mystical writing is found in T. A. Birrell, "English Catholic Mystics in Non-Catholic Circles," *Downside Review* 94 (1976): 60–81, 99–117, 213–28; David Rogers, "The English Recusants: Some Mediaeval Literary Links," *Recusant History* 23 (1997): 483–507.

10. Examples of Irish American printings of St. Francis of Sales include *An Introduction to a Devout Life* (Baltimore: F. Lucas, Jr., 1833); *The True Spiritual Conferences of St. Francis of Sales* (New York: D. & J. Sadlier, 1863); *A Treatise on the Love of God* (New York: P. O'Shea, 1861); and *The Consoling Thoughts of St. Francis of Sales* (Boston: Patrick Donahoe, 1874).

11. Thus Connary notes of Julian: "All of her life was centred fully with God in heaven. To live as she lived was for her xvi Revelations of pure heavenly love. Her whole Living power was then handsomely schooled by God in heaven endlessly. So are men schooled by God Himself for endless Eternity, if they are willing to be heavenly pure." From a note dated July 23, 1896, inserted between pages vi and vii in the *Revelations*.

12. On a note inserted in the *Spiritual Conferences* between page xlviii and the first contents page, dated May 14, 1890.

13. St. Francis of Sales, *Spiritual Conferences*, 25.

14. From a note dated May 28, 1882, and inserted between pages 330 and 331 of *The Council of the Vatican*.

15. Camus, *The Spirit of St. Francis de Sales*, 62.

16. It is instructive to note the specific titles into which Connary deploys his own epiphanic accounts. The *Spiritual Conferences* and *The Spirit of St. Francis de Sales* call particular attention to themselves in this regard: in the first we find the extraordinary narrative of the appearance of the Godhead in an Irish church (see the epiphany following chapter 4) and the account of the appearance of the Virgin and company. In the latter is related the appearance on a rainy day of the angels in celestial sunlight and the experience of a lamp of fire burning. In no other books in the library do we find the inclusion of two such accounts. Reference is made to similar descriptions inserted in *The Life and Revelations of Saint Gertrude* (a book that I have not been able to examine), and we find recordings also in the didactic religious treatises *The Sinner's Guide* and *In Heaven We Know Our Own*.

17. Derrida, "This Is Not an Oral Footnote," 197.

18. Julian of Norwich, *Revelations*, 6. The quotations from the *Revelations* that follow are from Connary's edition, published by Ticknor and Fields in 1864.

19. Ibid., 8.

20. The issue of dating Julian's Short Text and Long Text is considered in Nicholas Watson, "The Composition of Julian of Norwich's *Revelation of Love*," *Speculum* 68, no. 3 (1993): 637–83.

21. David Aers, "The Humanity of Christ: Reflections on Julian of Norwich's *Revelation of Love*," in David Aers and Lynn Staley, *The Powers of the Holy: Religion, Politics, and Gender in Late Medieval English Culture* (University Park: Pennsylvania State University Press, 1996), 83–84.

22. Berndt Hamm, "Normative Centering in the Fifteenth and Sixteenth Centuries: Observations on Religiosity, Theology, and Iconology," *Journal of Early Modern History* 3 (1999): 307–54. See also Hamm, *The Reformation of Faith in the Context of Late Medieval Theology and Piety*, ed. Robert J. Bast (Leiden: Brill, 2004).

23. Julian of Norwich, *Revelations*, 137.

24. Ibid., 152.

25. From a note dated January 29, 1889, and inserted before the end flyleaf.

26. Julian of Norwich, *Revelations*, 155–56.

27. Joan M. Nuth, *Wisdom's Daughter: The Theology of Julian of Norwich* (New York: Crossroad Publishing, 1991), 106.

28. Julian of Norwich, *Revelations*, 102. Nuth also cites this passage in *Wisdom's Daughter*, 106.

29. Julian of Norwich, *Revelations*, 156.

30. Written on the back of a letter received in 1889 from the Pilot Publishing Company and pasted onto page 214 of the *Revelations*.

31. Thus in the note dated February 9, 1890, between pages 20 and 21 of the *Revelations*: "Unfaithful human creatures find themselves to be unfaithful human creatures together, as one unhappy family of immortal creatures, as long as the one only True Living God can have power to be the best judge in the whole of His unfathomable unlimited creations. Long enough."

32. Julian of Norwich, *Revelations*, 22.

33. Ibid., 61.

34. See, for instance, Nicholas Watson's consideration of the theological and linguistic context of Julian's speculative salvation theology in "Visions of Inclusion: Universal Salvation and Vernacular Theology in Pre-Reformation England," *Journal of Medieval and Early Modern Studies* 27, no. 2 (1997): 160–66.

35. See, for instance, the important chapter 32 of the *Revelations*, where Julian engages with the topic of the possibility of the salvation of heathens. She concludes this chapter, "he shall make well all that is not well. But what the deed shal be, and how it shall be done, there is no creature beneath Christ that wot [knows] it, ne shall witt it till it is done." Julian of Norwich, *Revelations*, 72. See also the discussion in Frederick C. Bauerschmidt, "Julian of Norwich—Incorporated," *Modern Theology* 13, no. 1 (1997): 95–96. I have benefitted from Bauerschmidt's assessment of Julian's salvation theology in this part of my discussion.

36. Dated January 29, 1889, and inserted before the end flyleaf in the *Revelations*. John 6 contains the episodes of Christ's feeding of the 5,000 and walking on water, and it concludes with the discourse between Christ and the Jews on the bread of life. Here Jesus proclaims, "This is the bread which cometh down from heaven; that if any man eat of it, he may not die. I am the living bread which came down from heaven. If any man eat of this bread, he shall live for ever; and the bread that I will give, is my flesh, for the life of the world" (John 6:50–52).

37. Notes dated February 9, 1890, and March 2, 1897, and inserted between pages 20 and 21 of the *Revelations*.

38. Useful background can be found in *Religion and Public Life in New England: Steady Habits, Changing Slowly*, ed. Andrew Walsh and Mark Silk (Walnut Creek, Calif.: AltaMira Press, 2004); see esp. James M. O'Toole, "Catholics I—Minority Faith with a Minority Mindset," 41–60.

39. Note dated April 6, 1897, and inserted before the end flyleaf of the *Revelations*.

40. Julian of Norwich, *Revelations*, 71.

41. Ibid., 71.

42. Quoted from a note inserted in *Lives of the Fathers of the Desert* between pages 16 and 17.

43. Note dated April 6, 1897, and pasted in before the final flyleaf of the *Revelations*; Julian of Norwich, *Revelations*, 131.

44. Julian talks about sin as the absence of the good and as a "blindness" in chapters 47 and in those pertaining to her thirteenth vision (27–40). Connary talks often about man's "contrariness" or "contradiction."

45. "Statistical Summary: America's Major Wars," comp. Al Nofi, Louisiana State University, The United States Civil War Center, http://web.archive.org/web/20070711050249/http://www.cwc.lsu.edu/other/stats/warcost.htm.

46. Particularly penetrating analysis of the broader cultural implications of the destruction of the Civil War can be found in Drew Gilpin Faust, *This Republic of Suffering: Death and the American Civil War* (New York: Alfred A. Knopf, 2008), esp. chap. 6, "Believing and Doubting: 'What Means This Carnage?,'" 171–210.

47. Dated March 2, 1897, and inserted between pages 20 and 21 of the *Revelations*.

48. Faust, *This Republic of Suffering*, 173, 209. Faust also notes a turn among many Americans toward spiritualism and occultism for consolation and comforting ideas about heaven (178–88).

49. This note, dated April 24, 1893, is found in Philippe's *Six Hundred Thousand Combatants* between pages 14 and 15.

50. This note is dated May 16, 1894, and found between pages xx and 1 of Livingston's *Inquiry into the Merits of the Reformed Doctrine of "Imputation."*

Epiphany: "No Priest or Bishop in This Church but Himself Alone"

1. Julian of Norwich, *Revelations*, 189.
2. Ibid., 19.

Chapter 5

1. Frederick H. Wines, *Report on the Defective, Dependent, and Delinquent Classes of the Population of the United States, as Returned at the Tenth Census (June 1, 1880)* (Washington, D.C.: Government Printing Office, 1888), xix, xlii.
2. Ibid., xii.
3. Ibid., 8.
4. Joseph C. G. Kennedy, *Preliminary Report on the Eighth Census, 1860* (Washington, D.C.: Government Printing Office, 1862), 48. I also rely on Andrew Scull, *Madness: A Very Short Introduction* (Oxford: Oxford University Press, 2011), esp. chap. 3, "Madness Confined," 43–65.
5. Scull, *Madness*, 54–55.
6. Wines, *Report*, xlii. According to Wines's 1880 census report, the asylum of New Hampshire makes use of "night only" seclusion, and has a particularly high rate of "not secluded" patients, when compared with other institutions (82).
7. Ibid., 55. I rely on the description of New Hampshire Asylum for the Insane (in 1901 renamed the Concord State Hospital) on the Asylum Projects website, http://www.asylum-projects.org/index.php?title=Concord_State_Hospital. See also Simon N. Stone, "Psychiatry in New Hampshire—The First Hundred Years," *New England Journal of Medicine* 28 (1943): 595–605.
8. Wines, *Report*, ix.
9. The "Instructions to Enumerators" for the 1880 census provide the following guidelines: "Should any person persist in making statements which are obviously erroneous, the enumerator should enter upon the schedule of facts as nearly as he can ascertain them by his own observation or by inquiry of credible persons. The foregoing remark is of special importance with reference to the statements of the heads of families respecting afflicted members of their households. The law requires a return in the case of each blind, deaf and dumb, insane or idiotic, or crippled person. It not infrequently happens that fathers and mothers, especially the latter, are disposed to conceal, or even deny, the existence of such infirmities on the part of children. In such cases, if the fact is personally known to the enumerator, or shall be ascertained by inquiry from neighbors, it should be entered on the schedules equally as if obtained from the head of the family," http://usa.ipums.org/usa/voliii/inst1880.shtml.
10. Wines, *Report*, ix–x.
11. Ibid., viii.
12. Ibid., xli.
13. Ibid., xli.
14. Useful context and discussion of the association between immigrants and mental disorder can be found in John W. Fox, "Irish Immigrants, Pauperism, and Insanity in 1854 Massachusetts," *Social Science History* 15, no. 3 (1991): 315–36.
15. Francis A. Walker, *The Vital Statistics of the United States* (Washington, D.C.: Government Printing Office, 1872), 483. For the year 1870 New Hampshire has a registered 548 "insane." In the census of 1880 that number had doubled. Ibid., 473.
16. *Voices of Madness: Four Pamphlets, 1683–1796*, ed. Allan Ingram (Thrupp: Sutton, 1997), xiv.

17. From a note dated November 24, 1890, and inserted between pages 24 and 25 in *The Council of the Vatican*.

18. Undated note in *The Six Hundred Thousand Combatants*, between pages 70 and 71.

19. From a four-page note dated May 5, 1893, and pasted between pages xii and 1 of *The Lives of the Fathers of the Desert*.

20. Michel Foucault, *Madness and Civilization: A History of Insanity in the Age of Reason* (London: Tavistock, 1971), 100.

21. Ingram, *Voices of Madness*, xvii–xviii.

22. Foucault, *Madness and Civilization*, 125–26.

23. W. Julius Mickle, "Mental Besetments," *Journal of Mental Science* 42 (1896): 691–744.

24. Ibid., 712.

25. Ibid., 714.

26. Thompson, *History of the Town of Stratford*, 350–51.

27. From a letter transcribed and inserted between pages 246 and 247 in the first volume of Balmes's *Fundamental Philosophy*.

28. Note of July 31, 1894, in St. Francis of Sales, *Spiritual Conferences*, between pages viii and ix.

29. Note in *The Council of the Vatican*, between pages 24 and 25, dated November 24, 1890.

30. Fox, "Irish Immigrants," 318. Fox refers to Jarvis's study as "the first American study of the 'true' prevalence of mental illness in a general population," 318.

31. Thompson, *History of the Town of Stratford*, 350.

32. Foucault, *Madness and Civilization*, 91.

33. A body of recent scholarship examines the link between language, madness, and self-recovery. See, for example, Ingram, *Voices of Madness*, and G. Claridge, R. Pryor, and G. Watkins, *Sounds from the Bell Jar: Ten Psychotic Authors* (London: Macmillan, 1990).

34. Carlo Ginzburg, *The Cheese and the Worms: The Cosmos of a Sixteenth-Century Miller*, trans. John and Anne Tedeschi (Baltimore: Johns Hopkins University Press, 1980), xxi. The term "archive of the repression" alludes to Ginzburg's main sources for his study, which are two sixteenth-century inquisitorial records.

35. Ibid., 6.

36. Unlike Connary, Menocchio made strong pretensions to unorthodoxy, rejecting, for instance, sacred images and denying the soul's immortality and Christ's divinity. But like Connary, he advocated religious toleration and propounded an inclusive view on the availability of salvation.

37. Ginzburg, *Cheese and the Worms*, 36.

38. *The Cambridge Companion to Medieval English Mysticism*, ed. Samuel Fanous and Vincent Gillespie (Cambridge: Cambridge University Press, 2011), x.

39. O'Hanlon, *Irish Emigrant's Guide*, 168.

40. Vincent Buckley, "Imagination's Home," *Quadrant* (1979): 24.

41. Ibid., 25.

42. Dated July 11, 1896, and inserted between the end flyleaves in *The Dove of the Tabernacle*.

43. For full bibliographical references and more examples of Connary's books on Irish subjects, see the appendix.

44. According to the *Oxford English Dictionary*, the word "nostalgia" was coined by the German Johannes Hofer in his dissertation *Dissertatio Medica de Nostalgia, oder Heimwehe* (Basel: Jacob Bertschi, 1688). The phenomenon was analyzed as a disease manifested specifically in the overwhelming anxiety prevalent among Swiss mercenary soldiers fighting abroad.

45. For an argument along these lines, see the detailed sociological account by Fred Davis, *Yearning for Yesterday: A Sociology of Nostalgia* (New York: Free Press, 1979). I also draw on Svetlana Boym, "Nostalgia and Its Discontents," in *The Collective Memory Reader*, ed. J. K. Olick, V. Vinitzky-Seroussi, and D. Levy (Oxford: Oxford University Press, 2011), 452–57.

46. Davis, *Yearning for Yesterday*, 13.

47. Buckley, "Imagination's Home," 27.

48. Ibid., 25.

49. The theme of mourning and the sensitive issue of identifying battlefield dead receive extended discussion in Faust, *This Republic of Suffering*, esp. chap. 4, "Naming: 'The Significant Word Unknown,'" 102–36, and chap. 5, "Realizing: Civilians and the Work of Mourning," 137–70.

50. O'Hanlon, *Irish Emigrant's Guide*, 176–78.

51. Ibid., 171.

52. Ibid., 175.

53. Judging from the paper and typography, the poem is excised from the *Pilot*. No other source has been found for this poem.

54. The first recruiting station was set up in North Stratford in April 1861, and we know that the town furnished ninety-eight men (fourteen drafted and the rest volunteered) who were sent to the front in seven installments between 1862 and 1864. No member of the Connary family features among the list of recruited. As a selectman for the town of Stratford, Connary was comprehensively involved in the organization of recruitment. Records listing expenses for travel fares and subsistence in October 1863 and in early 1864 show that he traveled to towns in New Hampshire and Vermont (including Island Pond, Lyndon, West Lebanon, Lancaster, Concord, Northumberland, and Littleton), in connection with individual recruitment calls. Thompson, *History of the Town of Stratford*, 270–74.

55. The quotations are from a note dated April 6, 1897, inserted on an end flyleaf of Julian's *Revelations*. An inserted newspaper cutting in O'Leary's *History of the Bible* contains an article on the Americo-Liberian educator and politician Edward Wilmot Blyden, "perhaps the ablest negro in the world. He can read the Koran in Arabic, the Bible in Hebrew, Homer in Greek, Virgil in Latin, Shakespeare in English and Dante in Italian."

56. Note dated June 29, 1881, inserted after page 328 of Balmes, *Fundamental Philosophy*, vol. 2.

Epilogue

1. On the manuscript and publishing history of "Rome Unvisited," see *The Complete Works of Oscar Wilde*, vol. 1, *Poems and Poems in Prose*, ed. Karl Beckson and Bobby Fung (Oxford: Oxford University Press, 2000), 222–23.

2. Joseph Pearce, *The Unmasking of Oscar Wilde* (London: HarperCollins, 2000), 72.

BIBLIOGRAPHY

Aers, David, and Lynn Staley. *The Powers of the Holy: Religion, Politics, and Gender in Late Medieval English Culture*. University Park: Pennsylvania State University Press, 1996.

Ahearne, Jeremy. *De Certeau: Interpretation and Its Other*. Cambridge: Polity Press, 1995.

Allen, James Smith. "From the History of the Book to the History of Reading: Review Essay." *Libraries and Culture* 28, no. 3 (1993): 319–26.

Amsler, Mark. "Affective Literacy: Gestures of Reading in the Later Middle Ages." *Essays in Medieval Studies* 18 (2001): 83–109.

Andel, Pek van. "Anatomy of the Unsought Finding: Serendipity; Origin, History, Domains, Traditions, Appearances, Patterns, and Programmability." *British Journal for the Philosophy of Science* 45 (1994): 631–48.

Andrews, Martin. "The Importance of Ephemera." In *A Companion to the History of the Book*, edited by Simon Eliot and Jonathan Rose, 434–50. Oxford: Wiley-Blackwell, 2009.

Aston, Margaret. "Devotional Literacy." In *Lollards and Reformers: Images and Literacy in Late Medieval Religion*, 101–33. London: Hambledon, 1984.

Barney, Stephen, ed. *Annotation and Its Texts*. Oxford: Oxford University Press, 1991.

Bauerschmidt, Frederick C. "Julian of Norwich—Incorporated." *Modern Theology* 13, no. 1 (1997): 75–100.

———. *Julian of Norwich and the Mystical Body Politic of Christ*. Notre Dame: University of Notre Dame Press, 1999.

———. "Seeing Jesus: Julian of Norwich and the Text of Christ's Body." *Journal of Medieval and Early Modern Studies* 27, no. 2 (1997): 189–214.

Benjamin, Walter. "The Work of Art in the Age of Mechanical Reproduction." Translated by J. A. Underwood. In Walter Benjamin, *The Work of Art in the Age of Mechanical Reproduction*, 1–50. Great Ideas 56. London: Penguin, 2008.

Birrell, T. A. "English Catholic Mystics in Non-Catholic Circles." *Downside Review* 94 (1976): 60–81, 99–117, 213–28.

Borges, Jorge Luis. *Dreamtigers*. Translated by Mildred Boyer and Harold Morland. Austin: University of Texas Press, 2006.

Boym, Svetlana. "Nostalgia and Its Discontents." In *The Collective Memory Reader*, edited by J. K. Olick, V. Vinitzky-Seroussi, and D. Levy, 452–57. Oxford: Oxford University Press, 2011.

Brantley, Jessica. *Reading in the Wilderness: Private Devotion and Public Performance in Late Medieval England*. Chicago: University of Chicago Press, 2007.

Brewer, John. "Reconstructing the Reader: Prescriptions, Texts, and Strategies in Anna Larpent's Reading." In *The Practice and Representation of Reading in England*, edited by James Raven, Helen Small, and Naomi Tadmor, 226–45. Cambridge: Cambridge University Press, 2006.

Brown, Matthew P. *The Pilgrim and the Bee: Reading Rituals and Book Culture in Early New England*. Philadelphia: University of Pennsylvania Press, 2007.

———. "The Thick Style: Steady Sellers, Textual Aesthetics, and Early Modern Devotional Reading." *PMLA* 121, no. 1 (2006): 67–86.

Bryan, Jennifer. *Looking Inward: Devotional Reading and the Private Self in Late Medieval England*. Philadelphia: University of Pennsylvania Press, 2008.

Buckley, Vincent. "Imagination's Home." *Quadrant* (1979): 24–29.

———. *Poetry and the Sacred*. London: Chatto and Windus, 1968.

Cappon, Lester J., ed. *The Adams-Jefferson Letters*. Chapel Hill: University of North Carolina Press, 1987.

Certeau, Michel de. *Heterologies: Discourse on the Other*. Translated by Brian Massumi. Minneapolis: University of Minnesota Press, 1986.

———. *The Mystic Fable: The Sixteenth and Seventeenth Centuries*. Translated by Michael B. Smith. Chicago: The University of Chicago Press, 1992.

———. *The Practice of Everyday Life*. Translated by Steven Rendall. Berkeley: University of California Press, 1988.

———. "Reading as Poaching." In *The Practice of Everyday Life*, translated by Steven Rendall, 165–76. Berkeley: University of California Press, 1984.

Chartier, Roger. *The Order of Books: Readers, Authors, and Libraries in Europe Between the Fourteenth and Eighteenth Centuries*. Translated by Lydia C. Cochrane. Stanford: Stanford University Press, 1994.

Claridge, G., R. Pryor, and G. Watkins. *Sounds from the Bell Jar: Ten Psychotic Authors*. London: Macmillan, 1990.

Clark, Kelly James. "Spanish Common Sense Philosophy: Jaime Balmes' Critique of Cartesian Foundationalism." *History of Philosophy Quarterly* 7, no. 2 (1990): 207–26.

Colclough, Stephen. *Consuming Texts: Readers and Reading Communities, 1695–1870*. Basingstoke: Palgrave Macmillan, 2007.

———. "Readers: Books and Biography." In *A Companion to the History of the Book*, edited by Simon Eliot and Jonathan Rose, 50–62. Oxford: Blackwell, 2007.

———. "Representing Reading Spaces." In *The History of Reading*, vol. 3, *Methods, Strategies, Tactics*, edited by Rosalind Crone and Shafquat Towheed, 99–114. Basingstoke: Macmillan, 2011.

Connolly, Margaret. "Books for the 'helpe of euery persoone that thenkith to be saued': Six Devotional Miscellanies from Fifteenth-Century London." *Yearbook of English Studies* 33 (2003): 170–81.

Copeland, Rita. *Rhetoric, Hermeneutics, and Translation of the Middle Ages: Academic Traditions and Vernacular Texts*. Cambridge: Cambridge University Press, 1991.

Cormack, Bradin, and Carla Mazzio. *Book Use, Book Theory: 1500–1700*. Chicago: University of Chicago Library, 2005.

Cressy, David. "Books as Totems in Seventeenth-Century England and New England." *Journal of Library History* 21 (1986): 92–106.

Crone, Rosalind, and Shafquat Towheed, eds. *The History of Reading*. Vol. 3, *Methods, Strategies, Tactics*. London: Palgrave, 2011.

Cunningham, Bernadette, and Máire Kennedy, eds. *The Experience of Reading: Irish Historical Perspectives*. Dublin: Rare Books Group of the Library Association of Ireland and Economic and Social History Society of Ireland, 1999.

Curtius, Ernst Robert. *European Literature and the Latin Middle Ages*. Princeton: Princeton University Press, 1953.

Davis, Fred. *Yearning for Yesterday: A Sociology of Nostalgia*. New York: Free Press, 1979.

Denham, Scott, and Mark McCulloh. *W. G. Sebald: History, Memory, Trauma*. Berlin: Walter de Gruyter, 2006.

Derrida, Jacques. "This Is Not an Oral Footnote." In *Annotation and Its Texts*, edited by Stephen Barney, 192–205. Oxford: Oxford University Press, 1991.

Dewey, Bradley Rau. "Kierkegaard and the Blue Testament." *Harvard Theological Review* 60 (1967): 391–409.

Duffy, Eamon. *Marking the Hours: English People and Their Prayers, 1240–1570*. New Haven: Yale University Press, 2006.

Elfenbein, Andrew. "Cognitive Science and the History of Reading." *PMLA* 121, no. 2 (2006): 484–502.

Eliot, Simon. "The Reading Experience Database; or, What Are We to Do About the History of Reading?" Online at http://www.open.ac.uk/Arts/RED/redback.htm.

Eliot, Simon, and Jonathan Rose, eds. *A Companion to the History of the Book*. Oxford: Wiley-Blackwell, 2009.

Fanning, Charles. *The Irish Voice in America: 250 Years of Irish-American Fiction*. 2nd ed. Lexington: University Press of Kentucky, 2000.

Fanous, Samuel, and Vincent Gillespie, eds. *The Cambridge Companion to Medieval English Mysticism*. Cambridge: Cambridge University Press, 2011.

Faust, Drew Gilpin. *This Republic of Suffering: Death and the American Civil War*. New York: Alfred A. Knopf, 2008.

Foucault, Michel. *Madness and Civilization: A History of Insanity in the Age of Reason*. London: Tavistock, 1971.

Fox, John W. "Irish Immigrants, Pauperism, and Insanity in 1854 Massachusetts." *Social Science History* 15, no. 3 (1991): 315–36.

Garvey, Ellen Gruber. *Writing with Scissors: American Scrapbooks from the Civil War to the Harlem Renaissance*. Oxford: Oxford University Press, 2012.

Genette, Gérard. "Introduction to the Paratext." *New Literary History* 22 (1991): 261–72.

———. *Paratexts: Thresholds of Interpretation*. Translated by Jane E. Lewin. Cambridge: Cambridge University Press, 1997.

Gillespie, Vincent. "Lukynge in Haly Bukes: *Lectio* in Some Late Medieval Spiritual Miscellanies." In *Spätmittelalterliche Geistliche Literatur in der Nationalsprache*, edited by James Hogg, 1–27. Analecta Cartusiana 106. Salzburg, 1984.

Ginzburg, Carlo. *The Cheese and the Worms: The Cosmos of a Sixteenth-Century Miller*. Translated by John and Anne Tedeschi. Baltimore: Johns Hopkins University Press, 1980.

———. *Clues, Myths, and the Historical Method*. Translated by John and Anne Tedeschi. Baltimore: Johns Hopkins University Press, 1989.

———. "Microhistory: Two or Three Things that I Know About It." Translated by John and Anne Tedeschi. *Critical Inquiry* 20, no. 1 (1993): 10–35.

Grafton, Anthony. "Is the History of Reading a Marginal Enterprise? Guillaume Budé and his Books." *Papers of the Bibliographical Society of America* 91 (1997): 139–57.

Grafton, Anthony, and Lisa Jardine. "'Studied for Action': How Gabriel Harvey Read His Livy." *Past and Present* 129 (1990): 30–78.

Greenblatt, Stephen, ed. *Cultural Mobility: A Manifesto*. Cambridge: Cambridge University Press, 2010.

Greetham, David C. "Review of H. J. Jackson, *Marginalia*." *Papers of the Bibliographical Society of Canada* 40, no. 1 (2002): 61–73.

———. "What Is Textual Scholarship?" In *A Companion to the History of the Book*, edited by Simon Eliot and Jonathan Rose, 21–32. Oxford: Wiley-Blackwell, 2009.

Grounds, Amelia. "Evolution of a Manuscript: The Pavement Hours." In *Design and Distribution of Late Medieval Manuscripts in England*, edited by Margaret Connolly and Linne R. Mooney, 118–38. Woodbridge: Boydell & Brewer, 2008.

Gumbrecht, Hans Ulrich. *The Production of Presence: What Meaning Cannot Convey*. Stanford: Stanford University Press, 2004.

Hagberg, Garry L., and Walter Jost, eds. *A Companion to the Philosophy of Literature*. Blackwell Companions to Philosophy 44. Chichester: Wiley-Blackwell, 2010.

Hamm, Berndt. "Normative Centering in the Fifteenth and Sixteenth Centuries: Observations on Religiosity, Theology, and Iconology." *Journal of Early Modern History* 3 (1999): 307–54.

———. *The Reformation of Faith in the Context of Late Medieval Theology and Piety.* Edited by Robert J. Bast. Leiden: Brill, 2004.

Hanna, Ralph, III. "Annotation as Social Practice." In *Annotation and Its Texts*, edited by Stephen Barney, 178–84. Oxford: Oxford University Press, 1991.

———. "Miscellaneity and Vernacularity: Conditions of Literary Production in Late Medieval England." In *The Whole Book: Cultural Perspectives on the Medieval Miscellany*, edited by Stephen G. Nichols and Siegfried Wenzel, 37–52. Ann Arbor: University of Michigan Press, 1996.

Harte, Liam. "Migrancy, Performativity, and Autobiographical Identity." *Irish Studies Review* 14, no. 2 (2006): 225–38.

Hind, George. "Hugh Paulinus Serenus Cressy." In *The Catholic Encyclopedia*, vol. 4. New York: Robert Appleton, 1908. Online at http://www.newadvent.org/cathen/04486b.htm.

Holloran, Peter C. *Boston's Wayward Children: Social Services for Homeless Children, 1830–1930.* Rutherford: Fairleigh Dickinson University Press, 1989.

Howsam, Leslie. *Old Books and New Histories: An Orientation to Studies in Book and Print Culture.* Toronto: University of Toronto Press, 2006.

Ingram, Allan, ed. *Voices of Madness: Four Pamphlets, 1683–1796.* Thrupp: Sutton, 1997.

Jackson, Heather J. "'Marginal Frivolities': Readers' Notes as Evidence for the History of Reading." In *Owners, Annotators, and the Signs of Reading*, edited by Robin Myers, Michael Harris, and Giles Mandelbrote, 137–52. London: British Library, 2005.

———. *Marginalia: Readers Writing in Books.* New Haven: Yale University Press, 2001.

———. *Romantic Readers: The Evidence of Marginalia.* New Haven: Yale University Press, 2005.

Jeffrey, David Lyle, ed. and trans. *The Law of Love: English Spirituality in the Age of Wyclif.* Grand Rapids, Mich.: W. B. Eerdmans, 1988.

Johns, Adrian. *The Nature of the Book: Print and Knowledge in the Making.* Chicago: University of Chicago Press, 1998.

Kelly, Stephen, and John Thompson, eds. *Imagining the Book.* Medieval Texts and Cultures of Northern Europe 7. Turnhout: Brepols, 2005.

Kempe, Margery. *The Book of Margery Kempe.* Edited by Barry Windeatt. Cambridge: D. S. Brewer, 2004.

Kennedy, Joseph C. G. *Preliminary Report on the Eighth Census, 1860.* Washington, D.C.: Government Printing Office, 1862.

Kivy, Peter. "The Experience of Reading." In *A Companion to the Philosophy of Literature*, edited by Garry L. Hagberg and Walter Jost, 106–19. Blackwell Companions to Philosophy 44. Chichester: Wiley-Blackwell, 2010.

Lacombe, Michele. "Frying Pans and Deadlier Weapons: The Immigrant Novels of Mary Anne Sadlier." *Essays on Canadian Writing* 29 (1984): 96–116.

Lees-Jeffries, Hester. "Pictures, Places, and Spaces: Sydney, Wroth, Wilton House, and the *Songe de Poliphile*." In *Renaissance Paratexts*, edited by Helen Smith and Louise Wilson, 185–203. Cambridge: Cambridge University Press, 2011.

Lerer, Seth. "Histories of Reading." *Raritan* 20 (2000): 108–26.

———. "Medieval English Literature and the Idea of the Anthology." *PMLA* 118, no. 5 (2003): 1251–67.

Lock, Charles. "Book History and the Metonymies of the Text." In *Movable Type, Mobile Nations: Interactions in Transnational Book History*, edited by Simon Frost and Robert W. Rix, 137–56. Angles on the English-Speaking World 10. Copenhagen: Museum Tusculanum Press, 2010.

Machan, Tim William, ed. *Medieval Literature: Texts and Interpretation*. Medieval and Renaissance Texts and Studies 79. Binghamton, N.Y.: Center for Medieval and Early Renaissance Studies, 1991.

———. *Textual Criticism and Middle English Texts*. Charlottesville: University Press of Virginia, 1994.

McCoy, Beth A. "Race and the (Para)Textual Condition." *PMLA* 121, no. 1 (2006): 156–69.

McDonald, Peter D. "Ideas of the Book and Histories of Literature: After Theory?" *PMLA* 121, no. 1 (2006): 214–28.

McGinn, Colin. *Mindsight: Image, Dream, Meaning*. Cambridge: Harvard University Press, 2004.

Merrill, Georgia D. *A History of Coös County, New Hampshire*. Syracuse: W. A. Fergusson, 1888.

Merton, Robert K., and Elinor Barber. *The Travels and Adventures of Serendipity: A Study in Sociological Semantics and the Sociology of Science*. Princeton: Princeton University Press, 2004.

Mickle, W. Julius. "Mental Besetments." *Journal of Mental Science* 42 (1896): 691–744.

Myers, Robin, Michael Harris, and Giles Mandelbrote. *Owners, Annotators, and the Signs of Reading*. London: British Library, 2005.

Nichols, John G. "Ezra Pound's Poetic Anthologies and the Architecture of Reading." *PMLA* 121, no. 1 (2006): 170–85.

Nichols, Stephen G. "On the Sociology of Medieval Manuscript Annotation." In *Annotation and Its Texts*, edited by Stephen Barney, 43–73. Oxford: Oxford University Press, 1991.

Nord, David Paul. *Faith in Reading: Religious Publishing and the Birth of Mass Media in America*. Oxford: Oxford University Press, 2004.

Nuth, Joan M. *Wisdom's Daughter: The Theology of Julian of Norwich*. New York: Crossroad Publishing, 1991.

O'Connor, J. B. "Ven. Louis of Granada." In *The Catholic Encyclopedia*, vol. 9. New York: Robert Appleton, 1913. Online at http://www.newadvent.org/cathen/09385b.htm.

O'Hanlon, John. *The Irish Emigrant's Guide for the United States*. Boston: Patrick Donahoe, 1851.

O'Toole, James M. "Catholics I—Minority Faith with a Minority Mindset." In *Religion and Public Life in New England: Steady Habits, Changing Slowly*, edited by Andrew Walsh and Mark Silk, 41–60. Walnut Creek, Calif.: AltaMira Press, 2004.

Pantin, William A. "Instructions for a Devout and Literate Layman." In *Medieval Learning and Literature: Essays Presented to R. W. Hunt*, edited by J. G. Alexander and M. T. Gibson, 398–422. Oxford: Clarendon Press, 1976.

Parkes, Malcolm B. *Pause and Effect: Introduction to the History of Punctuation in the West*. Aldershot: Scolar, 1992.

Pearce, Joseph. *The Unmasking of Oscar Wilde*. London: HarperCollins, 2000.

Perry, Ryan. "'Some Sprytuall Matter of Gostly Edyfycacion': Readers and Readings of Nicholas Love's *Mirror of the Blessed Life of Jesus Christ*." In *The Pseudo-Bonaventuran Lives of Christ: Exploring the Middle English Tradition*, edited by Ian Johnson and Allan Westphall, 79–126. Turnhout: Brepols, 2013.

A Pictorial History of the Town of Stratford, New Hampshire, on the Occasion of Her 200th Birthday: 1773–1973. Stratford, N.H.: Bicentennial Committee, 1973.

Price, Leah. "Reading: The State of the Discipline." *Book History* 7 (2004): 303–20.

———. "Reading Matter." *PMLA* 121, no. 1 (2006): 9–16.

———. "When to Read Was to Write: Review of *Used Books: Marking Readers in Renaissance England*, by William H. Sherman." *London Review of Books* 30, no. 19 (2008): 35–37.

Raven, James, Helen Small, and Naomi Tadmor, eds. *The Practice and Representation of Reading in England*. Cambridge: Cambridge University Press, 2006.

Reinburg, Virginia. *French Books of Hours: Making an Archive of Prayer, c. 1400–1600*. Cambridge: Cambridge University Press, 2012.

Rhodes, Neil. "Status Anxiety and English Renaissance Translation." In *Renaissance Paratexts*, edited by Helen Smith and Louise Wilson, 107–20. Cambridge: Cambridge University Press, 2011.

Rice, Nicole R. "Devotional Literature and Lay Spiritual Authority: *Imitatio Clerici* in *Book to a Mother*." *Journal of Medieval and Early Modern Studies* 35, no. 2 (2005): 187–216.

———. *Lay Piety and Religious Discipline in Middle English Literature*. Cambridge: Cambridge University Press, 2008.

Rogers, David. "The English Recusants: Some Mediaeval Literary Links." *Recusant History* 23 (1997): 483–507.

Roure, Lucien. "Visions and Apparitions." In *The Catholic Encyclopedia*, vol. 15. New York: Robert Appleton, 1912. Online at http:www.newadvent.org/cathen/15477a.htm.

Scase, Wendy. "Reginald Pecock, John Carpenter, and John Colop's 'Common-Profit' Books: Aspects of Book Ownership and Circulation in Fifteenth-Century London." *Medium Aevum* 61, no. 2 (1992): 261–74.

Scott-Warren, Jason. "Unannotating Spenser." In *Renaissance Paratexts*, edited by Helen Smith and Louise Wilson, 153–64. Cambridge: Cambridge University Press, 2011.

———. "Words in Edgeways: Review of H. J. Jackson's *Marginalia*." *Cambridge Quarterly* 31, no. 4 (2002): 364–69.

Scull, Andrew. *Madness: A Very Short Introduction*. Oxford: Oxford University Press, 2011.

Sherman, William H. *Used Books: Marking Readers in Renaissance England*. Philadelphia: University of Pennsylvania Press, 2008.

Slights, William W. E. *Managing Readers: Printed Marginalia in English Renaissance Books*. Ann Arbor: University of Michigan Press, 2001.

Smith, Helen, and Louise Wilson, eds. *Renaissance Paratexts*. Cambridge: Cambridge University Press, 2011.

Snart, Jason. "Recentering Blake's Marginalia." *Huntington Library Quarterly* 66 (2003): 134–53.

———. "Review of H. J. Jackson's *Romantic Readers: The Evidence of the Marginalia*." *Studies in Romanticism* 47, no. 2 (2008): 257–61.

Somers, Amos N. *The History of Lancaster, New Hampshire*. Concord, N.H.: Rumford Press, 1899.

Spalding, Mary Caroline, ed. *The Middle English Charters of Christ*. Bryn Mawr College Monographs 15. Bryn Mawr: Bryn Mawr College, 1914.

Stallybrass, Peter. "Afterword." In *Renaissance Paratexts*, edited by Helen Smith and Louise Wilson, 204–19. Cambridge: Cambridge University Press, 2011.

———. "Books and Scrolls: Navigating the Bible." In *Books and Readers in Early Modern England: Material Studies*, edited by Jennifer Andersen and Elizabeth Sauer, 42–79. Philadelphia: University of Pennsylvania Press, 2002.

Stoddard, Roger. *Marks in Books, Illustrated and Explained*. Cambridge, Mass.: Houghton Library, 1985.

Szabo, Liz. "'My Heart Bleeds to Tell It': Women, Domesticity, and the American Ideal in Mary Anne Sadlier's 'Romance of Irish Immigration.'" Online at http://xroads.virginia.edu/~hyper/SADLIER/Intro.htm.

Taylor, Andrew. "Into His Secret Chamber: Reading and Privacy in Late Medieval England." In *The Practice and Representation of Reading in England*, edited by James Raven, Helen Small, and Naomi Tadmor, 41–61. Cambridge: Cambridge University Press, 2006.

Thompson, Jeannette R. *History of the Town of Stratford, New Hampshire, 1773–1925*. Concord, N.H.: The Rumford Press, 1925.

Tribble, Evelyn B. *Margins and Marginality: The Printed Page in Early Modern England*. Charlottesville: University Press of Virginia, 1993.

Wakelin, Daniel. "William Worcester Writes a History of His Reading." *New Medieval Literatures* 7 (2005): 53–71.

Wald, James. "Periodicals and Periodicity." In *A Companion to the History of the Book*, edited by Simon Eliot and Jonathan Rose, 421–33. Oxford: Wiley-Blackwell, 2009.

Walker, Francis A. *The Vital Statistics of the United States*. Washington, D.C.: Government Printing Office, 1872.

Walsh, Andrew, and Mark Silk, eds. *Religion and Public Life in New England: Steady Habits, Changing Slowly*. Walnut Creek, Calif.: AltaMira Press, 2004.

Walsh, Francis R. "Who Spoke for Boston's Irish? The Boston *Pilot* in the Nineteenth Century." *Journal of Ethnic Studies* 10, no. 3 (1982): 21–36.

Watson, Nicholas. "The Composition of Julian of Norwich's *Revelation of Love*." *Speculum* 68, no. 3 (1993): 637–83.

———. "Conceptions of the Word: The Mother Tongue and the Incarnation of God." *New Medieval Literatures* 1 (1997): 85–124.

———. "Visions of Inclusion: Universal Salvation and Vernacular Theology in Pre-Reformation England." *Journal of Medieval and Early Modern Studies* 27, no. 2 (1997): 145–87.

Watson, Rowan. "Some Non-textual Uses of Books." In *A Companion to the History of the Book*, edited by Simon Eliot and Jonathan Rose, 480–92. Oxford: Wiley-Blackwell, 2009.

Westphall, Allan F. "'I Am Here': Reading Julian of Norwich in Nineteenth-Century New England." *Mediaeval Journal* 3, no. 2 (2013): 137–68.

———. "'Laboring in my Books': A Religious Reader in Nineteenth Century New Hampshire." *The Library: Transactions of the Bibliographical Society* 13, no. 2 (2012): 185–204.

Windeatt, Barry, ed. *English Mystics of the Middle Ages*. Cambridge: Cambridge University Press, 1994.

Wines, Frederick H. *Report on the Defective, Dependent, and Delinquent Classes of the Population of the United States, as Returned at the Tenth Census (June 1, 1880)*. Washington, D.C.: Government Printing Office, 1888.

Winship, Michael. *American Literary Publishing in the Mid-Nineteenth Century: The Business of Ticknor and Fields*. Cambridge: Cambridge University Press, 1995.

INDEX

Amsler, Mark, 96
appropriation (reading as appropriation),
    12–13, 44, 80–81, 83, 167–68, 183

Balmes, James
    Fundamental Philosophy, 27–29, 109, 167;
        Connary's enhancement of, 28–29,
        90–92, 102, 103, 105–6, 107–9, 121, 148,
        177–79, 209 n. 11
    *Protestantism and Catholicity Compared in
        Their Effects on the Civilization of
        Europe*, 28
Benjamin, Walter, 208 n. 6
Bernard of Clairvaux, Saint, 121, 166
Bible, 73–74, 87, 88, 144, 168
    Bible quotations by Connary, 48–49, 119,
        144, 209–10 n. 23, 212 n. 36
Bloomfield, VT, 5, 58

Bodenham, Elizabeth de, *Mrs. Herbert and
    the Villagers*, 36
    Connary's enhancement of, 64–65, 101
book as metaphor, xiii, 100–101, 133
book enhancement
    as diary records and family history, 32,
        56–60, 66–67, 161, 170–71
    as a form of authorship, 21, 116
    as guide to reading aloud, 16, 95–97, 106
    as associated with holiness and salvation,
        86–87, 99–106, 107, 114, 184–87
    as associated with location, 1–2, 18, 87–89,
        108–9, 137–38
    material dimensions of Connary's book
        enhancement, 43–66, 123–27, 165–66
    as moral exhortation, 51–53, 60–62, 90–99,
        114–16, 119, 130–31, 135–37, 161–63, 175,
        183
    as newspaper and magazine clippings,
        51–56, 171, 185–87
    as poetry, 44, 46, 53, 54, 133, 171, 177–79,
        180, 184–87
    as prayers, 60–66
    as preaching, 161–65

as reading plans, 66–71
as reading for entertainment, 56, 81–82
as social in orientation, 11, 49, 77–78,
    89–99, 114–17, 161–62, 183, 184
book of hours, xii–xiii
booklouse, x
Borges, Jorge Luis, 7, 201–2 n. 8
Boston Pilot, 33, 46, 51, 53, 127, 185
Boston Weekly Globe, 33
Boudreaux, Florentin J., *The Happiness of
    Heaven*, 179
    Connary's enhancement of, 179, 180
Breckenridge, John, and John Hughes,
        *Controversy between Rev. Messrs. Hughes
        and Breckenridge, on the Subject "Is the
        Protestant Religion the Religion of
        Christ?,"* 37–38
Brown, Matthew, 12–13, 81, 87
Buckley, Vincent (Australian poet), 170–71,
    172

Camus, Jean-Pierre, *The Spirit of St. Francis
    de Sales*
    Connary's enhancement of, 22, 53, 84, 90,
        94, 95–96, 135, 143
catchword, 96
Catholicism, 128, 163–64, 166–67, 185–86
    Catholicism in New England, 4–5, 12, 128,
        144, 201 n. 5
    Connary's Catholicism, 20, 28–29, 64, 72,
        135–36, 170–71, 201 n. 5
    Recusant Catholicism, 126, 128
Certeau, Michel de, 80–81, 82, 183
Chardon, Guillaume, *Memories of a Guardian
    Angel*, 36–37, 166
    Connary's enhancement of, 37, 51–53,
        90–91, 147, 151, 174
Christ, 26, 40, 46–47, 49–50, 61, 62, 75, 85,
    110, 138, 141–43, 147
    as a book, xiii, 100
Civil War, American, 4, 146–48, 164, 174–75,
    179, 215 n. 54
Coleridge, Samuel T., 8, 9, 10

Previously published titles in the Penn State Series in the History of the Book

Peter Burke, *The Fortunes of the "Courtier": The European Reception of Castiglione's "Cortegiano"* (1996)

Roger Burlingame, *Of Making Many Books: A Hundred Years of Reading, Writing, and Publishing* (1996)

James M. Hutchisson, *The Rise of Sinclair Lewis, 1920–1930* (1996)

Julie Bates Dock, ed., *Charlotte Perkins Gilman's "The Yellow Wall-paper" and the History of Its Publication and Reception: A Critical Edition and Documentary Casebook* (1998)

John Williams, ed., *Imaging the Early Medieval Bible* (1998)

Ezra Greenspan, *George Palmer Putnam: Representative American Publisher* (2000)

James G. Nelson, *Publisher to the Decadents: Leonard Smithers in the Careers of Beardsley, Wilde, Dowson* (2000)

Pamela E. Selwyn, *Everyday Life in the German Book Trade: Friedrich Nicolai as Bookseller and Publisher in the Age of Enlightenment* (2000)

David R. Johnson, *Conrad Richter: A Writer's Life* (2001)

David Finkelstein, *The House of Blackwood: Author-Publisher Relations in the Victorian Era* (2002)

Rodger L. Tarr, ed., *As Ever Yours: The Letters of Max Perkins and Elizabeth Lemmon* (2003)

Randy Robertson, *Censorship and Conflict in Seventeenth-Century England: The Subtle Art of Division* (2009)

Catherine M. Parisian, ed., *The First White House Library: A History and Annotated Catalogue* (2010)

Jane McLeod, *Licensing Loyalty: Printers, Patrons, and the State in Early Modern France* (2011)

Charles Walton, ed., *Into Print: Limits and Legacies of the Enlightenment, Essays in Honor of Robert Darnton* (2011)

James L. W. West III, *Making the Archives Talk: New and Selected Essays in Bibliography, Editing, and Book History* (2012)

John Hruschka, *How Books Came to America: The Rise of the American Book Trade* (2012)

A. Franklin Parks, *William Parks: The Colonial Printer in the Transatlantic World of the Eighteenth Century* (2012)

Roger E. Stoddard, comp., and David R. Whitesell, ed., *A Bibliographic Description of Books and Pamphlets of American Verse Printed from 1610 Through 1820* (2012)

Nancy Cervetti, *S. Weir Mitchell: Philadelphia's Literary Physician* (2012)

Karen Nipps, *Lydia Bailey: A Checklist of Her Imprints* (2013)

Paul Eggert, *Biography of a Book: Henry Lawson's "While the Billy Boils"* (2013)